CARRIAGE DRIVING

CARRIAGE DRIVING

A LOGICAL APPROACH
THROUGH DRESSAGE TRAINING

Updated Edition

HEIKE BEAN and
SARAH BLANCHARD

ILLUSTRATED BY JOAN MULLER

HOWELL
BOOK
HOUSE

Howell Book House

Published by Wiley Publishing, Inc., Hoboken, New Jersey

Published simultaneously in Canada

For general information about our other products and services, please contact our Customer Care Department within the United States at (800) 762-2974, outside the United States at (317) 572-3993 or fax (317) 572-4002.

Wiley also publishes its books in a variety of electronic formats. Some content that appears in print may not be available in electronic books. For more information about Wiley products, visit our web site at www.wiley.com.

Library of Congress Cataloging-in-Publication Data:

Bean, Heike.
  Carriage driving : a logical approach through dressage training / Heike Bean and Sarah Blanchard : illustrated by Joan Muller.
       p. cm.
Includes bibliographical references and index.
  ISBN 0-87605-898-5
  ISBN 0-7645-7299-7 (paper: alk. paper)
  1. Driving of horse-drawn vehicles. 2. Driving horses—Training. 3. Carriages and carts.
I. Blanchard, Sarah. II. Title.
SF305.B36   1992   91-37323
636.1'4—dc20   CIP

Printed in the United States of America
10 9 8 7 6 5 4 3 2

CONTENTS

PREFACE

As all forms of driving increase in popularity, there has been a great need for a book that focuses on the step-by-step training of the driving horse.

This is a practical book, written for all driving enthusiasts, from novice to advanced, and for their horses. You won't find much here about style and beauty, and we don't address the subject of correct appointments or examine the hundreds of different styles of horse-drawn vehicles.

We are solely concerned with the correct training of the driving horse, the use of the right equipment and how these affect your horse's well-being and progress in training from the first lessons right up to competition. The beginning driver should be able to use this as a complete manual for training a sound, safe driving horse; the advanced trainer should find thought-provoking discussions of the way a horse should be trained; and we hope everyone will be able to use this as a reference manual for new ideas and answers to problems.

Limited space prevents us from covering all topics as thoroughly as we would like, but we hope that, through this book, you will come to a new understanding of your wonderful equine partner—and that both of you will benefit.

HEIKE BEAN
SARAH BLANCHARD

UNDERSTANDING YOUR HORSE

Our horses are made up of the same materials as we are—blood and bones, tissues and skin—yet they are very unlike us. The evolutionary processes that have shaped the horse (the hunted herd animal) are very different from those that have produced the human (the cave-dwelling hunter). To successfully communicate with our horses, we must always keep these differences in mind.

• THE NATURE OF HORSES •

Our domesticated horses are very close to their wild ancestors and even closer to their present-day feral cousins. Horses are far better equipped to live in the wild than in our enclosures and buildings, yet they do manage to live with us, and even thrive, in relative harmony.

We seldom make it easy for them, however. The same abilities and instincts that make it possible for horses to survive in the wild are those that often seem to cause what we think of as problems in our domesticated horses. To the horse, however, it is we who create the trouble with our unnatural demands.

Our horses' physical structure and natural behavior patterns can work either in our favor or against us; it all depends on how well we understand their needs and instincts, and how skillfully we adapt these traits to our own training goals.

The horse's basic nature dictates both the things he will easily learn and the things he will never learn. In your day-to-day relationship with your horse, you are his teacher (whether you want to be or not); for him to succeed as your willing partner, he must also acknowledge you as his superior. If you don't understand his social nature *and* his physical capabilities, you will never be a good trainer.

The horse is not a piece of sports equipment, and he has not been put into this world simply to be our slave and servant. To gain his cooperation and trust, we must learn as much as possible about him.

The Horse as a Herd Animal

First and most important—especially from the horse's point of view—the horse is a herd animal, accustomed to living in a social hierarchy. In the herd, every animal has its place. That place is determined by heredity (dominant mares tend to produce dominant foals), character (active animals are generally more dominant than placid animals) and physical strength. A herd member is usually very content in his place in the pecking order, as long as he feels that the dominant partner or partners are clearly in charge. However, as soon as he senses weakness in his superior, the horse will challenge the relationship and perhaps fight for a new position.

This trait is vital in herd life. Each herd member must understand and accept the hierarchy, but each must also challenge any sign of weakness. For the herd to survive, the strongest and most attentive animals must always be in charge, to guide and protect the group.

Although the horse has been domesticated for thousands of years, this instinct remains strong. Every horse needs to understand his place in the herd, even when some of the herd members are human. In his relationship with people, your horse will create a hierarchy, whether or not you realize (or appreciate) the implications of this.

We can use this trait to our advantage, of course, since the horse that fully accepts his trainer as his superior will be quite willing to learn and obey. The horse that does not respect his teacher will constantly challenge the relationship. If you do not know enough about reading your horse's likes, dislikes and intentions, he will have no inclination to learn anything from you, and will (literally) walk all over you.

As a herd animal, the horse is also very aware of the general mood of the herd. Fear is quickly transferred from one to every other member of the herd, even when the individual herd members do not know what the cause of the trouble might be. In a relationship with humans, this means that a horse very quickly picks up the emotions of the handler—and he often acts accordingly. A good trainer always practices self-control and always understands how he truly feels. It is nearly impossible for a trainer to mask fear or indecision from his horse. On the other hand, a calm, unhurried partner (horse or human) can help to instill calmness and confidence in a young or worried animal.

With any horse, we must remember that these are built-in behavior patterns. These instinctual reflexes stem from the horse's success at survival through many thousands of years; although much of our training involves adapting the horse's behavior for our own purposes, we will never entirely eliminate the patterns.

An Animal of Prey—Not a Predator

The horse, after all, is an animal of prey, programmed to run away at the slightest sign of danger. Any wild horse that ignores a rustling in the bushes becomes a predator's lunch. In his natural environment, the horse who survives is the one who pays attention to danger signals and is always ready to flee.

The horse is superbly constructed for running away. He has survived because he has managed to avoid being eaten. Keen hearing and a sharp sense of smell; eyes that can scan a wide area and work together or separately; and powerful hind legs for running are all important adaptations keyed to survival through flight. The herd members help, also, by giving every horse many extra pairs of eyes and ears to locate danger.

Gender as a Factor in Behavior

Many people do not realize that mares are really more dominant, by nature, than stallions. The lead mare of a herd is the group's social director and protector, determining when and where to travel, eat or rest. Mares are accustomed to bossing their own foals and everyone else who is lower in the pecking order.

The stallion's role in a herd is also that of a protector, but for different purposes. The herd is his harem, and he is always alert to any threats to his role as dominant male. When there are no threats to his sexual dominance, he is quite willing to be told what to do by the mares. This is why mares can give us more trouble than stallions in training.

Mares have earned the reputation for being stubborn, sulky, grouchy and strong willed. This behavior is the product of hormones and protective instincts, not merely bad temperament or nastiness. The mare, after all, must always be ready to protect her foal, detect approaching danger, guarantee the food supply and maintain the pecking order. Like a human mother, the mare must worry about several things at a time—and paying attention to her trainer isn't always going to be at the top of her list of "things to do." Although a mare is usually quite placid during her receptive cycle, many mares become extremely balky. It can be very difficult to convince a mare of a trainer's superiority. Mares are more subtle than stallions in their resistances, but far more persistent.

Stallions often seem far more concerned about preserving their male egos, but once they accept the trainer as the dominant partner, they are usually quite easy to deal with. They may test you occasionally, but are generally less intense and far more open than mares in their resistances.

Logically enough, geldings are the easiest to train. With very few exceptions, they make the most reliable driving horses because the trainer does not have to contend with fluctuating hormones, maternal instincts or "herd sire" egos.

Living Conditions

Although each animal is different, every horse deserves to be treated according to his equine nature. Among other things, this means that we should give him living conditions as close to his natural state as possible.

From the horse's point of view, the best possible living conditions include a run-in stall or shed, hay or grass and water available more or less all the time and the company of other horses. His herd instincts call for a social life; his need to move around demands access to a large paddock or pasture; and health requirements dictate that his intestines should have a fairly steady flow of low-protein fodder.

Why is the horse's social life so important? Aside from the sense of security he receives from a herd (no matter how small it is), the horse needs physical contact with his own kind, just as we do. When horses are bored, they often play together or groom each other. If a horse is kept alone (and in a stall for most of his life), he is unhappy, bored and probably well on his way to developing what we call "behavior problems" and "stable vices."

Horses that are accustomed to living according to their nature—choosing to go in or stay out in the rain, roll in the mud, eat frequently and be with their friends—are usually an absolute pleasure to work with. They live a contented life without exhibiting any stallbound anxieties or an overabundance of pent-up energy. As much as possible, try to make your horse's life comfortable for him. In return you will enjoy an animal who is mentally and physically healthy and balanced, ready to work with a calm mind.

You may not be able to give him his version of the ideal life, but please don't lock him in just because it rains. He may truly enjoy standing out in the rain and snow sometimes, especially if his coat has been left as nature intended it. Don't clip him and cover him with endless layers of blankets just so he'll look prettier, and don't decide that a heated stall is the place your horse wants to live simply because *you* don't like working in the cold.

Creating Trust Through Communication

To convince a horse to stay with us instead of running away, we must instill in him a large measure of confidence in us. We need his great trust and obedience. We must patiently but firmly convince him that certain things are not a danger to him, that he can rely on us and that we will always help him. This trust cannot be based on rough handling, ignorant treatment or fear. Fear will always cause the opposite reaction: the horse will always try to run away.

Human reasoning won't always help you to understand your horse. (Humans are hunters, and horses were hunted by us for food long before we thought to harness their energy.) Attempting to communicate with a horse on purely human terms just won't work. You must try to meet him on his terms, using your body language and knowledge of equine logic to teach him and let him know that you are the dominant herd member.

Establishing Dominance

How is this dominance established without destroying trust? When corrections and control are necessary, think of what people do to a horse, and think of the horse's reaction. Beating the horse with a whip or yanking on his head with a chain over his nose will more likely confuse, frighten or anger him than get his attention and submission. He does not understand this language. A threatening gesture of your body, however, combined with a firm command and a quick slap on his neck with your hand or a push with your fist into his ribs, will quickly get his attention and respect. (Does this sound "brutal"? Think of how another horse would communicate dominance when challenged. This is language he understands and can immediately accept.)

The trainer's first goal in communication, then, is to instill both trust and respect. There are horses who seem to have been born with an eagerness to please and a willing disposition; others will challenge you constantly. There are also horses whose trust may be won only with great patience and understanding. And there are horses who, because of a history of bad experiences with people, will never quite lower their guard and place their faith in their handlers.

Sometimes a horse seems to cease listening to his trainer; this may happen because the trainer is saying nothing important or comprehensible to the horse. When the trainer asks a horse to perform a specific task, he must be very clear about what it is he wants, and he must also convey a conviction of purpose to the horse. The driver cannot say, "Well, maybe we'll just drop down to a walk somewhere around here," and let the forward momentum disappear until the horse has fallen into some sort of walk. Clarity and consistency are vital in all stages of training and handling horses.

Horses will always have the same basic needs and instincts, but because every horse is an individual with a unique personality, he must be understood as such. Training techniques that work with one will not work with another. Some horses can't stand a loud word, while others don't seem to notice you until you yell at them. Some are very spooky by nature, and some don't seem to be bothered by anything. Many horses need a very sensitive approach from their trainer, while others don't seem to care what approach the trainer uses. The methods and approaches that work with your particular horse may be very different from those preferred by another driver or trainer. You must let your horse teach you what works, and be prepared to learn as well from every other horse you work with.

•   THE LOGIC OF HORSES   •

We often assume that horses are stupid animals, because their reactions to certain situations don't seem to make any sense to us. We think, for example, that a horse is acting "dumb" when he is afraid of an object that he's seen every day in the same place but that has now been moved to a new location. That's not dumb, it's smart and alert. Every change in a horse's surroundings could mean danger to this prey animal, and he's acting purely out of instinctual self-preservation.

Have you ever thought about how quickly horses can figure us out, and how long it takes us to understand them (assuming we ever do)? Don't most problems occur because of *our* failure to understand the horse, and not the other way around? A horse can learn the verbal commands for "walk," "trot" and "whoa" in just a few training sessions. How many of us understand their language when they nicker to each other?

What does it feel like to be this animal of flight, who must submit to being strapped to a carriage and controlled through a piece of metal in his mouth, doing things and going places he would never dream of doing on his own?

An incredible learning and adaptation process must occur as we train our horses. They must possess an amazing willingness to please for us to achieve all this.

We often say horses "can't reason." They cannot reason in the abstract as we can, but any sensitive, experienced horseperson can tell you about the horse's superb ability to remember and to learn when information is presented clearly and logically. It is this logic—based on the horse's ability to connect a stimulus with a desired response—that makes it possible for us to train horses. They also exhibit a genuine sense of humor and an ability to play—which can either entertain or frustrate us, depending on the circumstances.

Reinforcement in the Learning Process

Horses learn through positive and negative reinforcement and very quickly adapt to the situation in which they are placed. This means that a trainer must be ready to react quickly also, to be sure that the response the horse gives is the correct one. Any challenge to your dominance—no matter how subtle—must be corrected immediately. Proper behavior must be rewarded equally as quickly.

If the first correction is simultaneously applied physically (with a slap and a threatening body gesture) and vocally (with a loud command), soon the verbal command plus the gesture, and eventually only the verbal command by itself, will be sufficient. Thus, the focus of the discipline is shifted from actual physical punishment (slaps) to a form of mental discipline (gestures and words).

You should always try to dominate your horse mentally rather than physically, for two reasons. First, this is the way herd members assert their dominance (threats and gestures seldom lead to actual violence); secondly, *you* know the horse is physically stronger than you are, but you don't ever want the horse to realize this, or you will lose your superior status—especially if you are working with a stallion. (A mare will often assume that you are inferior to her—and you may never be able to convince her otherwise—but the consequences probably won't be as severe as if a stallion gets the upper hand.)

It is very important in training that the first correction make a big impression and that the horse does not feel you back down at any time. This doesn't mean that we shouldn't be nice to our horses, because they do deserve our friendship and trust. However, we must be firm about what behavior is desirable and what is not—and we must never weaken the border between the two.

On the other side of the coin, positive response must be generously rewarded. Every time the horse comes close to doing what you want, make a big fuss over him, tell him what a smart and good guy he is, pat him and scratch him in his favorite place. Some people will give food rewards also. Personally, we don't like food rewards, as some horses get to expect them and can become quite obnoxious about it. It is better to reward horses with rubs and pats and kind words. Then they look to please the trainer and are pleased when the trainer is pleased.

Your goal must be to establish a partnership based on mutual trust and love, with the horse looking up to his trainer as his master but also as his friend.

When Not to Punish

One of the most difficult things for a trainer to learn is when not to punish. You must never punish a horse when he is afraid, does not understand your request or is incapable of performing the task. If the horse is disobedient because he is being obstinate or is challenging your authority, he must be corrected, and quickly—but if you are not sure of the cause of the problem, you must give the horse the benefit of the doubt.

You may have asked for something unreasonable or impossible at the horse's present level or at any level of training. The horse may be in physical discomfort because of sharp teeth or poorly fitted tack.

Some horses—like some children—have a very short attention span, and after a while they simply stop listening to the teacher. Forcing them to pay attention and comply with your demands will only produce stubbornness and fear.

Remember also, that a horse's brain has very few connections between its two halves. Each training procedure must be repeated on both sides, and you should not punish the horse who has learned to accept something from one side, but then acts confused or fearful when you repeat the same exercise on the other side.

It is apparent that training a horse is a very complex task, similar to teaching a child. The teachers who instruct our children must go through a formal educational process and be tested for their knowledge and teaching abilities. People who train horses are not required to go through any similar qualifying program of instruction. Our horses are living beings also, and we must give due respect to their very complex and alien intelligence if we hope to have them as our partners. We should try to deal with our horses with understanding and as much justice as possible.

EQUINE MECHANICS

Trainers of human athletes must learn about the human body in general—its parts, functions, abilities and limitations—and must also know about the specific characteristics of each person they train. Anyone who drives a horse in harness (whether or not he thinks of himself as a "trainer") should also understand the basics of the horse's body mechanics.

There are any number of excellent books available on the subject. Many, however, go into more detail than many drivers need or want—and many books fail to properly relate the horse's structural parts to his abilities and functions. Knowing the name for a part doesn't always help you understand what it does, how it works or why it's there—and this is the sort of knowledge we need to acquire before we can train our horses correctly.

• A PRODUCT OF THE ENVIRONMENT •

Put very simply, form follows function. Since the horse is a prey animal, natural selection has equipped him with a perfect body for evasion and fast escape from predators. His instincts for flight are matched by his ability to flee.

Horses evolved as browsers and grazers on open plains. They have long heads and long legs so they can see above the grass while grazing; long necks to reach the grass and trees; a large digestive system to handle all that plant food; movement-sensitive eyes on the sides of the head for good all-around vision (but poor binocular and distance vision, as the horse doesn't need to judge distance as well as a predator must); and ears that can swivel to collect sounds from any direction.

The horse is naturally heavier in front than behind. He has a set of front legs with very little muscle attachment and very few angulations, providing a straight-up-and-down support for his body weight. His hind legs are long, very angular and heavily muscled to propel his body forward with great strength and speed.

Because of this arrangement, the front legs cannot originate forward movement—they simply move out of the way of the hind limbs and touch the ground to provide support for the body mass. The front legs are perfectly suited to bearing the weight of the horse's body, but they were never designed to bear the. *additional weight* of pulling a vehicle.

The horse's neck is a very important balancing tool, moving to compensate for shifts in the body's center of gravity. The length, shape and attachment of the neck to the torso determine—to a great degree—the quality of the horse's balance and movement. (More about this later.)

Since all these elements of the horse's form have to do with his balance and movement, we have to understand the impact that the construction of his body has on our training considerations.

• ADAPTATION THROUGH TRAINING •

Training a horse does not just mean teaching him certain behavior patterns; instead, it involves the gradual development of his whole body and his mind. This means a horse will have to learn, both mentally and physically, to control his body and perform maneuvers that he normally would not do on his own. Just as we train a human athlete through exercise, repetition and "body-building," we must gymnasticize the horse's body through a carefully structured program. Unless the trainer knows how the equine body works, and what the horse's individual needs are, training will not be entirely successful.

Dressage training (whether under saddle or in harness) is the only kind of training that does not have a certain performance or behavior pattern of the horse as its goal. (Note that we are referring to dressage *training*, not dressage competition—which does have a performance goal. This is addressed in Chapter 14.) Unlike jumping, reining, racing or saddleseat performance, the goal of dressage is simply to educate the horse's body and mind to best cope with human demands of any kind. It is a never-ending training because a horse can be endlessly improved.

To improve the horse with continuous training—rather than breaking down his body and "using him up" with inappropriate exercises or work— knowledge about the body functions is essential.

•   BALANCE, COMFORT AND STRESS   •

Understanding the horse's balance is a key factor in successful training. Physical balance is important to all animals, including people; when we are in balance, we relax and feel comfortable. When balance is disturbed, tension and possibly fear result. When we (or our horses) lose our balance, we struggle to regain it, and we cannot relax until we do.

As trainers, we must be aware that there are two different kinds of balance available to any horse. The first is the balance that is natural for him, that he offers on his own; the second is the balance we would like him to acquire so that he can work more efficiently for us.

The horse's natural balance is "front and heavy." This means that he carries more of his body weight in front than in the rear. Most horses also carry more weight on the left shoulder than the right because of their natural crookedness. (See Chapter 10, The Lateral Bend, for a complete discussion of this.) Each horse's natural balance will also be determined by his individual conformation: very heavy in front because of a low-set, heavy neck and rump-high hindquarters, or relatively light in front because of a high-set, well-shaped neck and higher withers.

The balance we would like him to be in is very different from the one he offers naturally. We would like him to be light in the forehand and to shift so much weight backwards onto his haunches that eventually he carries at least as much weight behind as in front—even more, if possible. (This is a key element of collection.) And we want him to distribute his weight evenly onto both sides of his body. (See pages 159–164) for illustrations of the progressive changes in balance.)

To proceed from the horse's natural balance toward the one we call "good balance" is a very difficult task for the horse, and it can frighten him if we introduce it in the wrong way. Much of the rushing and tenseness we see in horses during training comes from displacing the horse's natural balance *without* gaining his trust and showing him the better alternative.

In classical training, it has been understood for hundreds of years that only relaxation and willing submission to the trainer will improve the horse's balance and allow him to learn. To be relaxed the horse must be comfortable, and to be comfortable he must be shown how to adjust to the demands of carrying or pulling added weight.

If we ask the horse to handle additional weight by putting inappropriate stress on his front legs, sooner or later he will break down. The front legs,

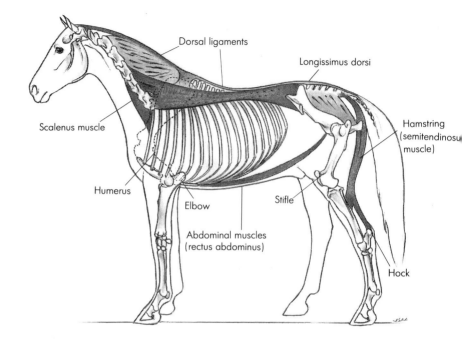

The well-built horse exhibits good bone and perfect angles in the joints of all four legs. His neck is set on high and flows smoothly into the withers: showing a long upper curve and short bottom line, it narrows sufficiently toward the clean throatlatch, with the head set on in an open angle. His withers are well developed, reaching far into his back; a perfectly placed loin coupling gives him a short, broad and strong back; a deep hip and a moderately sloping croup angle give him lots of power; and a deep ribcage allows plenty of room for heart and lungs. A humerus of good length forms a 90-degree angle with his shoulder, and a point-of-shoulder set fairly high allows for maximum freedom of the shoulder movement. His hamstring muscles reach far down to his hocks and will make flexing the haunches easy for him.

Note how the dorsal ligaments stretch along the top of the horse's spine, acting like the cables of a suspension bridge. The longissimus dorsi is the large back muscle stretching from the lower vertebrae of the neck to the hip. The scalenus muscle (not actually visible from the exterior) enables the horse to raise and lower the root of his neck. The abdominal muscles contract to shorten the horse's bottom line. The hamstring muscles play an important part in flexing the joints of the hindquarters.

perfectly designed for the horse's purposes, were not built to be artificially loaded. For this reason, it is important to shift weight—his own as well as that of his burden—back onto the muscle-packed hind legs as soon as possible in the training process. This is an early, continuing, and absolutely vital goal.

As the horse learns to make this shift in balance, he will become lighter on his forehand and more agile. As the correct muscle groups are strength-

Here we have a less advantaged specimen. He has an overall lack of bone in his legs; his left fore is overly straight while his right front leg is buckled over in the knee; he is sickle-hocked and club-footed behind, while his front feet have too little heel.

His neck is set very low, with a dip in front of the withers, a long and bulging bottom line and a short topline (a typical ewe neck). The throatlatch is thick and bulky, and the head connects to the neck at a 90-degree angle, producing a "hammerhead." His withers are underdeveloped and don't reach at all into his back; his loin coupling is far to the rear, thus causing a long and weak back. The depth of his hip is not too bad, but because he is rump-high, it will be hard for him to shift any weight back. The severe angles of the hind limb (from the exaggeratedly sloping croup down to his sickled hocks), in combination with a poorly developed hock joint and lack of bone, predispose him to weakness of the hind limbs.

His humerus is fairly short and almost horizontal, thus creating a low point of the shoulder, and this—together with a very upright shoulder—will not allow him much shoulder freedom. His weak and poorly muscled gaskins, together with the other weak parts of his hind legs, will make true flexion of the haunches very difficult for him.

ened, our training makes the horse capable of dealing comfortably with his burden.

From Pushing to Carrying Power

This is a worthy goal and sounds very logical, but we are faced with one particular problem: The horse's hind legs were not designed to carry weight, they were designed to push. However, since there are so many large muscles in the hindquarters—and muscles can be adapted through training—correct and progressive training can convert part of the pushing power into carrying power.

To create this change, it is necessary to strengthen the hind legs. This can only happen after we first place them under the horse's body, as far forward and as consistently as possible. The horse's physical structure allows for this, fortunately, but normally he does not do this on his own. He just doesn't need to bring them this far under his body in the course of free, unburdened movement.

The Importance of Stretching the Topline

The hind legs cannot move into this placement until one other thing happens: The horse's spine must be totally stretched and relaxed. It is this vital physical element of the horse's training that is so often ignored.

The dorsal ligament stretches from the horse's poll, over his withers and along the spine, with the withers acting like the support of a suspension bridge. Any shortening of this ligament will stiffen the spine and block the hind legs from swinging under. Also, since the largest and most important back muscle—the longissimus dorsi—attaches in the front to the lower vertebrae of the neck, any incorrect elevation of the neck or any stiffening through the lower neck and jaws will affect this back muscle by contracting and stiffening it, thus also preventing the free swing of the hind limbs.

Once the topline is stretched and every joint in the horse's body is allowed to work freely, success will happen quite quickly. Any tension, on the other hand, will result in stagnation or regression. Through proper training techniques, the horse's hindquarters and back will increase in strength. The horse will be able to "coil" his back, shorten his abdominal muscles and compress all the angles in his haunches, gradually taking weight off the front end. At all times, it is important for the horse to stretch the topline and contract the bottomline. Only this will lead to, and be the proof of, collection.

Any faked collection, where the horse is forced into a high neck position while the back is inverted and the bottomline lengthened, will result in tension—and will block out proper hind leg engagement. Thus, no shift in balance to the rear can take place; on the contrary, the horse's front end will be weighted even more because the hind legs are completely prohibited from stepping under the body mass.

Mental Relaxation

Notice what happens when a horse is excited, tense, frustrated or nervous: The head goes up, the body becomes stiff, the topline shortens as the back

True collection. The horse has lowered his hindquarters and fully stretched his topline; his neck is fully elevated from its root. His bottom line is very short, the hocks are well engaged and his shoulders exhibit great freedom of movement. This horse appears relaxed and confident.

"Faked" collection. This horse's neck and head are carried higher than those of the horse in the preceding illustration, but note how his withers are pushed down and his front end is heavily weighted. His hindquarters are not lowered at all, and there is no engagement of the hind legs. His topline is shorter than his bottom line, and his lower neck is bulging. Note also the tension exhibited by the stiffly held tail and the worried expression on his face.

muscles contract and the horse thinks only of avoiding what hurts or frightens him.

The tension may be the result of genuine fear or pain, but it can also come from something as simple as youthful exuberance or intense curiosity. When your horse's attention is drawn away (to another horse, something moving in the distance, the jacket hanging in the doorway), what happens? His head goes up, because he is attempting to focus his vision on the thing that interests him. A horse who is giving his trainer his entire attention does not raise his head to view something in the distance. The horse who is relaxed and trusting will keep his attention on his trainer, focus on the task at hand and ignore distractions.

A young or green horse, of course, cannot do this until he has had sufficient training and exposure to a variety of situations. How many times have you seen a young horse who is beautifully behaved and relaxed at home become a silly, spooky, inattentive—and possibly clumsy or dangerous—animal at a show or carriage rally? It is *absolutely vital* (for everyone's safety) that a potential driving horse be exposed to as many different environments and strange sights as possible, at a young age and *before* he's hitched to a cart. (See Chapter 7, Basic Ground Training.)

A horse must never be punished for his curiosity or his fear of a new object, but must be allowed to investigate, put his fears to rest and then attend to his job. This is as much a part of training as the physical work and every bit as important.

• CONFORMATION CONSIDERATIONS •

Each horse is unique, both in his temperament and in his physical build. Any willing, sound horse can be driven, and good conformation is not as important in a driving horse as it is in a riding horse. Still, the conformation of the individual horse plays a large part in our approach to his training.

A horse with less-than-perfect conformation may make up for his faults with a great disposition, but many disposition problems can also stem from physical problems. You must make an honest assessment of your horse's physical attributes before you put him to a particular task or try to map out your performance goals. If the work you demand is too hard or painful for your horse, a nice horse's willing attitude will soon change to stubbornness and hostility. Nearly every horse can happily pull a light cart on straight roads and flat trails; if, however, you are asking for precision ring work and taxing cross-country courses, you should have a horse with the physical abilities to handle this difficult work.

To properly assess your horse's suitability, it is important to understand how every part of his body influences the whole and how variations from the ideal will affect his performance.

• THE NECK •

The shape of the neck and its position on the horse's body play an often-underestimated role in the training process. Too many trainers are concerned only with the "engine," or hindquarters of the horse, not considering where the power produced from behind goes. All power should arrive at the horse's mouth (the bit), and from there the trainer determines how much of the power he will use for forward motion and how much of it he will keep in the horse to give his movement more strength and eventual collection.

Evasions and Obstructions
This flow of energy to the bit from the hindquarters can only happen successfully when there are no obstructions in between—and many, many obstructions can happen in the neck.

This horse's conformation does not suggest that he will be easily able to produce a short bottom line and a stretched, arched topline. However, patient and correct training turned him into an animal whose conformational problems are not obvious when he works.

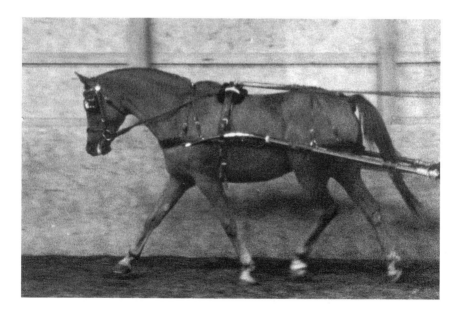

With his very mobile and flexible neck, every horse has endless evasion possibilities. Each evasion prohibits the direct flow of energy from the back to the front. There can be lateral (side-to-side) evasions, and there can be longitudinal (back-to-front) evasions.

In a lateral evasion, we think of a loss of power to one side or another, at some point along the spine. Whenever the entire length of the spine (from tail to poll, as seen from above) is not totally straight on a straight line—or parallel to the arc of a curved path—power will "run out" at the point of the break. The horse that bulges a shoulder, cocks his head, overbends in the neck or doesn't bend at all through his turns is practicing a lateral evasion. (See pages 143–146 for a discussion of straightness.)

In a longitudinal evasion the topline is not correctly stretched and the horse may evade, for instance, by trailing his hind legs, hollowing his back, stiffening his jaw or bulging through his lower neck. This last evasion is very common and seldom given the attention it deserves.

Any bulge—no matter how slight—in the lower line of the neck is an immediate indication that the topline is not stretching correctly and the horse is not engaging his hindquarters. Over time, the bulging in the lower neck and slackening of the upper neck muscles can become habitual, as the wrong muscles are being encouraged or allowed to develop.

The Shape of the Neck
Complicating the natural flexibility of the neck, however, there can also be problems in conformation. If a horse has a natural ewe neck—a neck set low onto his chest, with a short top curve and a long underline—it will automatically be difficult for him to properly relax and shorten the underside of the neck, while lengthening and stretching the top. The ewe neck puts his natural balance more onto the forehand and makes the weight shift to the rear more difficult. (See illustrations on pages 13 and 17.) Expert training will be able to slowly change the muscles of the ewe-necked horse, but any minor mistakes in training will worsen the condition. This is shown in the illustrations on pages 163–164.

An overly long neck, simply because of its length and weight, will shift the horse's natural balance more to the front. The horse with a long neck may also have a tendency to "curl up" in front, flexing at the fourth vertebra instead of at the poll. (When the horse is correctly stretched, the flexion occurs at the poll. In a trained horse, the poll is always the highest point of his spine.)

A very short neck does not help the horse find a good natural balance, because it provides too little counterweight for his body. To work forward

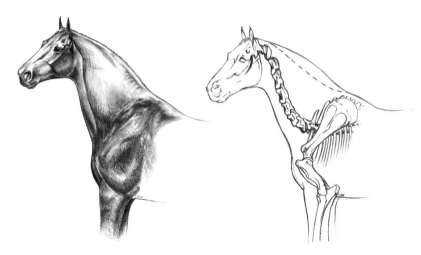

Although this horse has a very impressive-looking neck, it still is a ewe neck. His stallion crestiness almost hides the short upper line, but the skeletal picture reveals the true conformation.

and downward correctly, these horses will sometimes put the head far down and lie on the bit to compensate for the lack of neck length. Their longitudinal balance will often remain very precarious as a result.

How the Neck Functions

How does the properly functioning, correctly muscled neck of a schooled horse work? In the walk, as the horse steps forward, the neck should move with a telescoping gesture, first reaching and stretching and then contracting, but without lifting. The neck should rock back and forth, but not up and down. In the trot, the top of his neck is in an almost continuous stretch and arch; in the canter, it again stretches and contracts. This motion seems to originate right in front of the withers, but it actually begins at the root of the neck (at the seventh vertebra), as muscles contract and relax. The correct elevation of the neck—the lengthening of the top and the shortening of the lower curve—is produced by the contraction of the scalenus muscle.

The green horse, on the other hand, will not be able to arch his neck until the correct muscles strengthen and develop. In the green horse, you can't expect any elevation of the neck, but you should look for a total stretching and reaching to the bit forward and downward.

When you are driving the horse, you cannot see the bottom of the neck. You can, however, see the top. Many horses, when they are incorrectly contracting the topline, show wrinkled skin just in front of the withers. This is a very visible indication of bad neck posture. The horse with a bulging lower neck will also feel stiff and resistant in your hands, and his back may

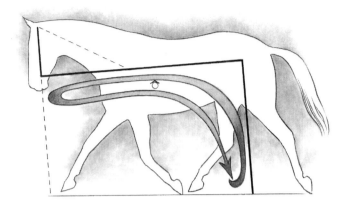

A horse in the early stages of training on the bit, stretching well through the topline. Note the "power line" that begins at the point where hind-leg movement originates: it continues through the point where front-leg movement originates, and meets the bit in an uninterrupted line. This allows the horse's energy to be recycled and permits the horse's center of gravity to be raised—which results in a raised and relaxed back, freedom in the horse's shoulder and front-leg movement, freely swinging hind legs, and a lightening of the forehand. Although the horse's overall balance is still front-heavy, he is well balanced within his present abilities and *not* working on the forehand.

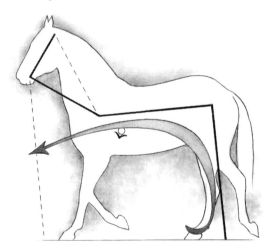

The same horse, above the bit, showing a tense and shortened topline. As a result, the horse's back is hollow and stiff, his center of gravity gets pushed down and the front leg movement is hindered through this additional weighting. The power produced no longer meets the bit; the created energy cannot be recycled and runs out into nothing. The hind legs cannot swing freely under the body anymore and can no longer support the horse's weight, thus pushing the horse even more onto his front legs. Now the horse is truly working on the forehand—even though his head and neck are carried a lot higher than in the previous illustration.

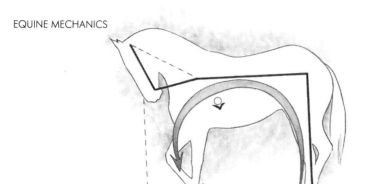

The same horse, behind the vertical and behind the bit. Again, the energy produced does not meet the bit in a straight line and cannot be recycled and fully used by the horse's body. By coming behind the bit, the horse has given up any bit contact; the energy seems to vanish into nothing. Although the back is not as hollow, it still is very rigid because of the cramped head and neck position. The hind legs therefore cannot swing under, and will only continue to push all the horse's weight onto his forehand. The front-leg movement is very restricted because of this weight (plus the tightness of the neck).

The horse can also be behind the vertical, but still apply pressure on the bit; if the horse is producing a lot of unwanted energy—especially if he is coming behind the vertical because the driver must hold him very strongly—we will get an "avalanche effect": The horse is basically always falling forward; if he were a ball, he would roll faster and faster. In an attempt to find his balance, he tries to get out of his own way in front but cannot. Because of the front-end heaviness and restriction, his steps are very short and quick, causing his hind legs to move quicker and quicker. The horse will then continue to rush even more—and fall forward even more.

appear hollowed. If it seems that you have to hold him back all the time, to convince him to keep his head down, you will also know that the neck is not working as it should. The horse should feel as if he is seeking the bit and reaching for your hands, looking for the support and guidance you give.

Sometimes, even knowledgeable spectators can be fooled by a horse who appears to carry his head and neck correctly but is actually failing to stretch the topline and work through the entire length of his spine.

The way the head attaches to the neck is of great importance. To follow through on our stretched topline and contracted underline, where do we want the head positioned? Seen in profile, the only acceptable position for the head of a schooled driving horse is *slightly ahead of the vertical* or *at the vertical—never behind it.* Green horses will often carry their heads very much in front of the vertical. They cannot be asked to work with the head near the vertical right away, as the correct muscles must be developed first.

When the topline is stretched and the neck and head are in the correct position, all energy created from behind will be transmitted to and caught by the bit, as illustrated at the tops of pages 20 and 22.

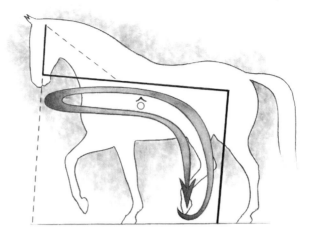

The horse in an advanced stage of training; here, he is correctly on the bit. More of his weight is balanced on his hind legs rather than on his front legs, his haunches are more flexed, his loin is coiled, his back is raised and his topline is stretched to the utmost. He has gained greater freedom of shoulder movement and travels in an "uphill" manner. All his energy is recycled, and a good part of it is used to lift his own center of gravity more off the ground, thus making his movement appear light and easy.

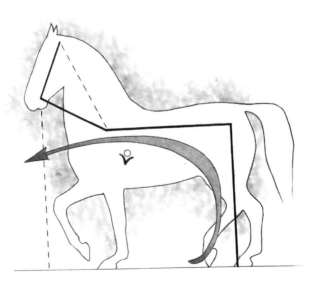

The same horse above the bit; he now closely resembles our low-level horse above the bit. Although his body may now be stronger (if it has been worked correctly at least part of the time), the same problems remain. No lowering of the hindquarters is possible, and his center of gravity continues to be pushed down toward his forehand. He is still working on the forehand.

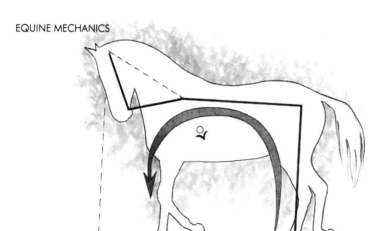

The same horse behind the bit. Although the overall carriage of his front end may be somewhat higher than that of the low-level horse and the problem may be less apparent, he has still given up the rein contact and the energy is lost. His hindquarters cannot be lowered because he lacks both available energy and relaxation through the topline. Just as with the lower-level horse, an "avalanche effect" can occur here if the horse is behind the vertical but also putting pressure on the bit; he will fall forward continuously and rush.

We can imagine the horse's body as a leaf spring that, due to the created energy, is coiled upward. This coiling can only occur when both ends of the spring are held in. If the rear is not pushed in, no energy is created; but if the front is not held in the right place with enough secure pressure, the "coiling" and containment of energy will not work either.

If the head is high and considerably in front of the vertical, energy will "run out" underneath. If the head is too low and tucked behind the vertical, energy will "run down" into the ground. Only when the horse accepts all the energy in his mouth and yields to the bit with soft jaws (which means reaching for the bit and seeking its support without leaning on it) can we bring all his energy under control and utilize it to best advantage.

THE THROAT, POLL AND ANGLE OF THE HEAD TO THE NECK

The horse with less-than-perfect conformation may find it difficult to meet these goals, and we should examine how his head and neck are joined before we set our training goals. We might have to compromise, and we may have to be prepared for a more difficult road ahead. A hammerheaded horse (whose neck and head naturally form a right angle) is likely to drop his head behind the vertical and come behind the bit easily. A horse with a thick neck coupling and/or a lot of bulk behind the jaws (sometimes caused by protruding glands and a narrow throatlatch) will find it hard to soften in the jaw and flex sufficiently through the poll. (See illustrations on pages 13 and 17.)

Ideally, the head should be set onto the neck at an open angle, with wide-spaced jaws and a "clean" throatlatch. The less bulk in the throatlatch the better.

• THE BACK, LOIN AND CROUP •

The back transmits the power from the hind end to the front; its length, shape and width greatly influence the degree to which this power is transmitted.

A long, weak or narrow back—perhaps swayed by age or bad training (the use of checkreins will cause a swayed back!)—is a very weak link in a chain that must be uniformly strong. Any form of weak back will prevent the horse (at least to some degree, and, in some cases, totally) from shifting weight back onto his quarters, since coiling his loin will be very hard—if not impossible—for him.

The placement of the loin coupling and the length of the pelvis are also important factors in determining the amount of power the horse can give. If the loin coupling is far to the rear (giving a long back and short, shallow hindquarters), the back will be weak and it will be difficult to bring the hindquarters underneath the body.

The horse with a short pelvis (the distance from the hip to the point of the buttock) will have less angulation in his hind limbs and, again, will find it difficult to bring the hind legs under the body and compress them. Especially if the short pelvis is combined with a very straight ("tabletop") croup, the horse will not have much ability for collection. The ideal pelvis is long and deep and has a moderate slope toward the tail.

To engage the hindquarters, the back must be able to coil. This cannot happen in a horse with a weak back or poor coupling of the back to the hindquarters.

The horse who stands rump-high has another problem. The higher the rear end (compared to the height of the withers), the more weight the horse will naturally bear on his front legs, and the more he has to flex his haunches when he tries to shift weight back. He can only compensate for this conformation problem if he has an extremely well placed loin coupling, with a deep pelvis and overall strong hind legs.

The ideal back is a little higher (about one inch) in the withers than in the croup. The horse gives the impression of being built slightly "uphill."

The movement of the shoulder and point of shoulder during one stride. As the horse advances his front leg, the shoulder muscles alone must work to move the whole weight of the carriage for several inches during each stride.

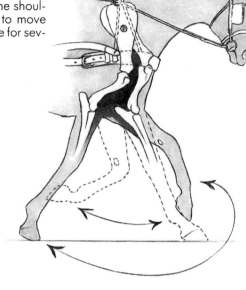

•   THE SHOULDERS   •

The horse's front legs and shoulders have no bony connection with the rest of his body. His ribcage is suspended between his shoulder blades in a sling made up of muscles and ligaments. The weight-bearing front legs—which must receive a great deal of concussion as they strike the ground—are thus better able to absorb shock than if they were attached directly to bone. However, the horse cannot brace his front legs against the rest of his skeleton the way he can brace his hind legs against the pelvis bone.

This is important to remember when you are driving your horse. Because of the way the horse's skeleton is constructed, the weight of the carriage rests at all times on the horse's chest, and thus on the bottom of his shoulder blades, just above the point of the shoulder.

To move forward, the horse must advance his front leg and also his shoulder blade. Therefore, when he is pulling a weight, he must displace the load, for a brief moment, solely through the movement of his shoulder. The hindquarters keep the whole mass (horse and carriage) moving by pushing, but in order to create a large stride in front and get his front legs out of the way of his hind legs, the horse's shoulder muscles must create an additional displacement of the load. (See illustration above.)

Evolution has not adapted the horse's shoulder for this purpose. This means that our training program and our driving equipment must allow for as much shoulder freedom and comfort as possible. Lightweight carriages and singletrees that allow for plenty of movement will make the horse's job easier, especially at the beginning of his training.

If we don't make these allowances, we will destroy the horse's shoulder movement. The muscles below the shoulder blade may tighten and go into spasms, and the pectoral (chest) muscles will stiffen and lose their elasticity. The horse will begin to move with short, choppy steps, and he will appear as if he is moving his front legs only from the elbow down. He may begin to forge with his hind feet, step onto the heels of his front feet, or compensate for the loss of front-end movement by shortening the stride of the hind legs, thus losing all the wonderful engagement and impulsion we are aiming for.

Collection, after all, can be developed only through correct strengthening of the horse's hindquarters through engagement and impulsion *and* a corresponding increase in the freedom of the shoulders. This will not happen if we block it early in the horse's training.

In riding we do not concern ourselves much with the strengthening of the shoulder muscles, but in driving the muscles of the shoulders are just as important as the muscles of the hindquarters. In all your driving, try to use the lightest possible vehicle with plenty of motion in the singletree to keep your horse's shoulders free. A horse with a large and naturally well-muscled shoulder will have it easier to begin with.

•   THE LEGS   •

All four legs should have sufficient bone to give an impression of strength and sturdiness, relative to the horse's build and type. The amount of bone in his hind legs, their proportion and angulation will also determine the amount of thrust he can produce.

Actually, it isn't quite accurate to speak of the density of bone as an indicator of stamina in the legs; the true measure of sturdiness is in the ligaments (which connect bones to bones) and the tendons (which connect muscles to bones). Since the ligaments and tendons are connected to the bones, the greater the surface area of the bones, the larger and stronger the ligaments and tendons can be. (Too-large bones, however, can make a horse's legs too heavy and cause him to move ponderously.)

The horse with very open angles in the joints of the hind legs will find it difficult to place his hindquarters properly underneath him, while the sickle-hocked horse (with excessively acute hind leg angles) may be predisposed to weakness and unsoundness. Sickle-hocked horses are especially prone to problems if this feature is combined with insufficient size of bone and joints. A very large, well-built hock joint—placed close to the ground—can compensate for sickle hocks.

In the front legs, a nicely angled shoulder (in the range of 90 degrees, measured by the angle between the humerus and shoulder blade), sufficient width to the chest and freedom of the elbows will give a horse agility. Good bone in the front legs, straightness (when viewed from the front and side) and correct pastern angles will reduce concussion and contribute to soundness. Avoid the horse who is very upright on his pasterns, or stands back at the knee ("calf-kneed"); this puts added strain on the tendons of the front legs.

The Feet

One of the worst, most frequent and most easily preventable problems is poor hoof angles. A hoof angle that does not match the other angles of the front leg (pastern and shoulder) can destroy the functioning of an otherwise good set of legs. A horse can easily be crippled through poor or neglected farrier work.

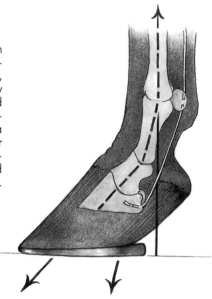

This is a foot we see very commonly on show horses. Note the broken axis between the long and short pastern bone, the run-under heels that don't give any support to the deep flexor tendon and the overly long toe, which creates a disastrously late breakover, putting a great deal of strain on the deep flexor tendon. Shoeing a horse this way predisposes him to navicular disease and constitutes physical abuse of the animal.

The clubfoot is the opposite of the artificial "show horse" foot. Again, we have a broken bone axis, but this time the strain is put onto the extendor tendon. The angulation of the bones allows for almost no shock absorption and all concussion is transferred to the joints, thus predisposing the horse to early arthritic changes.

The clubfoot can be caused by neglect and improper trimming, or it can be the result of injury or heredity.

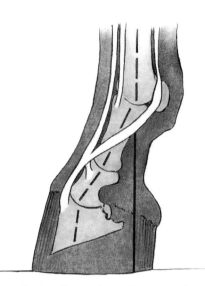

Many back and leg problems (including navicular disease) can be caused by toes that are left too long, by heels that are pushed under and allowed to wear too short or by simply letting the feet grow entirely too long—thus causing a much-too-late breakover at the toe.

Serious damage can also be done to bones and ligaments when borium or very severe studs are applied to shoes to give added traction or to prevent shoes from wearing out. When the foot strikes the ground, it must be able to slip slightly to minimize concussion. The "dead-stop" action of borium or sharp studs means that all the concussion of the unyielding ground is trans-

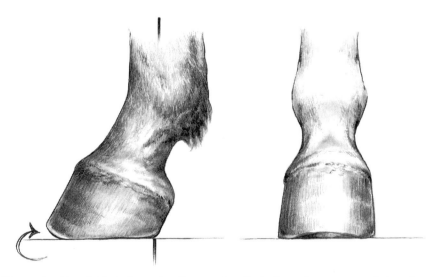

The unshod hoof. Note the naturally worn toe that allows for a very early breakover of the foot. The least possible strain is put onto the deep flexor tendon. Shoeing a horse should come as close as possible to the natural wear of the foot.

A properly balanced and shod hoof. The pastern bones and coffin bone have the same angle, and well-developed heels give plenty of support to the deep flexor tendon. Note, however, the late breakover as compared to the unshod hoof in the preceding illustration. If a horse has a problem with this, the shoe can be rounded up at the toe to simulate the natural breakover.

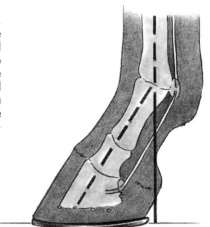

ferred directly to the feet and legs. To prevent unnecessary stress on the deep flexor tendon, a little wear on the toes of the shoes is desirable. The foot needs to break over easily in front as it travels; borium and large studs prevent this.

A better alternative is the "wida" stud. This is a small, round stud made of specially hardened steel. By drilling and tapping four holes in each shoe, and pounding in the wida studs, you will give your horse secure traction on pavement and ice, and the studs still allow for a bit of "slip" to prevent damage to legs and feet.

This foot is unfortunately an everyday sight. Not as severe as the "show horse" foot, it exhibits the same problems of a toe that has grown too far out (note the flair) and a heel that has been allowed to run under. Many farriers do not understand that, when trimming a shod foot, the toe has to be cut back as much as possible to make up for the lack of natural breakover wear. This will mean that as much of the toe has to be rasped off as would occur naturally. Large studs will also prevent any sliding motion as the foot strikes the ground, thus increasing concussion and tearing and inhibiting breakover of the toe even more.

An extremely useful type of horseshoe stud. These are wida studs, made of specially hardened steel; drilled and tapped into the shoe at four points, they provide excellent traction but still allow for slight "slip" when the foot strikes the ground.

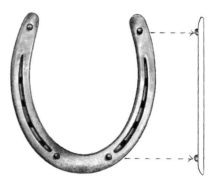

• THE SEARCH FOR THE "PERFECT" HORSE •

It is almost impossible to find a perfectly built horse, but as long as you recognize your horse's shortcomings and understand the need for progressive training, you can use (and transform, to a certain extent) your horse's body to its best advantage—and perhaps end up with an exceptional athlete.

This is what good driving—and dressage—is all about.

CHAPTER

· 3 ·

THE BIT

Many people seem to think that the bit is merely an instrument for braking and steering—to stop the horse or tell him which way to go.

Ideally, the bit serves several purposes, especially in driving, where it is our only constant and direct physical connection with the horse.

• THE PURPOSES OF THE BIT •

The bit is the continuous goal toward which the correctly trained horse is always working. This means that the horse is concerned with nothing else when he is moving forward. He is not making any decisions on his own, but submits completely to what the bit tells him to do. He uses it for direction and support. Through the bit, the driver asks the horse to move more forward, extend the strides, collect and so forth.

The bit determines the length and the shape of the horse's frame—from the long, low frame of the beginning driving horse and the relaxed horse walking on a long rein, right up to the highest possible collection of the advanced driving horse. In other words, it determines the amount of longitudinal flexion and also the degree of lateral flexion (bending) through turns.

Last, though certainly not least, the bit does also tell the horse where to go, at what speed to travel and when to stop.

To serve all these functions, it is vital that the horse trust the bit, be comfortable with it and respect it. To use the bit properly, the driver is required to have educated, sensitive hands and a total understanding of what the different types of bits and various rein actions mean to the horse.

• CHOOSING THE RIGHT BIT •

Every horse is different and therefore no one bit can accommodate all horses. A horse should always be started in the least severe bit possible, however, and he should be given plenty of time in his groundwork to understand the basic actions of the bit. Before he is hitched to any vehicle, the horse must learn the rudiments of longitudinal and lateral bending, and he must learn to steer reliably at the demanded speed. If, for whatever reason, the horse shows no respect for his bit during groundwork, he must not be hitched until the trainer has found a bit that does command the horse's respect as well as his trust. In driving, this is absolutely crucial.

Be sure that your horse's mouth is in good shape before you place a bit in his mouth. Regular attention from an equine dentist is vital (at least once a year; twice a year is even better). If mouth problems develop, check for physical problems before you tackle training corrections.

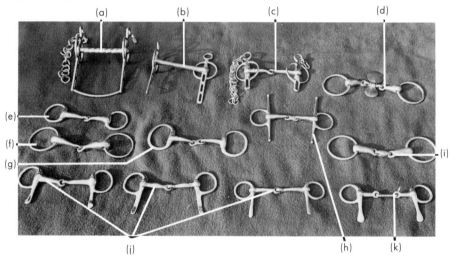

Different driving bits: (a) Fixed-cheek liverpool with a straight-bar mouth and bottom bar. (b) Swivel-cheek liverpool with straight-bar mouth. (c) Single-jointed liverpool with shanks cut off below the first slot. (d) Loose ring spoon snaffle. (e) Single-jointed eggbutt snaffle. (f) Single-jointed loose-ring snaffle. (g) Double-jointed eggbutt snaffle with very short link (our preferred bit). (h) Full-cheek double-jointed snaffle with fairly short link. (i) Loose-ring double-jointed snaffle with thick mouthpiece. (j) Three half-cheek single-jointed snaffles. (k) Half-cheek Dr. Bristol (compare this to the double-jointed snaffles).

The Snaffle Bit

All snaffle bits work by direct action on the corners of the mouth, tongue and bars (gums). Often, however, the specific action of different types of

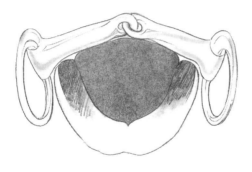

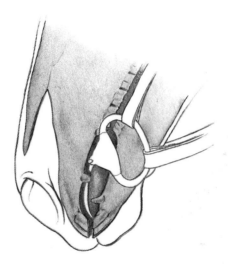

The single-jointed, hollow-mouth snaffle takes up a lot of space in the horse's mouth, and its single joint will very likely hit the horse's palate every time the reins are activated.

snaffles can have very distinct—and sometimes unintended—results.

We have found that the double-jointed, or French-link, snaffle (not a Dr. Bristol) is the best bit for starting a green horse. Many more experienced horses also go very well in this bit. If the horse does not respect the double-jointed snaffle, a broken liverpool bit is often very effective to remind the horse that the piece of metal in his mouth is to be respected. Even so, you should try to go back to the snaffle whenever possible, and we find that after a period of consistent, correct training, most horses can be worked with confidence in the French-link snaffle.

The traditional single-jointed snaffle bit, in all its various forms, has been in use for centuries, but it has several drawbacks. When rein action is

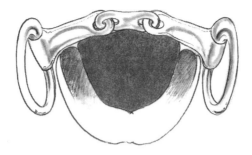

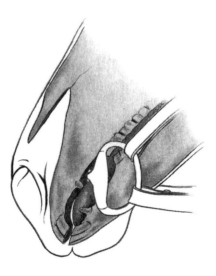

The double-jointed snaffle takes up a lot less space in the mouth, and conforms better to the shape of the horse's mouth. (Note also the position of the bit in relation to the canine teeth.)

applied, the single joint may be pressed against the roof of the horse's mouth, and the two halves of the mouthpiece may press onto the bars. Many horses are very uncomfortable with this "nutcracker action." If the horse tends to get above the bit, throwing his head up and hollowing his back in resistance, the single-jointed snaffle will only worsen this problem.

A double-jointed snaffle, on the other hand, allows the bit to conform to the shape of the horse's palate. This considerably reduces the pressure on the bars. There is no nutcracker action, no matter where the horse places his head.

It is very important that the center link of the mouthpiece be as short as possible (about one inch long) and lie flat on the tongue, not turned back at an angle as in a Dr. Bristol bit. The joints themselves should be quite small and smoothly made. If the centerpiece is longer, the joints are very easily pulled onto the sensitive gums. Large joints may also push up against the roof of the mouth.

A straight-bar or mullen-mouth snaffle does not allow for sensitive, one-sided rein action. Whenever one side of a bar bit is moved, the other side is moved also, usually pressing on the upper part of the gums, thus confusing the horse and causing him to tilt his head or throw it up. Of the two, the mullen-mouth bar bit is definitely better than the straight-bar, as the former does conform somewhat to the shape of the mouth.

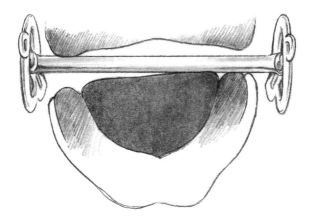

The straight bar bit. When one rein is pulled back, the bit presses on the lower gum on one side of the mouth (in this case, the right side) and touches the upper gum on the opposite side.

A trainer who uses a bar snaffle usually says that his horse has a very busy mouth and this keeps the horse's mouth quieter, because the horse cannot play with it as he can with a jointed snaffle. If the horse is fussing excessively with his bit, there are probably other problems that need to be addressed, and using a bar snaffle won't solve the problems but merely hide them. Also, a horse can take a very firm hold on a straight-bar and really pull against the driver if he wants to.

Another driving bit that has been recommended is the Hungarian double-ring snaffle. We have tried it, but do not see its advantages. With the double rings, there are too many possibilities for the skin at the corners of the mouth to be pinched.

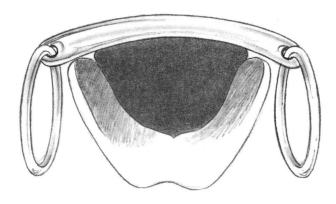

The mullen-mouth bit. This bit adjusts to the shape of the horse's mouth better than the straight bar.

How thick should the mouthpiece be? Although it is true that a bit with a thick mouthpiece is a mild bit—because the pressure is spread over a large surface area in the horse's mouth—many horses just aren't comfortable with a really thick mouthpiece. The smaller breeds, especially, often have very little room in the mouth, and a very thick mouthpiece may even prevent a small-mouthed horse from closing his mouth completely. The majority of horses seem most comfortable with a medium-to-thin double-jointed snaffle.

Always choose an eggbutt snaffle to prevent pinching the corners of the horse's mouth between the mouthpiece and the rings. (A loose-ring snaffle—or any bit with the joint right next to the corner of the mouth—can be made pinch-proof by wrapping the joints in latex.)

The Curb Bit

Any bit that includes leverage in its action is classified as a curb. While the snaffle bit acts only on the horse's tongue and bars, the curb—because of the leverage—applies threefold pressure: on the tongue and bars, on the poll and (by the action of the curb chain) on the lower jaw in the chin groove. The curb can be either a delicate instrument or a tool of torture; there have been cases where the severe use of a strong curb has broken a horse's jaw. (See illustration on page 41.)

Usually a curb bit is used for additional obedience to the bit and the control of speed, and—in an advanced horse—to allow for lighter rein contact in collection. A curb bit should not be used to force a horse into collection, as is unfortunately very widely seen.

There are many different types of curb bits, from mild to extremely severe. Uxeter kimberwickes should be included with the true curb bits because although they are quite mild, they do allow for a light curb action when the reins are attached to the lower slots on the rings. Kimberwickes are also available with a double-jointed mouthpiece, which makes them excellent for the horse that needs just a slightly sharper bit action to command his respect.

On a curb bit, should there be a connecting bar between the shanks or not? This really depends on the individual situation and the temperament of the horse. Generally, if you are driving a pair, the bits should have a connecting bar to prevent catching the cross rein on a bit shank. However, with the connecting bar, there is the chance of the horse catching himself on the tip of the pole or the end of the yoke and becoming really upset. Each driver must decide which arrangement is suitable.

Liverpools: Broken, Straight-Bar and Curved-Bar

The most commonly used curb bit in driving is the straight-bar or broken liverpool. The broken liverpool can—in its lightest adjustment—act like a regular, single-jointed snaffle. When the reins are attached to one of the slots with both reins in action, it performs very much like a regular curb. However, the real advantage of the broken bit is that when only one rein applies pressure, the other side of the bit is not affected. (True curb action occurs only when both reins apply pressure at the same time.) This unilateral-action feature means that it is a very nice bit for horses that need a little sharper control in their ringwork or in obstacle courses.

The disadvantage, again, is that it is a single-jointed bit and can press against the upper palate and the bars like any single-jointed snaffle. Also, when the reins are attached to the slots, the ends of the bit shanks may press against the horse's lower lips, inviting some horses to try to catch the ends of the shanks. (The mouthpiece of a broken liverpool should be a quarter to a half inch wider than other bits, for this reason.)

Some horses may also be annoyed or confused by the bit shanks pressing inward. Using a buxton-style bit with elbow joints eliminates this. Or, you may want to have the bit shanks cut off below the first slot, if you do not use the reins in the lower slots. With shortened shanks, we have had some nice successes in horses that do not respect the snaffle sufficiently, but find the straight-bar liverpool too severe and also dislike having the long shanks below their mouths.

The broken liverpool should not be used constantly (or, even better, not at all) with the reins in the second or third (bottom) slot. The severe leverage applied with the reins in the bottom slot puts a great deal of pressure onto the palate and bars, while pulling the lower bit shanks together in a nutcracker action. If you feel you need even more control with a horse (perhaps while driving on trails or competing on a cross-country course), try the straight- or curved-bar (mullen-mouth) liverpool.

Curbs with Ports

A very low-port mouthpiece is acceptable, and some horses even seem to like it—but we absolutely detest high-port bits as being unnecessarily cruel. Such a port not only squashes the horse's tongue and lets the bit drop down where it works on the sensitive gums, but it can simultaneously apply intolerable pressure to the horse's upper palate.

If a driving horse requires a high-port curb bit for control, do not trust your life to such an animal. Inflicting excessive pain on the horse's mouth does not make a horse safer to drive—instead, it makes him more unpredictable.

The horse certainly does have to respect his bit. Sometimes, this can only be achieved by letting the horse feel a certain amount of pain for a quick moment, to let him know it can hurt when he does not listen to the more friendly bit action. The horse must also learn to trust the bit, however, to like it, to accept it willingly and submit to it because he wants to and not because he is forced to.

If a horse really wants to bolt, no bit in the world will stop him. Only good training and the horse's trust in the driver will make a bit a safe means of control.

How Much Bit Is Enough?

For ringwork, nothing more severe than a broken liverpool, with the reins attached to the first slot, should be necessary. (The double-jointed Kimberwicke may be preferable.) If the horse is consistently ignoring the bit, something is very wrong either with the horse (physically or mentally) or with the training.

Some horses do have the ability to shut off pain totally. With this type of horse, the more pain you apply, the more they resist. You may even see a driving horse with a completely blue tongue—indicating that the blood flow to the tongue has been disrupted and the horse's feeling in that area has been numbed.

If a horse does not respect a bit with mild or moderate curb action, look for the cause before you reach for a sharper bit. Check for physical problems (a sore mouth, back, or shoulders, or perhaps a spavin), and try a milder bit to see if the curb action may already be too severe for him.

A bar bit always causes problems as soon as you ask your horse for turns and bending. Horses often object to the bar bit by rolling their eyes, gaping their mouths and laying back their ears. The horse who bends well in an unjointed bar bit probably has a mouth so well schooled that even the slightest indication of the driver's hands is enough to accomplish the turn— but then, the horse doesn't need a bar bit anyway. It is impossible to use a bar bit properly in bending a horse because rein action on one side of the bit directly affects the opposite side.

Straight-bar liverpools do have their place in driving. They can be very effective in controlling a strong horse on cross-country drives, where the horse is not asked to turn often. In such driving, safety always comes first. The curved bar is milder on the horse than the straight-bar mouthpiece, because the curved (mullen) shape conforms better to the palate, and when one rein is activated the other side of the bit is not as severely pushed up against the horse's gums.

• FITTING A BIT •

The bit must be neither too wide nor too narrow. The mouthpiece should not be visible on either side of the horse's mouth, but the corners of the mouth should not be pulled to the inside, either. Also, it is very important with curb bits that the upper shank (above the mouthpiece, where the cheekpieces of the bridle attach) is wide enough and does not pinch the horse's skin against the upper teeth on each side. Many horses need to have a bit with the upper shanks bent slightly to the outside.

Five-inch-wide bits fit most average-sized horses—but there are many average-sized horses that are not comfortable with five-inch bits. And different bits may require different widths for the same horse.

Fit the bit so that it is comfortable in the corners of the horse's mouth, neither too high nor too low. With a snaffle, look for one to two wrinkles in the corners of the horse's mouth. A curb can be fitted somewhat lower if the horse does not flex easily in the poll (but the mouthpiece must always be at least one finger's width above the canine teeth for a gelding or stallion and the small percentage of mares who also have canine teeth).

Pay particular attention to how close the bit lies to the upper canines, as these extend farther down into the mouth than the lower canines. Some horses have very little space in their mouths for the bit.

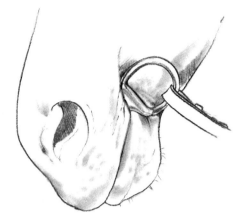

This bit is too narrow; it is pulling the corners of the horse's mouth to the inside.

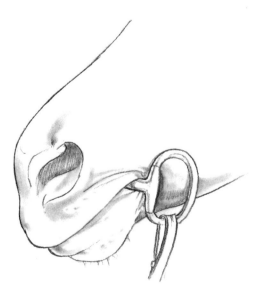

This bit is too wide. Although less aggravating for the horse than too narrow a bit, it will not conform to the mouth as intended.

Wolf teeth, also, may need attention. These small, false molars can seriously interfere with the bit. They can also be easily chipped and broken, leading to pain and infection. Equine dentists recommend that wolf teeth be removed whenever they appear, before they can cause any problems. Because wolf teeth have very shallow roots and are not true molars, they can easily be extracted by a veterinarian or equine dentist.

If your horse has learned the bad habit of putting his tongue over the bit, try adjusting the bit a little higher for a while. This, together with a snug noseband or a flash noseband—and, of course, proper training—should soon help him to forget this habit. It's not a good idea to use bits with rubber lollipops or spoons for this problem, as they tend to make horses even more nervous and mouthy.

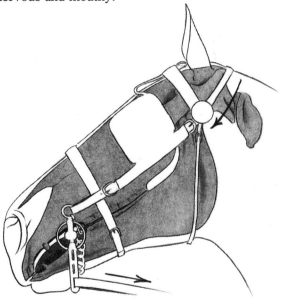

The curb bit applies pressure on the horse's poll, his tongue and bars, and his chin groove. This curb bit has been pulled beyond the 45-degree angle, causing the tongue to be squashed between the bit and the lower jawbone. Circulation can be cut off this way; if this happens, it causes the tongue to appear blue, and the nerves of the mouth go numb.

The Curb Chain

Always be sure the curb chain is turned so that the links lie flat and smooth against the groove of the chin. (For horses with very sensitive chin grooves, add a rubber or leather lining to the curb chain.)

The adjusted length of the curb chain (combined with the length of the bit shanks, from the mouthpiece to where the reins are attached) determines the severity of the curb action. The chain should be adjusted so that when the reins are taken up at moderate pressure, there is an angle of about 45 degrees between the shanks and the horse's mouth. Any shorter adjustment makes the bit intolerably severe; longer adjustments will either make the bit ineffective or pinch the tongue and gums very much like a piece of paper between dull scissors, and possibly cut off feeling.

If your reins are attached at the bit ring, not in the slots on the shanks, the bit will work like a snaffle, and the curb chain has very little or no effect. In this case only, the curb chain can be adjusted tight to keep it from dangling against the horse's chin and annoying him.

Remember: Each time you tighten a curb chain or change to a more severe bit, drive your horse from the ground *before* you hitch him. Find out how he will react before you put yourself or anyone else in jeopardy.

CHAPTER
· 4 ·

FINDING AND FITTING
THE RIGHT HARNESS

Choosing the right harness is vital. It can mean the difference between success and failure in driving. The "right" harness is one that can safely take the stress of driving, fits the horse properly to help him in his job and keeps its strength and value over time.

• NEW OR USED? •

When most people begin to drive, they look for a used harness. They may not be sure their horse will take to driving, and perhaps the investment in a new harness doesn't seem justified. This may work well if you only employ that used harness for groundwork and don't put any real strain on it.

However, when you hitch your horse to the carriage, it's a different story. It is very hard to find a used harness of good quality that has been maintained properly and will also fit your horse. A top-quality used harness in excellent condition won't be much cheaper than a new harness, anyway, because it has retained its value.

Most inexpensive used harnesses are not only inexpensive, they're cheap and dangerous. They are often of poor quality to begin with, or have been stored improperly so that the leather dries out and becomes brittle, or the stitching has rotted from mildew or over-oiling.

Remember that the life and safety of many people and your beloved horses are at stake. You must be certain that your harness is absolutely dependable. There is no excuse for an accident that occurs because of inferior equipment. Driving a horse is risky even under the best of circumstances, and every piece of equipment must be as safe and sturdy as it can be.

This doesn't mean, however, that you have to spend a fortune on a decent harness. Prices will vary, but you can expect to spend $400 to $500 (at 1992 prices) on a good new harness. Anything below this price should be avoided, since it is not possible to make a quality leather harness for less.

Of course, not every harness in this price range will be acceptable, either. Make a point of thoroughly inspecting the harness before you buy it, and be sure you can receive a full refund if it isn't exactly what you expected.

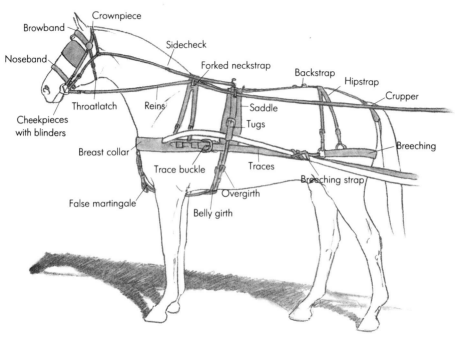

The single harness and driving bridle. This harness is of a good, sturdy weight and has a comfortable gig saddle.

Note, however, how the short sidecheck will inhibit stretch and relaxation of the topline. To avoid bothering the horse, it must be so long that he can fully stretch his neck and lower it to a degree where his nose would be at the same height as his point of shoulder.

What to Look For

First, the harness needs to be sturdy. Forget about the so-called show harnesses that are made only for light ring work. Look instead for a solid "using" harness with fairly heavy leather strapping, especially in the places where there will be a lot of stress, such as the traces, the breeching straps and the belly girth.

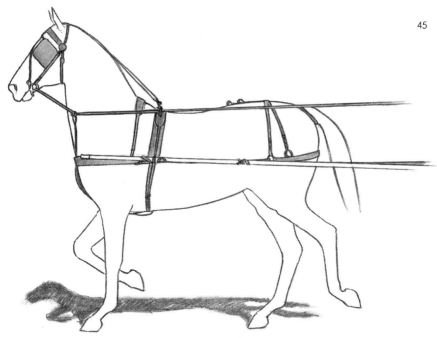

A typical "show harness" with overcheck and martingale. The horse's head and neck are locked into one place, and it is very apparent what damage the overcheck will do to the horse's physical development. The back is completely locked and true hind-end engagement is impossible. The hind legs can move up and down, but not forward. The harness itself would not be suitable for carriage driving, as it is too lightweight throughout.

Next, take a look at the buckles. Flimsy-looking buckles with thin tongues are very likely to give out in a moment of stress. Check the stitching: see if every stress point is thoroughly stitched and back-stitched to lock the threads securely. The thread should be heavy, pulled snugly through the needle holes, and not broken *anywhere*. The stitches should be spaced regularly and fairly close together. Very fine bridlework may have stitches as close as twelve to the inch; this will not be possible on heavier harness leather, but the stitches shouldn't be half an inch apart, either. If the stitching is uneven, irregular, or loose—even to the point where layers of leather are separating before the harness is ever put on the horse—send it back immediately.

It's always a good idea to take a more knowledgeable friend or trainer with you if you aren't sure of your own judgment in buying a harness. Buy only from a reputable harness maker, and don't be afraid to ask questions about the quality, the construction and whether the harness can be returned or altered if it doesn't fit properly.

There are harnesses made from nylon and biothane (a leather look-alike plastic), and these require little maintenance. We still believe, however, that leather is the most comfortable material next to a horse's skin. In cold temperatures, the synthetics often become stiff and difficult to work with.

One last consideration is color. Harnesses come in black or russet, with various types of trim or decorations such as patent leather on the saddle and blinders or a brass chain link on the browband. If you are not interested in showing, the color is unimportant. For shows, however—and for the tradition-minded pleasure driver—you should know that russet harnesses are used with natural-wood vehicles, while black harnesses are correct with painted vehicles or with natural-wood vehicles that have black appointments and trim.

•   WILL IT FIT YOUR HORSE?   •

Harnesses usually come in five sizes: small pony, pony, cob, horse and draft horse. Most harness makers will tell you how to measure your horse to determine the correct size. Use these measurements as guidelines, but until you actually try the harness on your horse, you won't know for sure.

Neck Collar or Breast Collar?

Before you lay out the money for a harness, you'll also have to decide whether it should have a breast collar or neck collar. This decision will be based on cost (the neck collar will always be more expensive), your horse's conformation, the type of vehicle he'll be pulling, and your own personal preference.

Neck Collars • A well-fitting neck collar allows the horse to better thrust his body into the load, and simultaneously gives him more freedom through the shoulders because it sits higher than the breast collar and does not constrict his chest. On the other hand, your horse may have a difficult time becoming happy with the neck collar because it may rub him uncomfortably. And, it is very difficult to get a neck collar that truly fits. Since your horse's neck muscles may change with work, the neck collar that fit him last year may not fit him now. And it probably won't fit any other horses in your barn, either—each will have to have his own.

How can you tell if a neck collar fits? A collar of the right size, when it is pressed or drawn strongly back against the shoulders, fits snugly enough against the side of the neck so that only the fingers, held flat, can be passed between the rim of the collar and the horse's neck. If there is too much space, the collar will press unevenly against the edge of the shoulder,

A properly fitted neck collar.

instead of distributing pressure along the neck and shoulder. This may be severe enough to cause a sore on the front edge of the shoulder. If the collar is too tight against the neck, it can restrict the circulation to the muscles, and can make some horses nervous with apparent claustrophobia.

The length of the neck collar (top to bottom) is right when a flat hand fits comfortably between the collar and the horse's windpipe. (Measured with a ruler, this space would be about two inches.) The correct length is very important. If the collar is too short, it can choke the horse under a heavy load, and it also moves the point of draft too high, possibly causing sores high up on the shoulders. Too long a collar will bring the point of draft too low and too near the point of the shoulder, which will sore the horse very quickly since it causes constant friction.

The collar should also be snug at the top where it rests on the neck. "Snug" means that there should be enough space on the sides to run the fingers clear to the collar cap at the top of the collar, but no more. Collars that are too narrow at the top will pinch the neck and chafe it, causing sores

This neck collar is too large, with too much space at the sides and bottom. It will rock on the horse's neck when he is pulling, and will chafe.

on the sides near the top. If the collar is too wide at the top, it will work from side to side, chafing the top of the neck.

The height adjustment of the hames can also have a major impact on the fit of the collar and the comfort of the horse. If the hames do not fit the collar and fall together with the true point of the draft, they can also cause sore shoulders.

Fitting a collar properly can be a complex task and is not a job for a beginner. It can also be difficult to locate a collar that fits your horse's particular shoulder and neck shape. One method of locating the right collar is to try on as many used collars as possible, find one that fits and then have that one reworked with new padding, stitching or whatever is needed to make it serviceable.

Too tight a neck collar; it isn't resting on the horse's shoulder and doesn't allow space for the windpipe.

Breast Collars ● The breast collar is less expensive and simpler to fit than the neck collar, but there are several points to remember to ensure your safety and the horse's comfort.

The breast collar should be at least two inches wide for ponies and smaller horses, and three to four inches wide for larger breeds, but it should never exceed four inches in width for any horse. If it is too narrow, the pulling pressure is spread over too small a surface area and it will cut into the horse's skin and muscles; if it is too wide, it will not allow enough space on the horse's chest to clear the point of the shoulder.

Be sure that the edge facing upward is nicely rounded and smooth, so it won't cut the horse. Cheap collars are sometimes made from a single, unfinished, rough-edged piece of leather. This can be very sharp.

Whether the traces are stitched directly to the breast collar or buckled on does not make much difference as long as the attachment is secure. The buckles, if there are any, must be sturdy, and the stitching must be strong and even. (Buckles in the traces do allow for more precise adjustment, since the holes for buckles at the collar end are spaced about two inches apart, while the holes at the singletree end of nonremovable traces are usually four inches apart—which may not accommodate the right distance from horse to carriage.)

Padding a breast collar is a very good idea, especially if the collar is made from fairly hard leather or if any rough stitching or wrinkles in a soft leather collar might chafe against the neck and shoulders.

The breast collar should be held in place with a neckstrap that offers a good width on top of the neck. The neckstrap should fork to provide two straps on either side, which prevents the breast collar from drooping down in the front. The rein terrets on the neck strap should be far enough apart (about ten inches) so there is not a severe break in the line of the reins as they run back to the saddle.

Conformation Considerations

Horses whose necks set on very low to the chest and shoulders may definitely benefit from the use of a neck collar instead of a breast collar. If the neck attaches to the body at the height of the point of shoulder, there is really no room for a breast collar. Either the breast collar will interfere with the horse's windpipe, or it will sit right on the points of the shoulders, which is also unacceptable because this greatly restricts the horse's movement. The higher the breast collar can be placed on the chest (without restricting the windpipe), the more shoulder freedom it allows the horse.

Some harnesses have curved breast collars, which may solve this problem, at least in part, because the downward curve at the front of the breast collar allows space for the windpipe. You can then set the collar itself higher on the shoulders. See an example of this on page 168.

You must take care that a curved breast collar is only used with a carriage that has a singletree with plenty of sideways movement. If the singletree has only a little play, the breast collar may move from side to side on the horse's chest with every step and will definitely be pulled to the side on the turns. A curved breast collar will cause the horse far more discomfort than a straight breast collar if the singletree action is restricted.

Some harnesses come with a "false martingale," a leather strap that runs from the bottom center of the breast collar, between the horse's front legs, to the belly girth. Its purpose is to keep the breast collar from slipping upwards. (See illustration on page 44.) It isn't really necessary in single driving, but false martingales are helpful in pair driving since the horse is hitched directly from the collar to the carriage. A false martingale does help to keep the collar of a pair harness from sliding up the horse's neck, especially if the pair harness is used without a breeching.

If you do use a false martingale to keep the collar in place, however, there is one problem: If it is tight enough to keep the collar down, it might also pull the belly girth too far forward, thus causing the girth to interfere with or chafe the elbows or elbow groove. Don't use a false martingale unless you feel the benefits outweigh the drawbacks.

This is a closeup of the harness seen in the illustration at the bottom of page 65. It has a wide, comfortable gig saddle. However, the overgirth that holds the tugs in place has slid off the belly girth and is in danger of pinching soft skin behind and below the elbow. The breeching is definitely too low, and will pull the horse's legs underneath him when he attempts to stop the cart.

The Saddle

As you examine a harness, check the construction of the saddle. Be sure the harness you purchase has a saddle with a stiff tree (unless you have a horse with absolutely no withers). We so often see saddles without trees

This shows how the short saddle of a medium-weight harness can press into the horse's back. (Compare this to the gig harness saddle in the previous illustration.) This needs padding.

lying right down on the horse's spine, and all of the shifting weight and the bouncing of the cart are transferred directly to the spine instead of being absorbed by the muscles on either side of the spine. In riding, we would never think of using a saddle that hits the horse's withers. It is a great failing that driving people (and especially harness makers) pay so little attention to this.

If a horse carries absolutely no weight on his back except for the weight of the shafts (as when he is pulling a four-wheel carriage), this is not as critical a consideration as when he is pulling a two-wheel cart, with the weight of the cart and driver resting right on his spine. This is why the most expensive two-wheel-gig harnesses feature such beautiful, wide, long, padded and tufted saddles.

Regular driving harnesses often come with a short saddle that—even with a stiff tree—does not always fit a horse's back properly and may need ample padding. The fleece saddle pads designed for this purpose may not be enough, either, especially on a long drive. A piece of soft blanket, carefully folded under the saddle, will do the job and protect your horse's back.

The Girth, Backstrap and Crupper

The belly girth should be sufficiently wide (at least two inches) to spread out its pressure and avoid cutting into the skin behind the front legs. Be sure that when the girth is tightened the buckles do not interfere with the horse's elbows, especially when either front leg is at its farthest back position. This can sometimes be a problem with the more expensive harnesses, since their girths are often elaborately worked, with many keepers and extra thicknesses of leather right behind the elbows.

Riders are always very concerned with the fit and the thickness of the girth on their horses. Many riding girths are shaped to avoid interfering with the elbows or pinching the loose skin in that area. Drivers should pay just as much attention to this as do riders.

If you are not sure whether your horse is bothered by his belly girth, have someone lead him while you walk beside him. Place your hand on the girth just below his elbow. You can easily feel if there is interference with the elbow.

Another problem can occur with the overgirth, which keeps the tugs snug. It is generally attached loosely to the belly girth, and it can sometimes slip off just enough to pinch the skin on the bottom of the belly. (See illustration on page 51.) The overgirth should be tight enough to steady the shafts, but it should not be so tight that it pulls the shafts together or transmits all of the motions of the shafts to the horse.

On some harnesses, usually the ones sold without breeching and intended for light show ring work, the tugs have no attached straps and are held down by a long, narrow leather strap that is loosely attached to the belly girth. This strap is designed to be wrapped several times around the shaft.

When it is used without breeching, this arrangement puts all the pressure of the cart directly on the saddle during braking and on a downhill slope. The movement of the carriage also pulls this tug-and-wrap strap arrangement into the horse's elbow groove. This is a totally unsatisfactory arrangement for carriage driving.

But even when it is used with breeching, a wrap strap can bother the horse. In case of a sudden stop or on a steep downhill grade, the shafts cannot slide in the tugs and the breeching cannot be adjusted tight enough to prevent at least some pressure on the saddle.

The backstrap should be attached so that it does not exert constant pressure onto the crupper and pull the saddle backwards, but it also should not be so loose that it lies slackly on the horse's back with the crupper dangling loosely below the dock of the tail.

The crupper should be snug but comfortable under the tail. Be sure there are no rough edges or wrinkles where it lies against the horse's sensitive skin. (If it is rough or uneven, it must be padded with some soft, wrinkle-free material such as doeskin or chamois. Also, make sure that there are absolutely no tail hairs caught between the skin and the crupper when you adjust it.) At least one buckle in the crupper-backstrap attachment is recommended for ease of harnessing and unharnessing.

The Breeching

The breeching is a vital component of a harness. Your safety depends on it. If the breeching breaks for whatever reason, and the cart hits the horse in the rear, disaster can occur.

Thimbles (thin straps that run from the saddle to little cups that slip over the ends of the shafts) are absolutely unacceptable. They are an unsafe alternative to breeching and are dangerous. In case of an abrupt stop or steep downgrade, they might simply break. Thimbles also put all the weight of the cart onto the saddle and possibly the horse's spine below the saddle. See page 72 for an example of this (and other problems with a less-than-ideal harness and hitch).

Good breeching is sturdy and properly adjusted. The correct position of the breeching on the horse's body is about one hand below the buttocks, where there is hardly any movement in the horse's leg. The illustration on page 44 shows a correctly adjusted breeching. If it is fixed higher, it may creep up under the horse's tail and cause him to panic; if adjusted lower, it pushes the horse's hind legs forward underneath him at the moment that he must hold up the cart's weight. This is especially bad on a downhill slope. Besides interfering with his job, it is very annoying to him—and it may be dangerous. Also, if the breeching is adjusted too low and you ask your horse to back up, he may very well become extremely upset, because it is very hard for him to move his legs against this unnecessary restriction. The photograph on page 51 shows an example of this.

The strap that holds up the breeching should fork into two pieces on either side to prevent it from drooping down behind. The proper length of this strap is also important. If it is too long, the breeching will always hang too loose and too low; if it is too short, the breeching won't lie flat on top of the croup, and it will exert a constant pressure on the backstrap. (See Chapter 8 for a detailed discussion of fitting and attaching the breeching.)

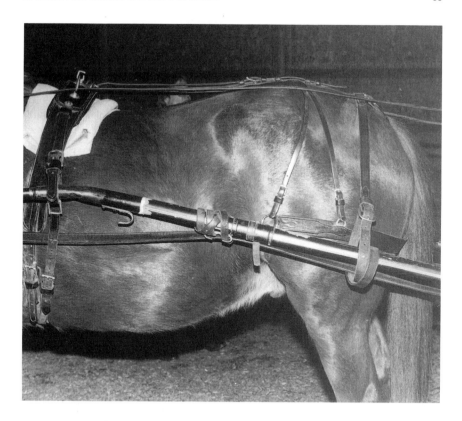

The adjustment of the kicking strap.

The Kicking Strap

One very useful and important piece of equipment (not normally sold as part of a harness) is the kicking strap. This is a strong piece of leather that is looped around one shaft, run over the horse's rump between the back-strap and crupper, and looped around the other shaft to prevent the horse from kicking up or bucking. Your crupper needs to have two buckle attachments to attach a kicking strap.

The kicking strap should be adjusted loosely enough so that it doesn't hinder the horse's normal movements, but tight enough to keep the horse's hindquarters from lifting. Whenever the horse tries to kick up, he pushes up against the kicking strap and is unable to lift his hindquarters any farther. This will usually discourage a green horse (or an older horse with bad habits) from trying to kick or buck again—especially if he is scolded verbally or spanked sharply with the whip at the same time.

Every novice driver should use a kicking strap while he learns to drive, as inexperienced drivers can easily confuse even a schooled horse and possibly induce a kick. And every young horse should wear a kicking strap, just in case he gets the urge to misbehave. The kicking strap can prevent a nasty accident that may occur when a horse kicks a hind leg over a shaft. If this happens, he can break a shaft and get hurt by the broken pieces, or panic and bolt.

The Driving Bridle

The Headstall ● The headstall seems to be rather an afterthought of harness makers. Many, many driving bridles—even those seen in top competition—are constructed with the blinder braces too short. The blinders then touch the horse's eyes or eyelashes. This is distracting, unnecessary and possibly dangerous. There is no reason for blinders and braces to be constructed this way.

If your driving horse really is spooky and distracted by everything behind him (and the general rule is "The less he sees, the better"), then be sure the blinders restrict his vision behind, *but don't let them touch his eyes.* We have found that most horses are much happier with a larger field of vision because they are able to see what they are doing around turns and obstacles.

The blinder height should be adjusted so that the middle of the cup lies beside the eye. Some trainers will advise you to place the blinder somewhat lower, so that the upper third of the blinder is next to the eye, but we have found that some horses will try to raise their heads so they can look backwards over the top of the blinder.

The shape of the cups—square, oval, round—is a matter of preference and does not affect their purpose or effectiveness.

For cross-country work, the best blinders are those called workhorse blinders, which allow the horse to see to the side and downward/backwards, but not straight backwards.

After you have adjusted the blinders, check to be sure that the ears are not hindered in their free swivel movement. There are curved crownpieces available that accommodate the ears nicely. These also work well for ponies with thick manes and small ears. (It can be very hard to keep a bridle on such a pony, and proper fit is crucial.)

If the browband is too short and pulls the crownpiece forward, this can also pinch the ears. A too-long browband will look awkward on the horse's forehead.

The throatlatch on a driving bridle should be fastened somewhat tighter than on a riding bridle, but not so tight that the horse's breathing is restricted when he flexes his poll. See page 168 for a too-tight throatlatch.

The Reins • The reins are about the only pieces of a harness that cannot cause direct discomfort to the horse by rubbing on him; however, it is still vital that you check them for sturdiness and safety.

Be sure all stitching is secure, especially where the rein lengths are pieced together. There should be a generous overlap of these pieces.

The buckles at the bit end should be sturdy with strong tongues, and the leather should look very "healthy." It should be of equal thickness and be pliable; reject any reins that are dry, cracked or worn thin.

The width of the reins is strictly a matter of preference. If you have large hands, you will probably feel more comfortable with a wider rein; if your hands are small, a rein three-quarters of an inch wide should work well for you.

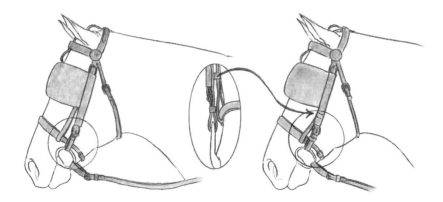

On the left: The raised noseband without a connection to the cheekpiece. There is a danger of the reins pulling the cheekpiece and blinder far enough away to allow the horse to look backwards, possibly frightening him.

On the right: A keeper connects the noseband with the cheekpiece. In our opinion, this is the best noseband solution.

Nosebands • There are many different kinds of nosebands, and they can be attached to the bridle in various ways. The best noseband attachment doesn't run through the cheekpieces of the bridle, but instead hangs on its own headstall. The noseband headstall then attaches to the regular bridle cheekpieces at its upper buckle, with a keeper farther down to hold the bridle cheekpieces and noseband headstall together. With this arrangement, the noseband fulfills its function of keeping the bridle from being

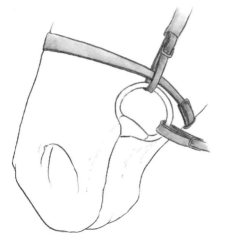

Here the noseband simply runs through the cheekpiece. It is an acceptable arrangement as long as the noseband does not have to be adjusted very tightly, as with a horse that likes to put his tongue over the bit. If there were enough space, a keeper could be added below the noseband to keep the noseband in a more stable position.

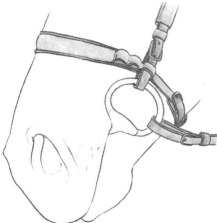

Here the cheekpiece runs through a loop of the noseband. This is an acceptable style when used with a curb bit. However, as shown here with a snaffle bit, it can have disastrous results. When a horse gets strong, lots of bit action backwards will be necessary. This noseband, however, limits the amount the bit can be pulled backwards—which means that the horse is then held back merely by the noseband.

pulled away from the horse's face, but the noseband itself doesn't create any unnecessary pressure points or interfere with the bit.

A noseband that runs through the bottom loop of the bridle cheekpiece just above the bit may squeeze the horse's cheeks inward against his teeth and cause discomfort.

Another type of attachment runs the cheekpiece through keepers on the noseband; this can create unnecessary bulk near the bit, especially on horses with small heads, and it can also limit the action of the bit (particularly if used with a snaffle bit).

We ran into trouble once on a group drive with our pair of pintos. They became rather strong, and suddenly it felt as if we were simply pulling on a log—very unusual for this pair. After the drive, we studied the bridle arrangement and realized that because the cheekpieces ran through the keepers on the noseband, there was very little bit action. This was fine for regular work, but when they became overeager and more control was required, we were simply putting pressure on the noseband when we tried to slow them down.

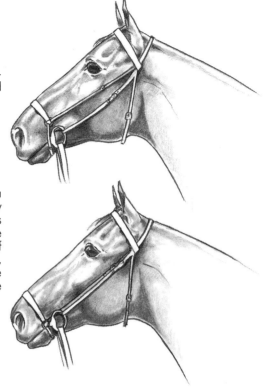

A properly adjusted dropped nose-band. It does not inhibit breathing, and it does not interfere with the bit.

A dropped noseband with too long a nosepiece. This causes it to rest too low on the nose. In this position, the horse's breathing is impaired and his skin will be pinched between the bit and the ring of the noseband. If adjusted any higher, the noseband ring would sit right on the bit ring, which would interfere with the action of the bit.

Recently, flash nosebands have become very popular for driving horses. Unfortunately, many people do not understand the proper use and adjustment of the flash noseband. The flash noseband is an alternative to the dropped noseband; both are designed to fit below the bit, to keep the horse from opening his mouth too far and evading the action of the bit.

Properly adjusted, the flash noseband is more humane and effective than the dropped noseband. The dropped noseband can never be closed snugly enough to be completely effective, since it sits too low on the horse's nose and inhibits breathing.

Another shortcoming of the dropped noseband is that because of the short distance from the noseband rings to the bit, it seems to jam the bit more into the corners of the horse's mouth than the flash noseband does. And, since the dropped noseband cannot be connected to the cheekpieces of the driving bridle, it does nothing to keep the bridle in place. With a dropped noseband, there is always the danger of pulling the cheekpieces and blinders off the horse's head; the standard noseband is designed to help prevent this.

For all these reasons, the flash noseband is a better choice than the dropped noseband if you have a horse that *temporarily* requires the use of this additional aid. By "temporarily" we mean a few months to perhaps two years at the most. If a horse still tries to open his mouth and evade the bit after two years of correct work with the flash noseband, there is definitely something wrong with either his physical condition or with his training.

Before we apply any kind of tight noseband, we must first analyze exactly why the horse is fussing and persists in opening his mouth. There are many reasons, and the most common are:

- Tooth problems such as wolf teeth, growth of a new tooth or sharp protrusions that need floating.

- A poor-fitting bit, or one that is too severe. Or, the driver's hands may be too restrictive.

- Pain in the horse's body. Back problems are frequently expressed through a fussy mouth.

Opening the mouth, putting the tongue over the bit, hanging the tongue out or grinding the teeth are usually symptoms of discomfort or pain. Once in a while, the fussy mouth is simply due to the horse's disposition. These are the horses that really benefit from a tight or flash noseband, and if this problem is not corrected early in their training, they can form terrible and sometimes irreversible bad habits.

If you have ruled out every possible source of discomfort and you are sure you are dealing with a playful, nervous, previously spoiled, or young and inexperienced horse, the flash noseband is of great value to teach him to keep his mouth closed and accept the bit.

To fit the flash noseband correctly, be sure that the raised noseband is adjusted as high as possible (no more than one or two fingers' width below the cheekbones) and that it is tight. If you have a horse that puts his tongue over the bit, you should not even be able to fit a finger between the noseband and the jaw. If the noseband is properly constructed—at least one inch wide, and lined or made of comfortable leather—it will not hurt the horse. Be sure the buckle does not press onto the jawbone. (Be aware that a young horse growing a new molar may object to a tight raised noseband. If this is the case, you must make allowances with the fit of the noseband until the tooth is completely grown in.)

This is a correctly placed flash nose-band. The raised noseband is set as high as possible without pressing onto the cheekbones, and it is snug enough to prevent any drooping. This keeps the flash noseband well above the soft part of the nostrils, and it does not inhibit breathing in any way. The buckle of the flash is placed where it can't pinch the soft skin near the bit or chafe the jaw in the chin groove.

This tight raised noseband will help considerably to keep the horse from opening his mouth wide. In many cases, this is sufficient. If you still think you need a flash attachment, be sure to use one that has a very short connecting strap. If the connecting strap is too long, it will allow the flash attachment to sit too low on the nose, no matter how well you adjust the raised noseband. With a correct short attachment, you can make the flash as snug as necessary without doing any harm to the horse, since the flash will run along a bony part of the horse's nose and not interfere with breathing.

This flash noseband connection is correct but the raised noseband is too low, so the flash noseband is still too low and inhibits breathing.

When you tighten the flash noseband, be sure the buckle does not interfere in any way with the bit or rest directly on hard bone. Adjust the flash so that the buckle rests either in the chin groove or above a nostril, and does not pinch or rest directly on a bony protrusion.

If the raised noseband is not tight enough or high enough, or the flash is connected to it with a long, buckle-in strap, there will be disastrous results.

This flash noseband is adjusted much too low. If it is buckled tight it will drastically inhibit breathing; if it is left loose, it will simply fall off. The raised noseband is drooping down because it is too loose and the buckle-on strap between the two nosebands is too long.

The flash will drop too low into the fleshy part of the nose, and if it is adjusted tight enough to prevent it from simply falling off, it will cut into the soft part of the nose, dramatically impairing the horse's breathing. More than once we have seen horses on the marathon course, nostrils flared to the breaking point and cut in half by a too-low flash noseband, expressions of panic on their faces. There is no excuse for treating any horse this way. Under these terrible conditions, the flash noseband is no longer the useful tool it was designed to be, but has been transformed into something even worse than any maladjusted dropped noseband.

Even when the flash is adjusted correctly, some horses will find it more of a bother than a help. Horses who produce excessive saliva, in particular, may become very nervous and fussy because of all the moisture that is produced. They may become extremely itchy and try to rub their mouths wherever possible, which can be very annoying as well as dangerous.

Before you put a flash noseband on your driving horse, first consider if it is really necessary. If you decide it *is* needed, take the trouble to ensure that it is correctly attached and adjusted. And when you no longer need it, take it off.

Checkreins

These are discussed at greater length in Chapter 6; all we say here is that they should not be part of a harness at all. Checkreins can create a great deal of discomfort and destroy whatever correct training a horse has had.

The only possible justification for a checkrein is on a horse that persistently attempts to eat grass while he is being driven. This, however, indicates a failure of discipline, which can be corrected by proper ground training.

• CARE OF YOUR HARNESS •

Harnesses should be cleaned regularly, but too much oiling can rot the stitching and weaken the leather.

Good harness care does not have to consume a great deal of time. After each use, clean the bit with a damp towel or sponge, and use another damp towel to remove any mud or caked-on sweat, especially from the belly girth, breeching and collar. A light application of saddle soap once a month will keep the harness supple; save the neatsfoot oil for the times when you've been caught in the rain or your harness has taken a real bath in a river. And when you do feel you need to use oil, apply it with a light touch and wipe off any excess.

If your harness is nylon or biothane, follow the manufacturer's instructions for cleaning. Every time you use or clean your harness, check it carefully for loose stitches or weak spots—and promptly make any necessary repairs or replacements.

Once you have found the right harness, you can turn your attention to the perfect vehicle.

CHAPTER
· 5 ·

CHOOSING THE
RIGHT CARRIAGE

When you go looking for a vehicle, it is very tempting to buy one of those pretty old carriages—either because it seems like a really good deal, or just because you've fallen in love with it.

You could be lucky. Without really being aware of what you are doing, you could get a useful, suitable vehicle. More likely, however, you will end up with something that is too large or too small for your horse, or is not in good repair.

WHY THE FIRST VEHICLE SHOULD BE A TWO-WHEELED CART

The first question you must answer is: two-wheel or four-wheel?

A two-wheeled vehicle is nearly always more suitable for a green horse and/or beginning driver. If the horse does something unexpected, the four-wheeled carriage is more likely to tip over, especially if the horse backs up at the same time; a four-wheeled carriage jackknifes very easily.

If you drive into a ditch or across a severe slope, the four-wheeled vehicle will turn over far easier than a two-wheeled cart, since the former is longer and gives the horse less leverage to help hold it up. A four-wheeled carriage also tends to be heavier than a two-wheeled cart.

On the positive side, the four-wheeled carriage is more pleasant for the horse, because it does not force him to carry the weight of it as a two-wheeled cart does.

Safety, however, outweighs comfort. For a first vehicle, purchase a sturdy two-wheeled cart. Wait until you and your horse are experienced before you tackle a four-wheeled vehicle.

This driver is sitting so low that he can't look over the back of his horse, but has to peer around the sides instead. The horse shows some tension in the lower neck, but appears to be otherwise relaxed and preparing nicely for a sharp turn to the right. The bridle should have a noseband; the breeching has dropped a little low. The harness is lightweight, but appropriate for the weight of the cart; however, wirewheeled vehicles are usually not allowed in pleasure shows. And the driver should remember to pick up his whip before he goes into the ring!

A lovely turnout. The driver would be able to see over her horse more easily if she could sit a little higher, which would be a definite advantage in a dressage or obstacles class. The sidecheck is adjusted quite long, but it will still prohibit a free, forward walk.

There are lots of options in the two-wheeled cart group. You can buy a light, wire-wheeled sulky-type cart, a meadowbrook high-wheeled cart, a gig, or any number of antique styles (such as a tub cart or governess cart).

Generally, steer clear of the antique carts. If you find one in really good condition, it will probably be very expensive. If it needs restoration, you will most likely spend a good deal of money on it—and you'll still have an old cart. Certainly, if you are starting a young or green driving horse, you need to have peace of mind regarding your equipment. Your cart should be solid and sturdy, and you should not worry about its surviving those sudden stops or the accidental collision with a big rock at the side of the road.

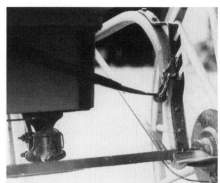

The seat height and weight distribution of this carriage can be adjusted by moving the shackles to one of three different slots, allowing it to accommodate horses from 14.2 to 16.2 hands. This picture shows the shackle set in the middle slot. (This is the same carriage shown in the illustrations on pages 200 through 223.)

Wire-wheeled carts with pneumatic tires are fine for ring work, since they are light and comfortable, but they are very dangerous for trail work. We have twice had a tire blow out on the trails, and this is not an enjoyable experience. Some horses absolutely do not like this sound! Of course, a blowout is most likely to occur far from home, so you can enjoy your walk home next to your horse.

If you plan to drive on the trails and dirt roads, choose something with sturdy wooden wheels and a solid, hard-rubber running surface on the rims.

Different carts will place you at different heights above your horse. You want to sit fairly high so you can have an unobstructed view of the ground in front of your horse—but if the seat is very high, the cart may tip easily on uneven ground.

The seat of a meadowbrook cart is fairly low (even though the height of the wheels may make it appear high), and you will find yourself constantly peering to either side of your horse to check for holes, rough ground, and obstacles. This can be dangerous. Meadowbrooks also tend to be rather heavy and uncomfortable for both horse and driver.

At the other extreme is the gig cart, which allows you to sit very high over your horse and gives you good visibility, but the height of the seat means the gig is less stable, with a higher center of gravity.

The best sort of cart is halfway between a meadowbrook and a gig. (Our road cart, shown in photographs in Chapters 11, 12 and 13, is a good example of this.) You may even be able to find a cart with an adjustable seat height. And for a truly sturdy, useful, inelegant all-purpose cart, you may want to take a standard breaking cart to a welder or carpenter and have the seat raised onto a platform to bring it to exactly the best height.

• FITTING THE CART TO THE HORSE •

Carts, like harnesses, usually come in five sizes: small pony, pony, cob, horse, draft horse. The main difference between the sizes is usually gauged by the diameter of the wheels, and by the length and width of the shafts.

The best way to find a cart that fits is to try as many as you can find (using someone else's well-schooled horse, if yours isn't well trained to drive yet!) and then locate something similar for sale. Take along a tape measure when you go cart hunting, because something that "looks about right" can prove to be very wrong when you finally hitch up. Carefully measure any cart that fits well with a horse similar in size, shape and conformation to your own.

Crucial Measurements
Here are some factors to consider when you measure a cart:

1. You know the height of the cart is right for your horse if, when two people are sitting in it and the horse is properly hitched, the seat is level and there is just a little weight in the tugs. If it feels like there is more than five pounds resting in each tug—or if the seat slopes forward, and raising the shafts a little by raising the tugs on the horse doesn't solve this problem—then the cart sits too high. This means that the shafts are set too high for that particular horse.

If there seems to be no weight in the tugs at all, and the shafts float up or hit the top of the tugs and the seat slopes backward—and lowering the shafts a little on the horse doesn't remedy this problem—then the cart sits too low for that horse.

Remember that the height of the seat or body of the cart is independent of the height of the shafts.

When you find a cart that seems to balance well for a horse of the same size and general shape as yours, get out your measuring tape and note the distance from the ground to the height of the shafts (when level); from the ground to where the shafts attach to the singletree; from outside hub to outside hub (the width); and from the ground to the hub of the wheel.

2. Are the shafts the right length? The shafts are right when the horse is neither too close nor too far away from the cart. The horse's tail should be 12 to 18 inches in front of the dashboard when he is moving forward, and slightly farther away when he is standing still (with his tail hanging straight down). The tips of the shafts should end at the point of the horse's shoulder.

The best shafts are those that bend downward and outward, beginning at the height of the tugs. With these curved shafts, there is no danger of the horse getting hit by the points of the shafts in turns. Some horses really hate to hit the shafts and will do everything possible to keep themselves away from them. (Usually, stock-made carts do not come with these nicely bending shafts, and they must be special-ordered from a carriage maker.)

Measure the length of the shafts from singletree to tips. It might be a good idea to draw a rough sketch of curved shafts, also, if you find a pair you like.

3. Consider the width of the shafts. Remember that we will ask our horse to bend through his turns, to maintain his balance, and to carry his hind legs properly under his body. If the shafts are not wide enough, he won't be able to bend. This is particularly important for ring work, where you will be asking for good bend through the corners and circles.

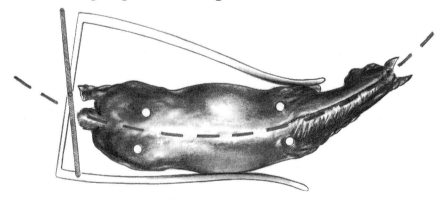

Wide enough shafts, plus plenty of movement in the singletree, allow for a correct bend through the turn. Note that the inside hind leg is tracking toward the inside front leg.

A horse that bends properly will conform his entire spine, from poll to tail, to the line of the track he is following. This means that the outside of his body becomes longer and the inside becomes shorter to accommodate the bend. Between shafts, the horse's inside shoulder must move closer to the inside shaft, while the outside of his barrel and hind end move closer to the outside shaft.

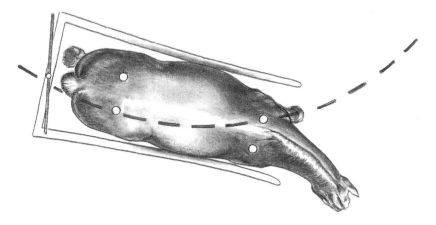

Too-narrow shafts and a too-limited movement of the singletree prohibit the correct bend. The horse is looking sharply to the outside and is falling badly over the inside shoulder; his inside hind leg is not tracking toward the inside front leg.

Although the shafts can pivot on the carriage, they always travel just a little behind the position of the horse—and, of course, the shafts themselves do not bend. The horse can bend only if the shafts are wide enough to allow him to move his barrel and hind end toward the outside. If the shafts are too narrow, he must travel with his inside hind foot farther to the inside, no longer stepping underneath himself, and giving up the correct bend. (See Chapter 10, The Lateral Bend.)

The best way to determine how wide the shafts should be is to drive an experienced horse in the ring, asking for a few 20-meter circles and watching how the horse handles himself through the circles and turns. If he seems to be restricted by the width of the shafts, if his outside hindquarters continually bump the outside shaft, or if he is unable to follow the arc of the turn properly, you will know that the shafts are too narrow. (You don't want the horse "swimming" in the shafts, either, since too-wide shafts are likely to catch on obstacles and are more difficult to fasten securely to the tugs.)

When you find shafts that are suitable, measure them and take notes.

An additional problem can be caused by too-limited movement of the

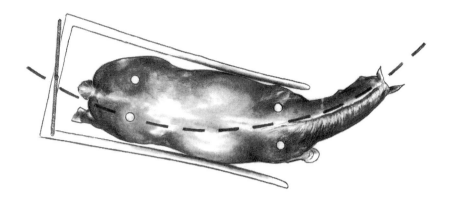

Another possible problem caused by too-narrow shafts and too-limited movement of the singletree: At first glance, this horse appears to bend, but his back
remains straight because of the lack of space. His neck is overbent to the inside,
causing him to fall over his outside shoulder. This can be a very dangerous
situation, especially in an enclosed area. The more the driver pulls on the inside
rein to keep the horse on the line, the more the horse can keep drifting to the
outside. In a fenced-in area, the horse will inevitably hit the fence.

singletree. Even if the shafts are sufficiently wide, the horse will not be
able to lengthen his outside trace sufficiently to achieve the bend if the
singletree can't pivot enough. This, in turn, will limit his shoulder movement.

4. Every vehicle, no matter how small, should be equipped with a brake.
This is a basic safety device and is discussed at length later in this chapter.

•   FOUR-WHEELED CARRIAGES   •

When you and your horse are both comfortable and confident with a two-
wheeled vehicle, you may want to move on to a four-wheeled carriage.

The first consideration is the weight of the vehicle. Four-wheeled carriages are generally heavier, and often have seating space for extra passengers. Take all of this into account when you try out carriages and be
sure you don't overload your horse.

Look for a carriage with a fifth wheel. With this type of carriage, the front
and back axles are not directly connected. The fifth wheel is a horizontal
"wheel" located on the front axle; it allows the front axle to pivot in a
complete 360-degree turn and is the safest type of four-wheeled vehicle.

If you cannot find a suitable carriage with a fifth wheel, at least find one

A fifth-wheel vehicle. The undercarriage in the front can be completely rotated on the fifth wheel, thus allowing for the tightest possible turns during driving. The horses can be literally beside the carriage, without upsetting it.

A cut-under vehicle that allows for quite a safe turning radius.

A farm wagon with a very limited turning radius. Note the mechanical brake.

that is cut under. In a cut-under carriage, there is no fifth wheel. The front and back axles are connected by a "tree" running from front to back under the body of the carriage, but the body is cut out on either side of the front axle so the front wheels can turn almost a full 90 degrees before they strike the tree.

A cut-under carriage is not recommended for an inexperienced driver, but it is still far safer than a vehicle on which the front wheels can't turn under the body at all. The worst type of carriage allows the front wheels to turn on only a limited arc before they strike the body.

A very lovely antique carriage with nicely down-curved shafts, but with a very limited turning radius. It is also fairly heavy for this young horse (a three-year-old Morgan mare).

As for the harness, hardly a worse choice could be made. There's no breeching; instead, thimbles are used. These are totally inadequate for the weight of the carriage. The saddle is resting fully on the horse's withers; when the carriage pushes forward onto the thimbles, all of its weight falls directly on the horse's withers. The breast collar is far too narrow, and the overall weight of the harness is much too light. The horse wears an overcheck, but this is at least long enough to allow for poll flexion. Note, however, how the horse's back is already swayed, even at this young age.

Her feet have been shod much too long, causing broken foot angles and a too-late breakover. This—combined with the light bone in her legs—will predispose her to leg problems down the road. Photo by Anthony Krulic.

If the carriage you are considering cannot make even easy turns without having the front wheels hit against the body, reject it. Even if the carriage is fitted with rollers against the body to prevent the wheels from locking when they strike, it's not safe. All it will take is one sudden shy sideways, and you'll be in serious trouble: The front wheels will lock, the carriage will tip, and your horse will panic. Carriages with this limited turning ability are generally cheap to purchase and are often purchased by first-time buyers who just don't know any better.

So often, we hear of people who have purchased a driving horse (or who have trained their horse to drive), who then proudly show off their new harness and handsome, dangerous, antique carriage. Many older carriages were made with a very limited turning radius—perhaps because it was cheap to make them that way, and perhaps because driving in the past required very little in the way of tight turns and precise handling. Whatever the reason, these carriages just aren't acceptable when safer styles are readily available.

• VEHICLE MAINTENANCE •

When you purchase a cart or carriage, ask about its maintenance. You will need to follow the same procedures for good maintenance, no matter what the vehicle's age. Once each year (generally in the spring, at the beginning of your active driving season), you should give it a thorough check-up. If you don't feel you can handle the job yourself (or won't know what to look for when you're looking at carriages for purchase), ask a mechanically oriented friend or knowledgeable carriage maker to help you.

To properly maintain a driving vehicle:

1. Have the wheels greased once a year. Jack it up, pull the wheels off, and use a suitable oil or grease for lubrication. (Use automobile wheel bearing grease for wheels with bearings, or 80-90 weight gear lube for rubber or leather washers.) While the wheels are off, check that the rubber is still secure in the channel of the wheel rim, or—if the rims are made of steel—see if there is enough steel remaining to protect the wood of the wheels.

2. Clean and condition any leather straps and pieces. Clean the entire vehicle thoroughly, so you can repair any damaged or cracked wooden parts.

3. Check and tighten all bolts. Replace those that seem weak or worn, or that won't tighten properly.

4. If you can get it out, remove the kingpin bolt that holds the singletree to the carriage or cart. Replace it if it shows any wear.

5. Lubricate the fifth-wheel mechanism if there is one. (Marine grease is good for this, because the fifth wheel is exposed to splashing from puddles and wet weather.)

6. Check the brakes. The brakes should move freely and grab evenly. If the brake system is hydraulic, be sure there is sufficient fluid in the master cylinder, and check the rubber hoses for cracking. (Any good brake mechanic can help you here.) Simple mechanical brakes should have their moving parts lubricated.

If the vehicle is driven often through water and mud, you'll have to check the lubrication and brakes more often, perhaps even once a month if you do a lot of driving.

• SLEIGHS •

For many people, there is the persistent dream of driving across snow-laden fields in a "one-horse open sleigh." We all know of people who have taken up driving just so they can fit themselves into this picture-postcard image.

Driving a sleigh *is* an incredible amount of fun with a safe horse in front of you. By the time you think seriously of putting your horse to a sleigh, he should be driving reliably and safely in a carriage. It is crucial that your horse listen well to you in driving, because a sleigh has far less maneuverability than a carriage.

Remember also that on firm snow, a sleigh runs along very easily. A spunky horse feeling a little too good in crisp, cold weather can be a real handful, and he'd better know how to listen to his driver and mind his manners.

On the other hand, pulling a sleigh through deep snow can be very taxing, so your driving horse must also be fit enough to handle the job without tiring. Many people make the mistake of letting their horses off work for the winter, and then expecting them to enjoy a lengthy sleighride when they're out of condition.

If, however, you are confident that your horse is reliable, go ahead and purchase the beautiful antique sleigh you've had your eye on. Just be sure it is in excellent repair and be particularly careful about checking the wood of the runners. Too often, there is dry rot in the runners or in the underside of the box, and a little bit of stress will break a key part.

Choose a sleigh of medium seat height. If you sit too low, you will have a hard time seeing anything, especially in deep powder snow. It can be difficult to spot ditches, rocks and other hazards in deep snow; if you can't look for them ahead of time, you'll be tipped over before you know it.

If you can find a sleigh with a short set of turning runners in the front, choose this one over one with a fixed pair of regular runners. Turning is much safer and easier on the horse with these turning runners.

We once broke a set of sleigh shafts in a field when the snow suddenly became deep and very firm. No matter how slowly we tried to turn, the runners were stuck so deep in the wind-packed snow that they couldn't slip sideways. There was no other way out of the field, however, and we had to keep trying to turn—and the shafts broke. This wouldn't have happened with short front runners that could pivot on the body.

A well-constructed, well-cared-for carriage or sleigh will give you many hours of pleasant and safe driving. Driving a horse is risky enough—don't add to the risk with poorly designed or badly maintained equipment.

• THE IMPORTANCE OF BRAKES •

Brakes have not been common in this country in the past, and there are still many carriages being built and driven without brakes—especially the two-wheeled carts.

The brake is an important safety device, but it also helps the horse by easing his burden on downhill slopes and whenever he must slow or stop the carriage. Before the automobile, when horses were used as real beasts of burden, it seems that few people really cared about making their horses comfortable in their work. Tight checkreins, cruel bits, and heavy, brakeless carriages were standard equipment. Today, there is really no excuse for careless, ignorant or dangerous treatment of our horses.

So, be sure your vehicle—two-wheeled or four-wheeled—has a properly designed brake.

Different Types of Brakes

Brakes can be either mechanical or hydraulic. A mechanical brake works through leverage and presses a block against the surface of the wheel. Wheels with iron rims usually have wooden brake blocks that need to be replaced periodically because they wear down. Rubber-rimmed wheels usually have steel brake blocks that do not need to be replaced unless they are damaged or badly rusted.

Although better than nothing, these mechanical brakes are very sensitive to moisture. When you drive in rain or through water, the brakes will grab only poorly—and sometimes not at all. It is also very difficult to have both brakes adjusted evenly, so that both wheels are braked evenly. Sometimes, one wheel becomes blocked and the carriage travels very crooked.

Hydraulic brakes work like car brakes. Both drum brakes and disc brakes are available. They are very much preferable to mechanical brakes, but there are some important points to keep in mind.

For hydraulic brakes to work well, the wheels must run absolutely round. For this reason, hydraulic brakes often cannot be installed on older vehicles, unless the axles and hubs—or the entire wheels—are changed.

Also, hydraulic brakes can be sensitive to water, although pumping on them a bit after you've gone through a stream will bring them back quickly (just as in a car). Another common problem with hydraulic carriage brakes seems to be that it is difficult to get all the air out of the lines. Again, if you step down on the brakes and there is no response, you must pump the pedal a few times to bring them back.

A foot pedal is always preferable to a hand lever for brake control, because the foot pedal keeps both your hands free for handling the reins.

Your horse certainly can (and must be taught) to hold up a carriage on his own. If the brakes give out, or if you must stop so suddenly that you have no time to activate the brake, you want a fully reliable horse who can sit into the breeching to stop the carriage to slow the descent on a hill. And there is some merit to the argument that holding back a carriage on a downhill slope without a brake will help strengthen a horse's muscles. But think of the strain on his joints. You want to keep your good driving horse sound for many years and the brake will help. Don't leave home without it.

How and When to Use a Brake
On hills, use your brake whenever the breeching starts to become taut. If the horse is trotting down a gentle slope and the breeching is not taut against his hindquarters, don't use the brake—it would only bother him. (If you are driving a green horse, however, always keep your foot on the brake, ready to use it quickly.)

When you are on a steep hill and must use the brake, use it only enough so that the breeching and the traces are both loose. If the traces are taut, you're making the horse pull downhill, which is certainly not necessary— unless you're trying to stop him. If the breeching is taut, you know you need to apply more brake.

You should also use the brake every time you stop your horse, especially if you are halting from the trot. It will make the stop quicker, smoother and more pleasant for the horse.

Use your brake also when your horse gets a little strong in the trot. Used with the reins, it will help slow the horse down without upsetting him or giving him the feel that something is wrong.

We once watched a man warming up his pair at a show; they were obviously doing very nicely, and the horses appeared strong but well under control. We then noticed that one hind wheel of the carriage seemed to block from time to time; a few minutes later, both hind wheels seemed to block. We were just about to inform the driver that something was wrong with his wheels, when we noticed that he was using the brake to slow his somewhat over-eager horses. Instead of pulling on their mouths, he just made them work a little harder, and this soon quieted them down. It was done with such subtlety that few people noticed anything at all.

Easing the Load on Hills

Many people are not aware of how much their fully loaded vehicle actually weighs. A meadowbrook cart weighs from 300 to 450 pounds; add the weight of two adults, and the total is equivalent to the weight of a small horse. Drive down a steep hill, and this load can suddenly become more than a small horse can handle.

There was a man who brought his 14.3-hand Morgan mare to our barn for training. He complained that the mare's hind feet always slipped when she went down hills. This had become such a problem that his wife would get out of the carriage at the top of the hill to lead the mare down.

When we checked his equipment, the cause of the problem was obvious. He had a heavy meadowbrook cart with no brakes, and the breeching on the harness was adjusted so low that the weight of the cart pushed the mare's legs right out from under her. To compound the trouble, he had her in a very short overcheck that caused her back to hollow badly; the breast collar was only about one inch wide, cutting into her neck when she went *up* the hills, and the saddle sat right on her rather prominent withers. This horse still tried her best to do what was asked of her. She was a true saint!

Once we explained to him what he was doing to his mare, he was very embarrassed and contrite, since he really did love his horse. He had relied upon another professional's advice as to equipment before he began driving and had felt he was doing the right thing.

If you drive without a brake, your horse's mouth must be the brake. This is so unfair to the horse. If your voice command is not sufficient to slow or halt your horse, you must pull on his mouth. If, however, you can slow or stop the carriage with a brake, you need to use the reins to stop only the horse.

Think about driving down a hill. If you have no brake, you must keep hanging on the horse's mouth just to keep everything under control; you may even have to slow to a walk as a safeguard. With a brake, however, you can slow the vehicle slightly with it, and your horse can keep trotting. Even if the horse shies, you are safer, because there is nothing pushing into him to make him more nervous.

In the countryside, you sometimes have to contend with dirt bikes coming up suddenly behind you—as you're trotting downhill—or you must steady the horse while passing a barking dog. These can be dangerous situations, especially with a green horse, and the brake will help to see you through more safely.

The Brake as an Educational Tool

You can also use the brake to educate the horse. If your horse likes to jig and rush toward home, without a brake all you have is your voice and rein action to try to correct him and get him to walk quietly. But the horse who jigs has probably already shortened himself up in the neck, and additional pressure on the bit is just going to make that problem more severe. But, if you have a brake, you can use it to teach him jigging is unpleasant. Instead of correcting him with rein action, just step on the brake to make pulling harder for him. This will often cure a jigging horse very quickly.

When your horse will not stand still but shifts back and forth—either from overeagerness, bad manners or an honest inability to hold a parked carriage steady on a hill—use the brake. Your horse will learn that when you tell him to stop, he must stop and stand. Pulling against a fully braked carriage will soon discourage him from moving off too soon—and you don't have to haul on his mouth.

Sleigh Brakes

And don't forget the brake on your sleigh, either. This is usually a forklike piece of heavy metal that can be pressed by a lever down into the snow. (If there is a brake on only one side of the sleigh, it may pull the sleigh crooked, but this is still better than no brake at all.)

Imagine what it would be like to be driving a heavily loaded sleigh down a steep hill, and suddenly discover that there is ice under the snow. Your horse is already having a tough time staying on his feet—and suddenly the heavy sleigh is pushing against his hindquarters. Perhaps there's even a snowmobile approaching from the rear. At times like this, a brake seems like a very good idea!

One word of caution about using your brakes: Just as when you are driving a car, a brake is only effective as long as the wheels are not completely locked. When the wheels lock, you skid. On a steep downhill grade, this can be very dangerous, as you can lose your steering and find yourself going sideways. Try never to brake to the point where the wheels lock up. And have your brakes carefully adjusted so they work equally on both sides of the carriage.

CHAPTER
· 6 ·

AUXILIARY REINS
AND THE WHIP

The minimum equipment needed to drive a horse—a harness and a vehicle—is seldom enough during the training process. Often, you will find the need for some sort of auxiliary reins to help the horse find his balance, learn the correct responses and use the proper muscles in his training.

Your whip is also a vital part of your communication system, and although it is technically considered an artificial aid, few people would think of setting off on a drive without one. Almost every form of driving competition requires the driver to carry a whip as standard equipment. Understanding the correct use of these additional aids is very important.

● AUXILIARY REINS ●

An auxiliary rein is any sort of rein that is designed to work with the regular reins and help the horse learn his job. Auxiliary reins are seen as training aids, and are generally prohibited from the show ring. (Checkreins and running martingales are allowed in some classes.)

Checkreins

The checkrein (sidecheck or overcheck) is the one auxiliary rein that specifically works *against* the horse's ability to pull—yet it is allowed, even *required*, in some driving classes.

While the overcheck rein does not allow for any flexion of the poll whatsoever (see page 45), and applies a constant pressure to the horse's upper gums through the action of the check bit, the sidecheck (if it is left long enough) does at least allow for flexion of the poll (see page 44). Depending on its length, it can allow the horse some measure of comfort. It also does not work on the upper gums but applies pressure instead on the corners of the mouth. The sidecheck is therefore a little more humane than the overcheck, but it is still a definite nuisance to the horse—and it prevents proper muscle development of the topline. Neither is ever needed in driving.

Checkreins were created in earlier times when someone decided it was fashionable and stylish to have driving horses carry their heads as high as possible, while appearing agitated and fiery. When tight checkreins were the fashion, no one seemed to consider the pain they were causing their horses. Because the checkrein caused the horse to travel with a hollow, locked back and stiff neck, the horse's ability to pull effectively was completely destroyed.

Compounding the horror of tight checkreins, drivers often felt the need to use severe bits with high ports and long shanks. Generally, the horse was so upset because of the tight checkrein that a regular, milder bit wouldn't work—and with his head so high in the air, a snaffle mouthpiece would get hung up on his lower teeth anyway.

Unfortunately, we can still quite often see this horrible combination of tight checkrein (both overcheck and sidecheck) and severe bit in the show ring today. This goes along with the desire to produce an "animated" driving horse. The show horse or fine harness horse, at least, is usually driven for only a short period of time on flat ground and hitched only to a light carriage.

But we also see "pleasure" drivers who hitch their horses to heavy carriages, attach the short checkreins and proceed to drive across the

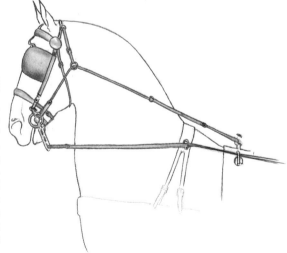

A short sidecheck used in combination with curb action is an absolute instrument of torture. If the horse tries to raise his head, the curb action will become even more severe; if he tries to lower his head to evade the curb pressure (or simply to relax), the sidecheck will prevent this. In addition, the sidecheck is hooked to the driving bit instead of to an additional checkbit—thus, the horse experiences pressure from different directions from the same bit.

countryside for hours at a time. We see this in carriage competitions and in certain parts of the country where the driving horse is still a rather common sight. These poor horses cannot relax, even for a minute, by stretching their necks. Often, they resort to all sorts of sideways evasions to ease their sore muscles.

Checkreins create ewe necks and swayed backs. Checkreins prohibit the stretching of the topline, the development of the carrying and pulling muscles and the engagement of the haunches. A horse that has learned to accept the reins correctly will always be a lot more manageable in any situation than a horse that has never truly understood the reins and bit because he's always been locked into a checkrein.

Why Do Drivers Use Checkreins?

If you ask drivers why they use checkreins on their horses, they will give you a variety of reasons:

1. The checkrein prevents the horse from bucking.
2. The checkrein keeps the horse from eating grass.
3. The horse looks "flashier."
4. It came with the harness.
5. The checkrein makes pair-driving safer, because it keeps the horses from possibly getting hung up on each other's reins when curb bits are used.
6. It helps to collect the horse.

The only acceptable reason to use a checkrein is to prevent a notorious grass-eater from indulging himself. (A young or weak person driving a strong, thick-necked pony might make a case for this argument.) If you do need a checkrein for this purpose, it should be a sidecheck, not an overcheck, and it should be adjusted just short enough to prevent the horse from getting his head to the grass. The horse should not feel the checkrein at any other time. It must be long enough so he can truly stretch forward at the walk, without any interference. If it is long enough for this, however, it will dangle and flop on his neck at the trot, and may annoy him. The bottom photograph on page 65 shows an example of this.

Of the two types of checkrein (overcheck and sidecheck), the sidecheck is the lesser of two evils. Use of an overcheck is never acceptable. The sidecheck at least allows the horse to flex his jaw, but the overcheck prohibits even this.

Every reason listed above (except for "It came with the harness") is a result of poor or insufficient training. The most misguided reason for using a checkrein is the belief that it helps to "collect" the horse.

Anything that is called "collection" created by a checkrein is merely an improper elevation of the head and neck. A checkrein always *prevents* any progress toward true collection.

When a sidecheck is combined with a curb bit (and the reins are attached to a lower slot in the shanks), the leverage of the bit is greatly increased. Caught between the checkrein and the leverage of the curb bit, the horse has no relief—and no way out of this forced position.

Checkreins are so commonly included as a normal part of a driving harness that many people assume they must use them. Don't let a harness maker tell you that you need a checkrein. Take it off; or, better yet, specify "no checkrein" when you order your next harness.

For the same reasons, you do not want or need a bitting rig—which is, after all, just a way to attach the checkrein and sidereins to the girth and crupper. Putting a horse into a tight bitting rig and leaving him in his stall for a couple of hours is nothing but torture and nothing good can come from it.

Sidereins

There *are* auxiliary reins that can help us in training. The major purpose of properly used auxiliary reins is to *lower* the horse's head and neck, teach him to reach for the bit and encourage him to become comfortable and secure with it. Sidereins can be beneficial, when correctly adjusted and used.

There are two basic types of sidereins: fixed (or standing) sidereins and sliding sidereins. The sliding sidereins are definitely preferable to the standing sidereins because they invite the horse to find his correct position and allow him a certain freedom of movement.

Fixed or Standing Sidereins ● Standing sidereins, which are fixed from the bit to the middle rings of the surcingle, often restrict the horse's ability to move properly. If they are fixed short enough to help the horse find a correct position for his head and neck, they are too unyielding and will bump his mouth at every step. At the walk, especially, when you want the horse to really use his neck in a rocking-back-and-forth motion, standing sidereins can be very restricting. At the trot, these sidereins are often so heavy they bounce around and jerk the horse more or less constantly, simply because of their own weight.

Even when standing sidereins have a rubber donut or elastic inserts, they limit the horse's movement too much. (Have you ever tried to stretch a siderein's rubber donut? Do you really want your horse to have to put that much pull into something before it gives him an "elastic" feel?) Sensitive

Standing sidereins in different lengths.

When these sidereins are adjusted long enough to give some support to a young horse's natural frame, they still don't give him enough freedom to stretch down. Also, they will not help at all in "showing the horse the way to the ground," which is so essential—especially for a horse with poor neck conformation or mental resistance.

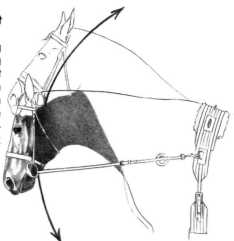

When adjusted to a length that will support a more advanced horse, standing sidereins allow for even less downward stretch and relaxation; however, the horse can still evade the contact upwards.

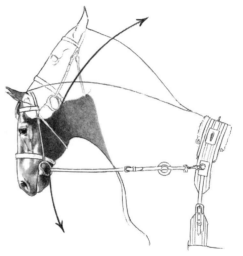

To completely eliminate the upwards evasion, standing sidereins must be so short that they pull the horse's head behind the vertical and create a break at the fourth vertebra. No downward relaxation at all is possible. This is a sure way of teaching a horse to go behind the bit or behind the vertical.

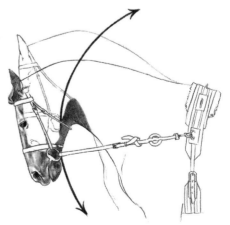

horses, in particular, are very bothered by them when the sidereins are adjusted short. If they are adjusted longer, the horse can easily escape their action by taking his head up, and he quickly learns all the tricks to avoid bit contact.

Standing sidereins do not do enough to encourage proper muscle development and willingness to reach for the bit. They limit the horse's motion and do not reward him for correct stretching of the topline. Far better than standing sidereins are what we call sliding sidereins.

Sliding Sidereins • These training reins have been used in Germany for many, many years on both riding and driving horses. They are the most useful form of auxiliary reins, as they very effectively help the horse find his balance, accept the bit, and stretch his topline correctly—without being restricted by the rigidity of standing sidereins, and without being bothered by the uneven motions of a driver's hands.

The green horse, or the horse with conformation problems (ewe neck, short neck, heavy jaw, bulging muscles at the bottom of the neck), soon learns to relax and let the sliding sidereins work for him. A beginning driver, also, gains confidence and valuable experience when the sliding sidereins are used because he can feel what it's like when the horse moves correctly. And the driver doesn't have to worry about bothering the horse's mouth with his less-than-perfect hands.

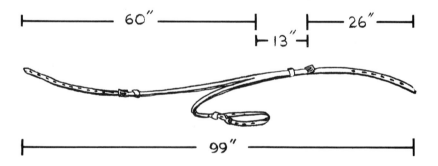

The original sliding sidereins, made from leather.

Sliding sidereins give a horse a continuous invitation to put his head down and lengthen his topline, but he doesn't get pulled down into position. He meets with serious resistance only when he tries to raise his head very high. Otherwise, he can find different comfortable positions depending on what he's doing—longer and lower at the walk, slightly higher at the trot.

Attaching the sliding sidereins. Note how the line passes through the neckstrap of the breast collar to prevent entangling in the shafts. It must be tightened firmly on the saddle so it won't slide down. If your horse insists on carrying his head severely to one side, you will have to fix the sidereins at the belly girth so they can't change in length. Make sure, however, that both sides are absolutely the same length when attached.

Because the sidereins "slide" through the bit at every step, they encourage a soft jaw and flexion without jerking the bit. A green horse finds comfortable contact and begins to develop his topline muscles correctly; the schooled horse can still benefit from occasional use of the sidereins as a refresher, or when some particular resistance has developed. And for the problem horse who has been in harness for some time and needs to have his muscles, his attitude and his behavior patterns completely rebuilt, the sliding sidereins are invaluable.

Sliding sidereins can be created for you by a local harness maker if you want proper leather ones. We began working with these, but then realized that they were very bulky and difficult to keep in place on the belly girth. (They do work well with a riding saddle.) For driving, we now prefer to use about 18 feet of lightweight nylon cord to fashion a simple set as shown in the illustrations. Loop the middle of the cord around the girth, pull it even, run each end through one ring of the bit and attach it to the girth band. Stand in front of the horse and adjust the two sides to be sure they are even.

This works well for ground driving, longeing and ponying, but an added precaution is necessary when your horse is hitched, to avoid the possibility of having the sidereins catch on a shaft. If you are using these sidereins while driving, run each end of the cord through the bight (endpiece) of the neckstrap (if you are using a breast collar) before attaching it to the girth band.

Here, the sidereins are adjusted too long and are not doing the job. Tension, a short topline and a long bottom line are all clearly evident.

Adjustment of the Sliding Sidereins ● It is very important to adjust the sliding sidereins to the correct length, which will depend upon the horse's conformation, his level of training and the sensitivity of his mouth. And be sure you introduce the sidereins while the horse is on the longe or in ground driving before you hitch him with sliding sidereins attached. Some horses will have a rather violent reaction at first to any sort of sidereins. Remember also that through the use of the sliding sidereins, you are rebuilding muscles, and this can be tiring. Limit the sessions with sliding sidereins to about 15 minutes at first.

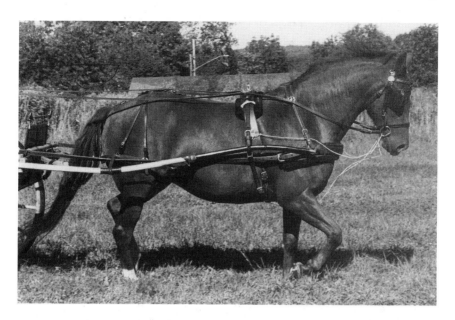

With the sidereins still too long, the driver is working to get the horse stretched down—but there's no success. The mare is now showing tension through her tight neck and back and short steps.

Adjust the sidereins just tightly enough so that the horse "arches" and lengthens his topline; by this, we mean that he yields in the jaw. If your horse is very ewe-necked or very stubborn, you may have to shorten the sidereins so that the horse goes almost behind the vertical for the first few times, so that his muscles have to give in. If this is necessary, however, you must keep the sessions with sidereins especially short at first—no more than ten minutes.

For the horse who carries his head severely and consistently to one side—and keeps pulling one side of the sliding sidereins tighter than the other—then the sidereins must be fixed to the center of the belly girth, and you must be very sure that both sides are exactly the same length.

Before you hitch a horse with sidereins attached, make sure that he fully accepts them during groundwork. Always have a helper with you in case they get caught around the shaft.

By guiding each siderein through the endpiece of the neck strap, between the buckle and the keeper (but not under the neckstrap itself, as this may be too tight to allow free movement of the sidereins), you will minimize the danger of having one catch on a shaft. Or—better yet—you can tape a small metal ring onto the neckstrap at the proper height, and run the siderein through that. When you hitch your horse with sidereins, use shafts

Here, the sidereins have been adjusted to ask the horse for stretching and re-laxation. The driver doesn't have to fight, the tension has disappeared and the horse's steps are long and powerful.

In this photo, the mare is giving in to the sidereins through the beginning of a bend. She's yielding nicely, showing softness through her jaw, neck and back.

Here, the mare is working to her full ability. Note her even shorter bottom line, her stretched-to-the-utmost topline, the increased coiling of the loin and the full acceptance of her own weight on the far-forward-reaching and well-flexed hind leg. You can almost see the recycling of power that takes place as she pushes all her energy toward the bit and accepts it with soft jaws and a light rein contact. When a horse is working this well, the sliding sidereins have no effect—but they also do not interfere in any way.

with a good downward/outward curve, or set straight shafts farther back than usual to keep them from catching. Even after you and your horse become accustomed to driving with sidereins, it is always advisable to have a helper on hand.

If the green horse is not confused by inept or heavy rein actions, he will readily accept the position indicated to him by the sliding sidereins, but even a severely spoiled older horse may come around in a very few minutes when put into sliding sidereins; often, such a horse will seem relieved, because he is no longer fighting with a driver who is trying to pull him into position. The sidereins give him a place to be comfortable, correct and left alone.

Some horses, of course, never need the help of the sidereins, or of any other training aid, while others will need them for quite a long time as a support during their early training or rehabilitation. Once the horse is reaching and stretching down to the bit on his own, and traveling in a relaxed, confident, forward manner, the sidereins can be gradually lengthened and then taken off entirely. If incorrect driving or an interrupted training schedule causes the horse to revert to wrong use of the neck muscles, go back to the sliding sidereins again. It's far easier on both the horse and driver to use this helpful training aid than to try to fight him into a correct frame.

If properly used, at the appropriate length, these sidereins will never pull a horse into a frame he is not able to work in. They will not make a horse hold himself. They will, however, help to build the proper muscles at the top of the neck, while the muscles at the bottom of the neck will go slack with disuse. Through this development, you can watch the muscles of the neck, back and hindquarters grow from week to week.

The use of sliding sidereins is not a shortcut in the horse's proper and correct dressage training. It merely assists the horse to understand how to use his body to his best advantage.

Other Auxiliary Reins

The *chambon* is another popular training aid, used by many riders and some drivers. The chambon does teach the horse to get his head down, but it doesn't really ask for any flexion at the poll. The horse can learn to get his head far down and still poke his nose out in front. It doesn't help his balance much, either, because there is no lateral support.

A variation on the chambon, the *gogue,* is a little more useful because it does ask for poll flexion, but the action of the bit is upwards against the horse's mouth—not at all what he will be asked to accept when the gogue is removed. Both the chambon and the gogue restrict the free, energetic motion of the head and neck that is so desirable at the walk. Inhibiting this motion will cause the walk to stiffen and shorten.

The use of *drawreins* has no place in training the driving horse. Because of the long, heavy reins used in driving, a driver can apply a dangerous and destructive amount of leverage with drawreins. Drawreins can never help the driving horse find acceptance of the bit.

Any sort of *tie-down* (or standing martingale) won't teach the horse anything useful. Since the tie-down attaches to the noseband, the horse isn't learning anything about bit contact. A horse who tosses his head up will continue to toss it as soon as the tie-down is removed. It is far better to determine the cause of the high head or the head tossing, and then use sliding sidereins, if necessary, to correct the problem.

The *running or forked martingale* is of no use at all. If it is adjusted short enough to have any effect on the horse (as it is designed to take the head down), it will create a break in the straight line of the reins, destroying the direct rein contact from the driver's hands to the bit. (See photograph on page 45.) If the running martingale is adjusted too long, it has no effect at all.

The running martingale is often seen in fine harness classes, used in conjunction with a tight overcheck. The running martingale prevents the horse from throwing his head straight up in the air in drastic reaction to the tight checkrein; used in this way, it may help prevent rearing. The horse that is locked in between a short checkrein and tight martingale has no more than two inches of vertical head movement available to him; often, the drivers are seen hanging onto the reins with their full strength, leaning backward in the carriage. This is the worst of driving scenarios—and is precisely the opposite of what can be achieved with the methods of humane training that we advocate.

With no overcheck, there's no need for a running martingale. If you feel your horse needs a running martingale because he travels with his head too high (even without an overcheck), use sliding sidereins instead for as many training sessions as needed to show him the correct position.

• THE WHIP •

Besides the reins and our voice, the only other communication available to us as drivers is the whip. It is vital that both the driver and the horse fully understand how the whip should be used; it is equally important that the whip be introduced to the horse properly.

The whip can convey to the horse many things. It can say:

> *Pay attention.*
> *Move forward.*
> *Go to the bit.*
> *Move sideways.*
> *Behave yourself!*

Because it can have so many meanings, depending on how and when it is used, it is very important that a driving horse be given the chance to fully understand all of these commands.

With some horses, it is easy to properly introduce the whip and teach them to respect it without fearing it. Many horses, however, either ignore the whip or are very afraid of it.

Introduce the whip early to your horse. In the beginning, just touch him gently with the whip, stroking and pressing it all over his body, being careful not to irritate or tickle him. You will be able to tell immediately whether your horse accepts, ignores or strongly dislikes the whip. Some horses will be quite concerned about it for a long time. Work carefully to reassure him, and spend a longer time on this lesson with the nervous horse than with the complacent one.

When the horse accepts being touched all over by the whip, he must next learn to move away from the whip, both to the side and forward, as we begin ground training. This is described in Chapter 7.

After the horse understands the use of the whip as an aid in longeing, you will carry a whip as you begin ground driving. If the horse is reluctant to move on or go by something that catches his attention, you will touch him with the whip to reinforce your verbal command. What amounts to the "correct touch" depends greatly on the individual horse's disposition and acceptance of the whip.

The whip should always be applied just behind the saddle, never on the croup or rump. Using the whip on a horse's croup will cause many horses to buck or kick up.

The whip is always used in conjunction with voice and/or rein commands, as a reinforcement. Whether you are asking for attention, more forward movement or prompt obedience will depend on the situation and the horse's response. To encourage forward movement, use the whip high up on his barrel or back. To ask him to move sideways, use it farther down on his barrel, about where a rider's leg would lie.

With a very sensitive, "hot" horse, you may run into a real problem at this point. He may not mind, initially, being touched with the whip, and he will yield to it when he is asked to move forward or away, but because the sensitive horse tends to be quick and nervous even in the best of circumstances, touching him with the whip to encourage him forward when he is being a little spooky may make matters worse. This sort of horse usually responds very well to voice, anyway, and will jump to carry out your commands—especially if you use a loud voice. With a very sensitive horse, you may find it difficult to use the whip tactfully for any sort of guidance.

A different sort of horse can present almost the same problem. This is the very calm, attentive, obedient horse who promptly does everything you ask—he's almost too perfect! What happens here is that you never find the need to touch him with the whip during his normal training. Then, often much later, you and he must face a frightening situation that he just can't quite cope with—and when you use the whip to encourage him, he's so unaccustomed to it that this unusual touch frightens him even more.

For these reasons, you must create in your groundwork specific situations where you do need to use the whip as a tool of guidance, communication and reinforcement. These contrived situations can be anything that will give your horse pause without terrifying him: perhaps asking him to leave a group of his friends, or insisting that he walk past something moderately scary. If he can feel the whip in an appropriate use during ground training, he will learn to respect it without fearing it.

Be absolutely sure that, when you touch him with the whip, it has meaning. Don't use the whip if he is already in the process of obeying your voice, and don't use the whip all by itself without giving some sort of verbal or rein command.

Once your horse is hitched to the cart, you may not have the chance (or need) to use the whip again for quite some time, as the cart itself is all a nervous horse can handle at first, and using the whip at any time might excite him just too much, creating a dangerous situation. You must always use your best judgment regarding the whip. With a nervous horse, you must always make the decision as to whether the use of the whip will help or harm a situation.

The lethargic horse, however, needs regular reminders that the whip must be respected. You will find a need for the whip early on with these horses, and you may have to use it strongly at first to make an impression on them. You must convey to them that when you ask they must respond, and the whip is a supremely useful tool to emphasize this. The lethargic horse may have a fairly insensitive mouth, and he probably doesn't mind being yelled at either, so the whip may be the only way to command his attention.

When you do use the whip on these laid-back fellows, be sure that you don't simply keep nagging at them and dull them to it all together. This can be very hard to do, as some horses seem to need whip encouragement at every other step, but try to get their attention quickly with a few sharp swats, rather than a lot of picky, gentle touches.

As for the type of whip, this is largely a matter of individual preference. It should be long enough to easily reach the horse behind his saddle, but not much longer, because you don't want to carry any more weight in your hands than is necessary. Very long whips can also be clumsy and inaccurate.

Our choice is the type with a fairly long, rigid shaft, tapering to a flexible braided thong that ends in a short lash. The length of the thong (measured from the end of the rigid shaft to the tip of the lash) is about 12 inches. Even for pair driving, we prefer to keep the thong and lash as short as possible—about two or three feet long.

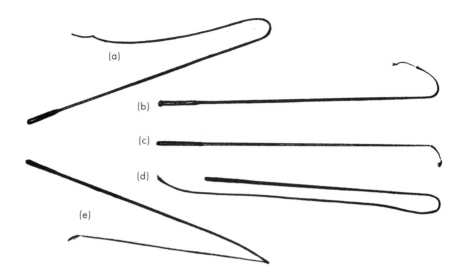

Different styles of whips: (a) English Gig Whip, Single. We like to use it for pairs, since the lash is long enough for use in a relatively short hookup. (b) Regular Single Whip with a 1-foot lash. We like this one for single driving; it is gentle and can be applied quickly and precisely without striking the horse with the shaft of the whip. (c) Regular Single Whip with a very short lash. With this type of whip, it is almost impossible to apply the lash without hitting the horse also with the shaft. (d) English Pair Whip. We don't like this long lash, as it is slow and inaccurate to apply and can easily become entangled in harness or wheels. (e) Another style of single or pair whip. We prefer the bow-shaped shaft-lash attachment to this kind (see the English Gig Whip) because it allows more precise control and use.

Avoid the type of driving whip with a thong and lash as long as—or even longer than—the rigid shaft. This sort of whip is fine as a longe whip, but in driving the thong will be difficult to control, blowing in your face, dangling over your passenger and often touching the horse exactly when and where you don't want it to. The long thong can also make a noise when it swings through the air, and sensitive horses hate this sound.

Having good hands in driving means more than just skilled reinsmanship. It also includes the judicious use of the whip as a delicate precision instrument.

CHAPTER · 7 ·

BASIC GROUND TRAINING

The better a horse's ground training, the more reliable and responsive he will be when he is driven. All work in harness begins on the ground.

The more time you spend *effectively* with your horse, the greater the mutual trust and communication will be between you. "Effectively" means that you don't merely play with your horse, but that you are always aware that you are the teacher and boss. You are continually teaching him something while you are handling him, and the horse learns to respect you as his superior. Trust and respect—combined with genuine affection—are the cornerstones of a successful relationship, and learning cannot take place if any of these elements is missing.

• LEARNING TO STOP AND STAND STILL •

Assuming that your horse leads fairly well, the first thing he must learn is to halt and stand still. At first he will learn to do this while you hold him and stay near him, but later he will need to learn to do this on his own.

You may be starting from scratch with a youngster, you may be training your good riding horse to drive or you may be looking for methods to improve the driving skills of an experienced horse. Regardless of your horse's age and background, the halt is something he must learn.

A good driving horse will stop whenever you tell him to, and he *will keep standing there* until you tell him to move, whether or not there is a person at his head to remind him of this.

How is this taught?

Begin simply. Try to reduce distractions as much as possible at first, so your horse will pay attention only to you. Lead your horse at the walk and give him the voice command to halt—usually the word "whoa." (You can use any voice command you wish, but be absolutely consistent about it.) If the horse does not obey you, repeat the word and at the same time give a pull on his halter, directing it straight back toward his chest. If he still does not listen, jump in front of him, push back against him and repeat the command.

Now, there are horses that will not be impressed at all by this. They will try to walk right through you. If this happens, move to the side and pull him quickly around you, interrupting his forward motion. Give him a strong jerk backward on the halter and an angry voice command; if necessary, add a sharp slap on the neck with your hand to get his attention.

Once he stands, pet him profusely and tell him what a smart guy he is, how good and bright. Don't expect him to stand for any period of time—at first, we want him simply to stop his forward movement on command. Repeat this lesson many times and in many familiar places: in your training area, when you lead him from stall to paddock or when you take him for a walk around the field. Keep doing this until he stops willingly each time you tell him "whoa."

When you ask him to step forward again, be consistent also. Use a definite voice command: "walk," or "come up," or whatever you wish—and combine it with a slight tug forward to let him know he is to move forward.

In the next lessons, you must ask him to stand for a period of time. You will have to be the best judge of how long and how often. For a nervous horse, learning to stand still for ten seconds can be a real achievement. The calm horse will be able to manage several minutes at a stretch. Be sure, however, that your horse has had a chance to stretch and play before you insist on his standing still for a long period—especially if he's young or the weather is nippy and he's just come out of his stall.

Regardless of how long it takes, work on this frequently. Your goal is to have your horse willing to stand still for as long as you want him to, and to stay there until you ask him to step forward.

When the horse will do this in familiar quarters, take him to places where he is less sure of himself and ask him to stand still for several minutes at a stretch. This will require more of an effort from him, as he must concentrate on you instead of on his surroundings. He must learn to rely on you for direction, and he must wait for your command before moving off.

Standing Still Without a Handler

Once you feel the horse is listening and responding well to these lessons, you can begin to teach him to halt and walk beside you without actually being led.

The best place to begin this work is in a small paddock or—even better—the aisle of a barn, with all the doors closed so he can't leave abruptly. If this is not possible, you can attach a fairly long, lightweight cord to his halter and tuck it in a pocket or through a belt loop, so it doesn't look as if you're leading him, but you can still catch him if you have to.

Have your horse haltered, but don't touch the halter. Ask him to move forward with you walking at his head, and then give the command to "whoa." Do this a few more times, staying near his head but making no leading motions unless he ignores you or turns away. If he's not listening at this point, go back to work with the lead rope—he's not ready for this step.

If the horse does well with you at his head, ask him to walk forward without you. Stay behind him or near his flank, and give the command to halt. Many horses will find out very quickly that you now have no physical control over them, and they'll try to get away from this silly discipline game by walking or even trotting away. Since he can't go far, however, it is easy to catch him.

If he tries to leave, catch him by the halter and energetically put him back into the place where you asked him to halt. Give him a good verbal scolding and try again. Of course, once he responds well you will praise him and pat him lavishly. Repeat the exercise several times.

Most horses catch on quickly, especially since a good scratch behind the ears and a few kind words are a lot nicer than angry scoldings.

As part of this training—and as part of their daily routine—we groom and harness all our horses in the aisle without tying them, and eventually without even haltering them. All our horses lead on our farm without a halter; we may place a hand on their cheek or hold a few mane hairs if necessary.

Once this level of "remote control" is reached, we teach them to trot on the leadline in respect to a voice command, and we practice voice transitions into the walk and the halt. After they have learned this, we teach them to back a few steps on command.

Of course, you can't expect perfection at this stage of training, and often you'll have to repeat each command several times, especially if the horse is still very young.

Expanding the Horizons

Once you have established this basic obedience, your horse should be quite manageable and safe to lead by halter and rope. Begin taking him on walks through the countryside. Don't use a lead chain over his nose unless it is absolutely necessary for your safety. You don't want the horse to submit to you through fear of being hurt, but because he respects you, trusts you and wants to listen to you.

If you are trying to reschool a spoiled, older animal with bad manners, you may have to use a lead chain over his nose on the first few walks, but try to adjust it so he won't feel it unless you absolutely must use it.

If your horse is well acquainted with the roads and trails around your stable, you may feel he doesn't need much of this work. Remember, however, that when you are driving, your only control over this horse will be through the reins, whip and voice. You want him to listen to you wherever you go, even though he cannot see or feel you on his back.

Introducing the Bit

Once your green horse is happy and relaxed on these walks, add a simple headstall (without blinders or reins) and a double-jointed snaffle bit. Slip the bit in quietly and make it as comfortable for him as possible. Don't put any pressure on the bit as you lead him. Keep your leadline attached to the halter, and just let him carry the bit to become accustomed to it.

Ponying

Now it is time to begin ponying him. Use a solid, quiet, experienced fellow for ponying your youngster, and begin with quiet trips around a paddock or field so that you, your riding horse and your green horse all become accustomed to this new activity. Pony the young horse by leading him from the halter, never from the bit, and try to keep him traveling with his head about even with your knee.

Move back onto the trails and quiet roads as soon as you feel comfortable with this, and remember to continually reinforce your verbal commands. (Your riding horse must comply, also, or there will be confusion!)

Whenever the three of you come to something scary or startling, give your youngster plenty of time to figure things out—but also insist, gently but firmly, that he must eventually step over logs, white lines in the road and puddles. Plan your travels carefully, giving him a chance to meet and deal with cows, barking dogs and traffic under safe circumstances. Remember, this is your future driving horse, and he needs to learn about *everything* that you will encounter when driving.

Sometimes you will not be able to convince him that an object is harmless—but you *can* convince him that he must still listen to you and go by there in a decent manner, without rearing, bolting or jumping to the other side of the road.

This is extremely important in a driving horse, since there is no way that you will be able to show him all the scary things in the world before you drive him. He will have to learn to deal with new scary things in a manageable way, and the earlier you teach him the better.

If you are not a good enough rider to feel comfortable with ponying your young horse, expand your walks to include comparatively safe roads with traffic and other hazards. Invite friends and their quiet horses to accompany you so your youngster will have some good examples to follow. If you do have an experienced friend with a suitable horse, ask him to do some ponying for you. Be sure, however, that the voice commands are kept very consistent and used correctly.

• INTRODUCING SURCINGLE AND SIDEREINS •

When you feel that the horse is comfortable with the feel of the bit in his mouth, you can add a surcingle and very loose sliding sidereins attached to the bit. The sidereins must be short enough so there is no danger of him tangling his legs in them if he puts his head down, but long enough so he can lift his head all the way up and doesn't become panicky from the restraint.

The "sliding" action of these sidereins on the bit prevents a horse from actually being jerked in the mouth if he does push his head out or up abruptly. Gradually, the very loose sidereins can be shortened a little, and the horse will quickly learn to accept the bit and chew on it.

Continue the walks and the ponying, and continue to reinforce the verbal commands. After the horse has become accustomed to the simple bridle, surcingle and sidereins, you can introduce the harness itself.

Some people make a big deal out of getting a horse used to the harness. Often, this step seems a lot bigger to the people than to the horse. Be sure every piece is introduced quietly, giving the horse the chance to look it over and sniff it, and be sure that once it is on his body for the first time, all dangling straps (like the overgirth that holds the tugs in place) are securely tied up to prevent them from tangling in his legs.

Begin with the belly girth, placing it carefully on his back after he's had the chance to sniff and examine it. Fasten the girth loosely, and then move to his tail to fasten the crupper. If you scratch his rump just above or beside the tail, your horse will probably be delighted, and will relax and lift the tail slightly. Calmly slide the crupper under the dock. Occasionally a horse will flinch a little at first and hump his back, but if you just keep scratching and talking, he should relax again. Fasten the girth snugly (he should be accustomed to this from the feel of the surcingle) and finish your preparations for the training session. Save the breeching for the next lesson.

When you do introduce the breeching, let it hang loose while you lead your horse, so he will become accustomed to the feel of being touched around his hind legs and having things flop around on his hindquarters. You might also let the breeching dangle loose sometimes during longeing or ground driving. This helps induce bucking and kicking if the horse is so inclined. That sounds strange, but you want the horse to do as many bad things in his groundwork as possible, where there is little danger involved, and where you can prove to him that this bad behavior doesn't lead to anything except punishment and your anger. When he does buck or kick, of course, you will use strong, angry words—plus gestures, slaps or a pull on the longe—to correct him.

When you are ready to exchange the open bridle for one with blinders, there should be no problem. Most horses seem to accept blinders readily, and don't seem concerned that their vision is restricted. The horse will probably try to turn around and look for the source of a strange noise behind him, but he shouldn't object to the blinders themselves. (The blinders, of course, must be positioned correctly and spread far enough apart so that they will never touch the eye or eyelashes.)

In our experience, only one horse would not accept the blinders. He absolutely refused to take a step forward. Further on in his training, it became apparent that he did not like any aspect of driving, and we gave up trying to put him in harness.

• EARLY GROUND DRIVING FROM THE HALTER •

Generally, a trainer will teach a young horse to lead and respond to simple voice commands before moving onto longeing when the horse is two years old or older. (Do not ask a horse younger than two to do any work at all on the longe; his legs cannot handle the strain.) Most people begin to long line and ground drive the horse only after he has become steady and obedient on the longe.

However, you don't have to wait until he's two to begin some simple ground driving. And some trainers do not like working their horses on the longe line at all.

If you have lots of time for your young horse and would like to do more than just pony him or lead him on walks (but you can't longe him yet because of his youth), you can begin to long line or ground drive him even

Here is a very young horse carrying a bit but being long-lined on the cavesson.

before he's learned to longe. If he's less than 18 months old, however, you should ground drive him with the reins attached only to the halter or cavesson—not to the bit. You will also have to introduce him to a surcingle.

This work can begin when he's a year old, but don't ask for any long training sessions. Begin with ten-minute lessons and work your way up to about 30 minutes in the ring, or up to an hour on the trails. (See the discussion of ground driving later in this chapter.)

Although ground driving him on the halter does not teach a horse to steer from the mouth, you can still teach him many good things this way. It will increase your horse's confidence because it requires him to move ahead of you instead of being led. Bold horses will love this; timid ones will want to turn around and look to you frequently for your help.

This sort of work will also help him learn to work on his own balance, and to move forward. In the beginning, you may find that your youngster can hardly go two steps in a row on a straight line, varying the length of his stride at every step. With experience, he will become accustomed to being controlled from behind. He will learn basic steering as he begins to respond from the pressure on either side of his head.

Before you begin this sort of "baby ground driving," your horse must lead well on the halter and listen to your commands. And when you first introduce this to him, stay very close to him, either just beside his hip or close behind his rump so that you can correct him quickly if he tries to turn around or begins to drift badly. If he doesn't understand at all, have a helper lead him for a few sessions while you hold the long lines behind him.

If you don't have a suitable place for longeing, or if you do not want to longe, you can skip longeing entirely and move on to long lining and ground driving. But this is only recommended if you are very athletic and can at least trot with the horse on long lines for a few minutes at a time.

Whatever course you choose, remember that your objectives will be the same. *Before* you hitch your horse to a cart, you will want him to show steadiness and rhythm in both the trot and walk, and you will want him to be calm, willing and obedient to your commands. This may be achieved without longeing, although it is more difficult. Remember, also, that the excellence of a driving horse depends to a great extent on the education of his mouth. You can ask him to carry a bit when he is about a year and a half old, and as soon as he is comfortable with the bit, you can begin to ground drive him with the reins attached to it.

•   BEGINNING ON THE LONGE LINE   •

All the ground training up to this point can be introduced to a horse of almost any age (including yearlings), but before you begin work on the longe your horse must be at least two years old. Horses younger than this cannot handle the physical strain to their legs.

Correct longeing will help you meet several objectives:

1. You will be able to refine your system of voice commands, enforcing the horse's response to a command the first time it is issued.
2. You can introduce the canter and will be able to ask the horse to back on command without your direct assistance.
3. Most important, the young horse will learn to work himself on the bit, learning to reach for it, respect it and become completely comfortable with it, while moving freely and calmly forward.

Equipment
The best longeing cavesson is a lightweight nylon one. Leather cavessons are usually very bulky, and unless you fasten them very snugly, they will slide across the horse's head and irritate the eye on the outside. Or you can simply put a comfortable halter on over the bridle and attach the longe line to the inside ring of the noseband. Since your horse already listens well to your voice and the halter, this should work just fine.

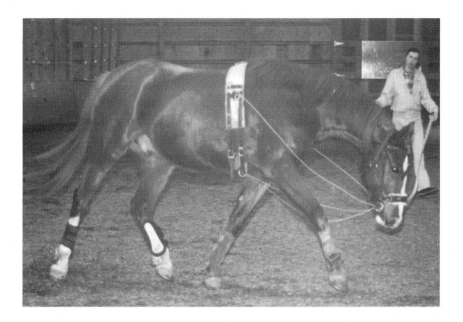

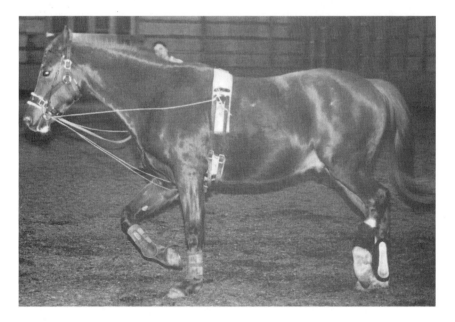

It is apparent in these two photos that the sliding sidereins allow the horse the full range of motion of his neck. As opposed to standing sidereins, these add no weight to his mouth and do not cause the horse to be jerked in the mouth as he moves.

Your longe line should be at least 24 feet long, *without* a chain. Cotton web is better than nylon, as cotton is less likely to cause chafing if it gets caught under a tail or fetlock, or is pulled sharply through your hands.

Use a training surcingle or the surcingle from your harness, and be sure your sliding sidereins are correctly adjusted. This means they should be fairly loose to begin with—just tight enough to keep the horse from traveling crookedly. You will shorten these sidereins gradually, over a period of time, depending on the horse's disposition, conformation, age and stage of training. Keep the equipment simple at first; later you can add the rest of the harness for your longeing sessions.

Not much can be accomplished by longeing without sidereins, because it doesn't teach the horse anything positive. Without sidereins, he will run around with his head in the air, falling over his inside shoulder, traveling with a stiff back and hind legs trailing behind him. Even when he is wearing sidereins, a horse usually doesn't truly bend in longeing, and the best you can hope for is that he will move straight in his spine. When a horse has spent a lot of time longeing, it becomes extremely difficult to teach him to bend later, in driving. This is why you should not overdo work on the longe. Spend only as much time as is necessary to achieve those intermediate training goals.

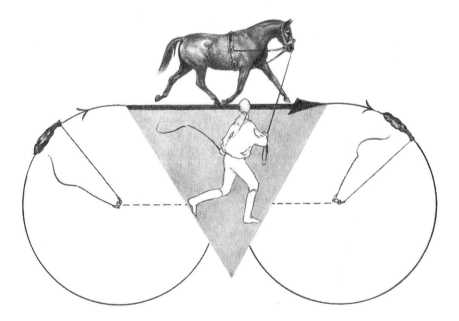

Teaching the horse to lengthen his stride at the trot on the longe.

Also, please don't depend on longeing as exercise for your horse. Moving constantly in a circle for long periods of time is very stressful on all his leg joints, especially for a youngster. If your horse needs exercise, be sure he spends plenty of time turned out with his buddies, or pony him around a large field. You can also "free-longe" him around an arena, encouraging him to move around you and use the entire space available. (But don't chase him wildly around a small space; you want him to work off his excess energy, not learn to run away each time you approach him. Use your regular commands and signals from your whip to encourage him forward.)

Keep your longeing sessions brief (no more than 20 to 30 minutes), and change directions every five minutes to avoid tiring him more on one side or the other. Longeing circles should be no smaller than 20 meters in diameter; larger is better. Avoid longeing in a small round pen, as you will need an area where you and the horse can travel in a straight line for a distance. By asking for some work on a straight line, along with your circles, you will give the horse a chance to relax his inside legs for a few minutes. This will help prevent tiring. It also encourages him to move forward more freely. If the horse is especially talented, you can also introduce a little lengthening in the trot along the long, straight side of your training area. The drawing on page 104 illustrates how to ask the horse for lengthening on the longe line. Chapter 12, Transitions, also discusses this in greater detail.

First Steps in Longeing

If your horse is listening well to you as you lead him, it is very easy to move on to longeing. All you really have to teach him is to understand the whip and to move around you.

Begin on either side. Hold him quietly in one hand by the halter or by the longe line close to the halter, and hold the whip (with the lash tucked up at first, not dangling) in the other hand. Touch him with the whip all over his body, moving quietly but firmly (some horses are quite ticklish!). Be sure to repeat this on his other side, until he agrees that this is not a scary object.

Next, hold him in the same manner, but tap the whip gently on the upper part of his hind leg (near the gaskin) to ask him to move away from it by crossing his hind legs and stepping sideways. As he moves, turn his head slightly towards you and encourage him with your voice, saying "Over," "Step," or whatever you choose. (Try to vary the sounds of your commands, so that your command to step to the side doesn't sound at all like your command for a halt. "Over" and "Whoa" sound very similar; "Step" or "Side" may work better.)

Later, you will also want to teach him to move away when you touch him on his barrel, where a rider's leg would lie. You will need this skill later when you encourage him to bend correctly through his turns.

Reward his first steps profusely with pats and kind words, and then ask for a few more steps. It is important to give the horse plenty of time to fully understand this, so he does not become frightened and try to run from it. Do not demand that he move sharply. You do not want a horse to leap away at the touch of a whip; you simply want him to acknowledge it as a command, and to oblige by calmly stepping aside.

Repeat the same exercise on the opposite side. Once he has grasped this command, let go of the halter and give him a little slack on the longe line as you ask him to step to the side, so he can move forward as well as sideways. Give him the command to walk. You will have to move with him, stepping backwards and to the side to establish a small circle.

Most horses grasp the idea quite quickly. If your horse keeps walking directly toward you, stop and repeat the first exercise again. You can also try making him stand in place while you move back to the center of your small circle; when you are in place, give him the command to walk on. If he still walks toward you, point the whip at his shoulder and wave it a little to tell him to move back out onto the circle.

Once the horse has learned to walk in a small circle in both directions, you can enlarge the circle and begin the walk-halt transitions, and then ask for transitions into and out of the trot. Use the full diameter of your longeing circle when he begins trotting, to minimize the strain on his legs. Do not ask him for trot work on anything smaller than a 20-meter circle.

One note about the trot: Some horses are bred to produce a gait other than a trot; nearly all the same training considerations will apply, no matter what the horse's natural "intermediate gait" may be. We have noticed that a horse who paces or does a running walk may begin to perform a very nice trot once he has learned to stretch his topline and lower his head. A horse that exhibits any intermediate gait other than a trot will be penalized in competitions recognized by the American Driving Society.

Canter on the Longe

It is very important that a driving horse learn to canter. Many trainers feel that the canter should be completely discouraged, but this is the wrong approach.

The canter is a natural gait for most breeds, and when a horse becomes excited and tries to get away from something that frightens him, he will usually try to do this at the canter. If you do not ever allow your horse to canter, and he spooks and bolts one day in harness, neither he nor you will know how to handle it. In addition to being frightened by an object or noise, he will also be scared because he will think he is doing something bad.

Since the uneven motion of the canter is very different from the steady rhythm of the trot, your horse will also find this frightening unless he has been properly introduced to it in safe surroundings. If he has learned to canter on command, and to come down to the trot calmly when asked, the canter itself will not be a terrifying experience.

Cantering is also useful exercise to supple your horse's back, since the canter requires the spine to "coil." The trot, which uses diagonal pairs of legs, tends to flatten the horse's back instead.

Introduce the canter on the longe only after your horse is obedient to your commands for walk, trot and halt. It is easy for your horse to buck at the canter if he is so inclined, and you must reprimand any attempts of this sort.

After you have moved on to hitching and actual driving, it's a good idea to ask for the canter first in your ring (if it is fairly large), and later on a long stretch uphill on a wide, straight trail or dirt road. Once your horse is comfortable with this, you can introduce a canter on level ground. Don't, however, ask a driving horse to canter downhill. (He may find the temptation to buck too strong to resist!)

Backing
No horse likes to back up. It is a very obvious demonstration of his submission, and it is also quite hard on the hind legs, which are designed to push forward. (Try walking straight backward yourself, and you will feel different muscles come into use. Our legs are rather straight, and it is easy for us to walk backwards. The horse, with his very angular hind legs, finds it far more difficult.)

Backing up is essential for a driving horse. Your horse must be willing to back when asked. The horse who reins back on command, stepping straight and calm, can help prevent accidents and get his vehicle out of tight situations.

Some horses do, however, learn to use running backward as an evasion at times—and this can be even more dangerous in driving than refusing to back up at all. This is why your horse must learn to back on command for exactly the number of steps you ask for, but no more—and to move forward again immediately on command.

Begin asking your young horse to back in hand, a few steps at a time. This should be a part of his early halter training, even before you introduce the harness and the longe line. Gradually increase your requests from one or two steps backward, up to ten steps backward.

Although you should praise any early attempts to back—no matter how crooked they are—you will eventually want to stress straightness in backing, and for this purpose working alongside a wall or fence is helpful. Use your voice commands and backwards pressure on his halter, if necessary; try to avoid pushing on his chest, where the collar will press later. And remember to ask for the halt when you want him to stop backing.

A horse that backs correctly will use his legs in diagonal pairs, stepping back straight and picking up his feet in good-sized steps. He will not drag his feet through the footing.

The horse can only back properly and easily if his jaws are softly flexed and his topline relaxed. If this does not happen, he will stagger, toss his head up and throw himself to either side, or perhaps begin to rush backwards. Go back to asking for only a step or two at a time, encouraging him to relax and remain supple. Sliding sidereins are a great help here, because they encourage suppleness, relaxation and a stretched topline, while giving him lateral stability.

Once your horse backs in hand by voice command alone, you can introduce this as part of your work in longeing, and then in ground driving. Only when the horse backs willingly in ground driving and on the longe should he be asked to back when hitched to the cart.

When to Move On

Your work on the single longe line is well concluded when your horse walks, trots, canters, halts and backs up on command, traveling in either direction. (Some horses do not canter easily on the longe or in harness, and cantering is not absolutely necessary.) He should demonstrate willingness and relaxation, and should accept the bit, sidereins and harness with calmness and assurance. He should be able to balance around the arc of a 20-meter (or slightly larger) circle, and he should travel equally well in both directions. When you have reached this stage, it is time to move on.

Think of longeing as a transitional training stage. Your goal is to move on to ground driving as soon as you can. The next step toward that goal is longeing with two lines.

Work on the Double Longe

Working the horse with two longe lines is the next step toward ground

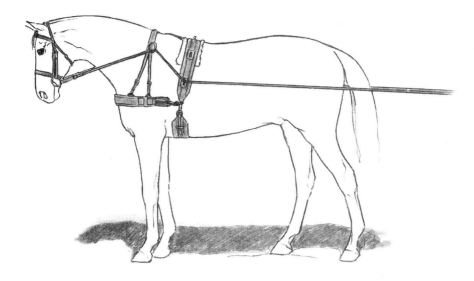

Rigging for long-lining with a breast collar. Although the reins do have the proper angle toward the bit (and will prevent pulling the horse together as in the following illustration), even this arrangement may be uncomfortable for sensitive horses. A pulley effect is created because of the sharp angle the reins make in passing from the terrets to the surcingle; there is also extra friction on the reins because of this.

driving. With two lines, we can teach him to steer and to associate bit pressure with voice commands that he already knows.

Until now, the single longe line has been attached to the halter or cavesson, but when we add the second longe line, we will attach the lines directly to the bit and ask the horse to begin accepting commands through his mouth. This will be a major adjustment for him, and it is important that we introduce these elements properly.

Do not proceed to longeing with two lines until your horse goes well on the single line (unless you have already been ground driving your youngster with the lines attached to the halter, as illustrated on page 101).

The first few times you attempt longeing with two lines, attach them to the side rings of your halter or cavesson. Then, if your horse becomes upset by the feeling of the lines around his body and hind legs, he won't jerk himself in the mouth in his efforts to avoid the lines. You want him to learn that it's okay if he gets tangled up a bit, and he doesn't have to panic. If this happens, you will firmly ask him to stand while you calmly sort everything out.

If he hasn't yet had the feel of a rein or longe line getting caught under his tail, you'll want to introduce this, also. When this happens, ask him to

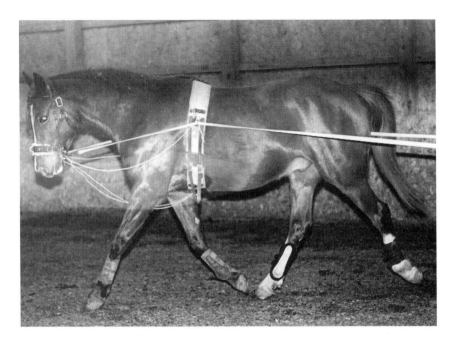

This shows our young horse in long lines. Although the lines are very light and are guided through the highest rings on the surcingle, he is still pulled together a little too much. This is a clear disadvantage of the long lines. For this reason, we prefer driving the young horse as soon as possible in a light cart, using sliding sidereins if necessary.

halt as you ease the line out from under his tail. This is bound to happen sooner or later, and you'll want it to happen first in ground work, *before* you hitch him for the first time. It isn't pleasant for a horse to feel a rein under his tail, but this is still another thing he must come to accept.

When he is comfortable with the feel of two longe lines attached to his halter, you can then attach them to the bit. Ideally, the reins should run from the bit through rein rings on the breast collar neckstrap, and from there down to rings set fairly low on the belly girth. (See illustration on page 109.) This approximates the feel of the reins the horse will receive when he's actually driving, but will keep the reins low enough so they don't get caught under his tail. This method, however, causes quite a bit of friction on the reins, and takes away much of the driver's direct feeling of the horse's mouth. By having the first few yards of the reins sewn round, and by dusting them with talcum powder, the friction can be minimized— but most people won't want to go to this much trouble to double longe one or two horses.

The most practical method is to run the lines from the horse's bit (or, at first, the halter) back through rings on the surcingle or belly girth to the trainer's hands, as shown on page 110. The placement of the rings on the surcingle is very important. You want the lines to be low enough to avoid getting caught under the horse's tail, but high enough so they won't pull the head way down.

If you place the lines too low (through rings very low on the belly girth or low rings on a surcingle), you'll have a great deal of leverage on his mouth, and it is very easy to cause the horse to overbend and quit his free forward motion.

If you don't have a suitable surcingle, one solution is to run the lines through the tugs of the harness. This should allow them to move freely at about the right height. When the lines are in this fairly low position, sidereins are not necessary unless your horse has a very bad ewe neck.

Some trainers place a lot of emphasis—and spend a lot of time—on double-longe work. Although this is a necessary step in the education of the driving horse, it has some serious drawbacks. For one thing, it is very difficult to rig the two longe lines in such a way that they do not apply too much pressure on the mouth. (This problem is shown clearly on page 110.)

So, while this step is necessary to help the horse understand the new demands placed on him, you will do best to keep it brief, be extremely careful about how the lines are handled once they are attached to the bit and move on to ground driving as soon as you can.

With the lines in place (first on the halter, and later on the bit), ask your horse to begin walking around you in a longeing circle. Take plenty of time for both of you to become accustomed to this new arrangement before you begin to direct him through the lines. Gradually, as you work him through his walk, trot, halt and reinback, you will add the rein commands to the voice.

Steering—From Longeing into Ground Driving

When he is comfortable with this, you can begin steering him. From your longeing circle, simply direct him to walk forward on a straight line, perhaps following a fence or wall, and then ask him to turn again. Make your turns large and gradual, and give him plenty of time at the walk to find his balance. You should be walking with him, behind him but slightly to one side so he can keep you in view easily. As you change directions, cross over to his other side. (This means you will not have to travel as many steps, as well as helping him keep you in sight.)

Do not rush this part of your horse's training. Spend a lot of time at the walk and practice many turns and walk/halt transitions. When you feel he is very responsive at the walk, move on to the trot, making sure that you do not hang on his mouth in an effort to keep up. For the trot, use plenty of 20-meter circles interspersed with straight lines. If you become tired, ask for a smooth transition to the walk *before* you are out of breath! It is very important that your horse listens well to your voice commands, and that you *use them*, so you do not have to pull at his mouth all the time for the downward transitions.

As soon as your horse steers well with the reins running along his side, you can move them to the terrets. This will introduce him and you to the actual feel of the reins when you are driving.

Some trainers like to keep the horse at this stage of training for a very long time, and will try to teach bending, collection, extension and movements such as half passes, serpentines and so forth. This is not necessary, although complex work on long lines can be of great benefit in the hands of highly skilled, very knowledgeable dressage trainers (who are also very fit and can keep up with the horse without hanging on his mouth!), but there can also be a great danger in this sort of work when it is incorrectly done. Many horses end up nervous, stiff and unable to bend correctly as a result of "too much too soon." Often, the so-called collection that is achieved in long lines with these horses is merely an incorrect "pulling together."

True collection is impossible for young, green or unmuscled horses to accomplish, and they shouldn't be asked to try. A horse that has been *ridden* correctly and consistently for two years, and is well muscled, may be able to offer real collection in long lines.

So, do not ask for tight circles or any attempt at "collection" from your green horse. You cannot ask a horse to bend correctly by turning him in small circles that destroy the free forward movement.

Your goal at this stage of the training is to make your horse obedient and responsive without destroying his movement and *his willingness to stretch into your hands*.

With practice and agility, you'll probably be able to negotiate a smooth change of hand at the trot from one 20-meter circle to another—and that should be about the limit of your ground-driving acrobatics. Once he's hitched and actually driving, you'll be able to strengthen the correct muscles, teach him to bend and perform smooth transitions and eventually ask for real collection.

What you *can* do while ground driving is to repeat some of the work you did earlier on your walks. Take your green horse out onto the trails for a "drive," and ask him to go over logs, through puddles and past scary things while you drive him from behind. Go visit the cows and travel down your safe roads. Be ready, however, to deal with any problems quickly and firmly. If he spooks at something, twists sideways or tries to flee, you may have to grab him very firmly on the mouth. If he stalls, you can introduce the whip as a strong driving aid, perhaps even using it as punishment if necessary.

Now is also the time to teach him to step to the side when you touch his barrel with the whip (if you haven't done this already). Hold him quietly in hand, tap him on the barrel (where a rider's leg would be) with the whip, and use your voice to ask him to step to the side. Once he understands this, you can ground drive him at the walk and ask for a little more bend through the turns by touching him with the whip on the inside of his barrel as you turn. He should move quietly but obediently away from the whip, stepping more underneath his body with his inside hind leg. (See Chapter 10, The Lateral Bend.)

Once he is comfortable with all of this, exchange his light open bridle for a regular driving bridle with blinders, and work him in this so he becomes accustomed to listening for your commands without always looking for you. He now has to learn that even when things happen back where he can't see you, he must rely on your voice and your hands for direction and security.

Ground driving is a vital part of the process, but it's not the end product. Besides, once he's confident and comfortable in his groundwork, you'll want to move on to actually hitching and driving him. Then you won't have to jog around behind him any more.

HITCHING

Your horse is doing well in his ground driving, and you feel that you are ready to introduce him to an actual vehicle.

There are a number of things the two of you must do before that happens, however.

• NOISE AND COMMOTION •

You cannot keep your driving horse forever sheltered from noises that may upset him. You must, in fact, go out of your way to introduce him to noises and ask him to accept them. He must be willing to trust you and behave reliably under any and all circumstances, or you will never have a truly safe driving horse.

Introduce your horse to all the noise-makers first when he is wearing an open, or unblindered, bridle. Many horses go into a real panic when something they cannot see makes a loud noise behind them. Others are more complacent and will react with calmness no matter what sort of bridle they are wearing.

A good first noise-maker is a wheelbarrow, as it sounds somewhat like a cart. Have a friend wheel the wheelbarrow behind you and your horse as you ground drive him at a walk around your training area. If he accepts this without fuss, put a rake or shovel in the wheelbarrow and continue driving him while the wheelbarrow clatters behind.

Next, have the wheelbarrow travel beside him, have it pass in front of him, come directly toward him, and so on. Continue with this until he is completely comfortable with it. Drive in both directions, asking him to turn, halt and walk on your command. Work him through the same routine with his driving bridle, also.

Be sure to work equally in both directions; a horse may accept a strange object when he sees it with his left eye, but will spook as soon as it approaches him from the right. This doesn't indicate a failing on his part, but is simply a function of his binocular vision and the fact that the two halves of a horse's brain exchange very little information.

More Noise

After the horse becomes bored with the wheelbarrow and rake, you must become creative. Only your imagination and a few necessary safety precautions will set the limit. Remember that you want to introduce your horse to successively more frightening noises and situations, but never in such a way that he will be hurt if he puts a foot wrong or gets too close to your contraptions. Be sure that your helper has clear instructions about what to do, where he should stand or move and how loud you want the noises to be.

Introduce horns, bells, rattles, someone banging on pie plates, yippy dogs, crinkling tissue paper, capguns and rattling plastic. Fire up a lawnmower, start a chainsaw and play Sousa marches at full volume on your tape deck. Work the horse quietly in his training area, first with an open bridle if he seems to need it, and then with his driving bridle. Repeat all the noises, first from a distance and then at closer quarters.

It's terrible, really, to have to put our horses through all this, but it is absolutely vital for everyone's safety.

Amazingly enough, nine out of ten horses that accept the wheelbarrow will also come to accept all of the other strange noises you can create. It is a good example of their ability to adapt to the environment, and their trust in us—the people they view as their superiors.

The Nervous or Panicky Horse

Some horses accept all this commotion easily, but others—especially those who have led a quiet, sheltered life—will react with anything ranging from high anxiety to sheer panic. These horses may try to bolt, rear or at least turn around to face their tormentor (especially if they are wearing blinders). Let your horse turn to face the wheelbarrow a time or two without scolding him. Then ask him to continue in his work, and be firm as you give him commands.

If he rears or tries to bolt, however, you must be sharp in your correction.

Now is the time to teach your horse that he must never get away from you, no matter what happens. If you do not establish this now, you will always have an unreliable horse. If your horse rears or shoots forward, you must give him a sharp jerk in the mouth and very angry words. If he is a very strong horse, you may have to switch to a more severe bit to enforce your commands. But he must *not* be allowed to rear, kick, bolt or leap sideways.

If he is so frightened that he becomes rooted in place but does not attempt to bolt, try leading him quietly around, reassuring him as you walk past the wheelbarrow.

Moderate nervousness is okay—some horses are nervous about loud noises for quite a long time—but as long as they listen to the trainer and are completely manageable, there is no reason to give up on them as driving horses.

The moderately nervous horse may well make a very good driving horse, as he is often very attentive and quick to learn. ("Moderately nervous" does not mean insane or unpredictable; he must still be easily controlled.) The best horse we ever drove was a total flake as a three-year-old, and even when he was a lot older, he could sometimes act in a way that could have frightened anyone that did not know him. However, he was so obedient, so easy to control and hold back, that he could have been driven in a halter. He was almost offended by even the gentlest bit, and anyone could have driven him anytime, anywhere.

The nervous horse learns to deal on a daily basis with scary things, and he becomes used to being helped through them by his trainer—if he fully trusts the trainer. The trainer learns, through experience, what the horse is capable of and how to prepare for difficult situations.

We've found that the really dangerous horses are the ones that seem to be bothered by nothing, yet have a relatively insensitive mouth and don't care about obeying, respecting or learning from their trainers. You cannot prepare them—or yourself—for every possible situation to occur. One day, however, you and this horse will be in a dangerous and scary situation, and neither one of you will know how to deal with it. Because this horse has not learned to trust and depend on his driver for guidance, you'll have serious trouble—probably resulting in a runaway.

By contrast, a very nervous horse is not what you want for a driving partner. A horse that does not accept the empty wheelbarrow after two or three training sessions will not make a reliable driving horse. He may still be quite suitable as a riding horse, but you may have to face up to the fact that this horse just won't be trustworthy in harness. There are quite a few horses that just are not able to become driving horses, and usually it is because they cannot accept this part of the training.

It is far better to realize this early, before you hitch him to the cart and suffer a crash. Your ground training has not been in vain, however, as you have laid an excellent foundation for all types of further training under saddle. It is not necessarily your fault that your young horse won't accept training as a driving horse; be prepared to deal with this and, if necessary, exchange him for one of more accepting temperament.

Be sure you thoroughly introduce your young driving horse to a wide variety of scary and startling sights and sounds.

• MORE SCARY STUFF •

Once a horse accepts noises, you can move on to ground driving him over, past and through all sorts of strange things. You've done a little of this in your walks and ponying on the trails, but now you will go out of your way to create situations that will challenge and confirm your horse's trust in you.

Ask him to walk over blankets, newspapers, plastic and canvas tarpaulins (especially black ones), plywood and old tires. Drive him past people holding umbrellas (and be sure to open one suddenly in front of him), blankets hung on a fence, trash bags and trash barrels (one with smoke coming out of it is even better); walk him between lines of sheets on clotheslines or strung up on ropes between posts. The more you show him, the better.

Next comes traffic. While you and your horse are driving along the road, have a friend come up close behind in a car and hit the brakes suddenly, honk the horn, pass rapidly (first with a margin of safety, then closer), speed directly toward you and swerve around. When he's comfortable with the car, go through the same antics with a tractor, motorcycle and bicycle (sometimes horses are suspicious of a bicycle because it *doesn't* make much noise!). If you have someone who can bring you a large truck and a nice yellow school bus, consider yourself lucky—and invite him over.

Strangely enough, most horses we have trained actually enjoyed all of this crazy stuff after they became used to it, and seemed to become quite proud of themselves. If you handle all of this "combat training" carefully and thoroughly, you'll have a solid, road-safe driving horse.

•   LEARNING TO PULL   •

The next step is to teach your horse to pull. This may be done before you work through the "combat training" or after. Almost every horse will be willing to pull, but not every horse will accept the noises and commotion as he needs to to become a safe driving horse. We also like to test a young horse with a training shaft early on, to see if he will be unduly bothered by it. If he can't accept being touched all over his sides and tolerate the feeling of a shaft next to his body, you won't want to spend all this time teaching him to drive.

To teach your horse to pull, you will need a helper and a spare singletree or a one-by-two about three feet long. Drilling a hole in each end of the one-by-two will make it easier to attach to the traces. First, lengthen the traces with rope so that you can attach the singletree or one-by-two about five to six feet behind the horse. Your helper will hold this at about waist height and follow behind as you drive your horse at a walk. Extending the traces with rope gives your helper plenty of clearance in case the horse bucks or kicks.

Walk the horse on, and have the helper gradually put more weight into the horse, adding more drag if the horse does fine and easing up if the horse gets nervous or "stalls." If they've gotten this far in their training, most horses will accept this without any trouble. The nervous horse will need a little extra time, and you should be very gradual in applying more weight to the traces.

Once the horse pulls quietly into a steady weight, ask your helper to pull harder, and then release the weight suddenly, so the horse feels a jerk against his chest. You want to simulate the effect of a carriage starting and stopping. Then increase the weight again, and ask the horse to pull forward out of the halt.

During these exercises, your handler should also allow the traces to touch and eventually almost slap the horse's sides and upper hind legs. (But don't actually hit the horse with the traces!) He must accept all these activities calmly and without any signs of anxiety before you can actually hitch him to the drag.

If you do encounter trouble and your helper has to drop the singletree suddenly, no great harm will be done. The piece of wood is light enough not to hurt the horse (or anyone else) seriously. The horse will probably get somewhat tangled up in the traces and perhaps the reins; however, after all the previous training, it is very unlikely that something like this will happen.

Introducing the Shafts

Once the horse is pulling willingly and quietly accepts the traces and the weight of the helper, you can introduce a shaft substitute. First, use a short piece of wood (your one-by-two will work) to rub and touch the horse's shoulders, sides and flanks; then introduce a rigid, fairly heavy pole about six feet long and two to three inches in diameter. (This doesn't have to be fancy; we use a sapling trunk with the bark peeled off.)

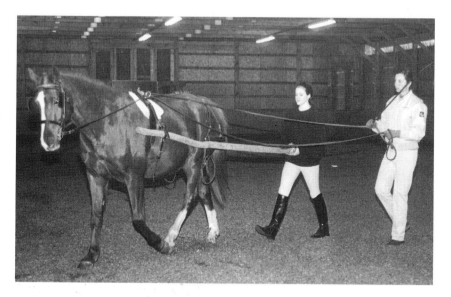

The young horse is introduced to a single "shaft." If he becomes upset, the helper can easily pull it out of the tug.

Let the horse look at it and sniff it. Place the pole against the horse's body so he can feel it along its width, move it up and down a bit, and then slip one end into the tug on one side. Drive him at a walk while your helper moves with you and supports the other end of the pole. If your horse is not concerned, proceed to some gradual turns. Be sure to follow the same routine with the pole on the other side, also.

●   THE DRAG   ●

The next logical step in your training is to introduce the drag. Through trial and error, we have found that the best type of drag is the one pictured here. This was created at home to meet the needs of different horses. There are horses that can deal with shafts touching them but don't like the noise of the drag; there are other horses that seem to pull willingly but don't like the feel of the shafts. This drag can be used in different ways to address these problems.

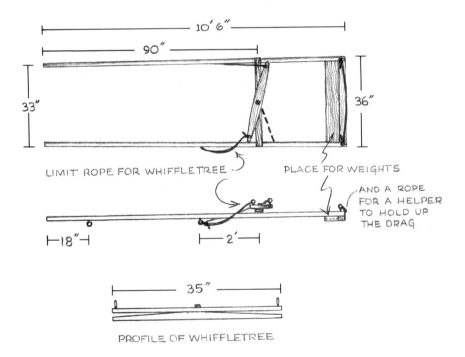

Our homemade drag.

A close view of the drag, with thin cinder blocks added for weight.

There is one drawback to this sort of drag. If a horse bucks or kicks, he can easily hook a leg over a shaft and panic. This happened only once to us: We had a badly spoiled older horse, who had been ridden for several years but had a known habit of bucking. This horse—a very intelligent Arab—was a quick learner in his groundwork and performed beautifully in the drag until one day he simply decided he was bored, and he bucked high and sideways, putting a hind leg over a shaft and getting tangled in the drag.

He could have panicked and tried to bolt, but instead he waited quietly until we were able to free him. He was fine after that, and never tried it again.

Although we have to remember that this type of drag has this drawback, it's still the best arrangement available. A horse that is inclined to buck in harness is going buck at some point anyway, and it's better to have him try it in the drag than when hitched to a carriage. The shafts of the drag are so low that there's less chance for serious damage—to the people, the horse or the equipment.

If the horse does get hung up through bucking and try to bolt, he will either learn that bucking is the wrong thing to do, or he will refuse to be placed back in the drag. If he totally refuses to accept the drag, you wouldn't have a reliable driving horse under any circumstances—and you might as well learn about this early, saving your time, your money and your health.

Nearly every driving horse experiences some sort of major or minor upset. The ones that are worthy of becoming driving horses are the ones that will go back and try it again for you; they learn from the upsetting incident and don't attempt the same behavior that caused the problem.

There are horses that simply cannot handle it when things go wrong. One horse that did not learn from a bad experience was a paint mare, who is no longer in our stable. She went through her driving training with flying colors and was driving well for two years. One day, while she was driving without blinders—which she very much enjoyed—she saw something absolutely horrible behind her (we still don't know what), and bolted. Seeing the cart bouncing behind her, she became even more panicky and began bucking and kicking. One hind leg went over a shaft, but she continued running and bucking. A wheel came off the cart and we fell out of the cart—fortunately without serious injury—while the mare ran into a newly plowed field and finally stopped from sheer exhaustion.

This mare later became nervous even if her tail got between her hind legs. After she bolted several more times while in harness, we decided it was not worth the danger and the trouble, and sold her as a riding horse. She was quite happy in her new job and gave no trouble.

So, if the bucking is going to occur, better to have it happen when the horse is in the drag than when you are in the carriage. The real advantage of the drag is that it simulates a carriage with a feel of the shafts, because he feels them against his body through the turns; and you can add weight to it, teaching him to pull. This will strengthen him and prepare him for the weight of the carriage, which is especially important for small or very young horses.

This type of drag should only be used on soft, fairly smooth footing. Don't try it on the road—the noise it creates is absolutely unbearable, not so much to the horse as to the driver's ears. Using it on a hard surface would also cause it to wear out quickly.

Attaching the Drag

If everything has gone well up to this point, it is time to attach the drag.

Give your horse a chance to thoroughly examine the drag before you bring it into position. It's a good idea to work him first without blinders, so he can see this thing that will be traveling behind him. When you and your helper bring the shafts up on either side of him, let them rub and touch his sides. Slip the tugs only a little way onto the shafts, and do not attach the

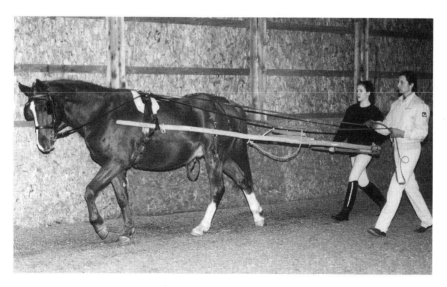

For the introduction to the drag, have your helper carry it. Again, it can be easily pulled from the tugs if necessary.

traces at all. Ask him to walk on, while your helper holds the drag up off the ground. The shafts of the drag will pull out of the tugs if the horse moves forward too quickly, so as long as he is quiet, your helper must walk along as pictured above, traveling at the same speed as the horse.

If your horse seems at all nervous about the shafts on both sides of him, don't slip the shafts into the tugs. Instead, take your unattached shaft substitute, obtain a second pole like it and slip these through the tugs instead of the drag shafts. Then walk the horse forward with your helper holding both poles, letting the poles touch him in the turns as they would if they were attached to the drag. If he shoots forward or sideways, or becomes very nervous, your helper can easily pull the poles out of the tugs and get out of the way. Once he accepts the two poles, go on to the drag.

When the horse is comfortable with the drag being carried behind him, remove the shafts from the tugs and have your helper pull the drag along behind the horse, so he can hear the sound it makes on the ground. If this does not bother him, you can then place the drag on the ground, slip the shafts back into the tugs, attach the traces and ask the horse to begin pulling it. Once he is actually hitched to the drag, it's a good idea to lead the horse, instead of ground driving him, to be in a better position to both control and reassure him. Another measure of control and safety is to attach a longe line to the halter and have your helper hold this, walking along as you drive him from the rear.

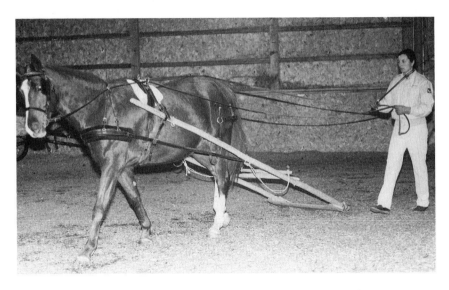

The young horse is hooked to the drag.

If you have been driving your horse with the lines run through the rings at the top of the saddle (which you should be doing regularly now), you may find that the extra effort of pulling the drag causes the horse to go crooked and wander. You can run the lines through the tugs (on top of the shafts) for a few sessions to regain the sideways stability.

Add weight gradually to the drag to simulate the weight of a cart, remembering that because the drag has no wheels it is automatically more difficult to pull than a wheeled vehicle. Try pulling it yourself to judge the amount of weight you should add, and adjust this to the size, age and fitness of your horse. The illustration on page 121 shows the simple method we use to add weight to the drag.

Keep your pulling sessions short at first: For a two-year-old, this should be just 15 minutes, no more than four times a week. An older horse can be worked a little longer and more often.

Once these lessons are going well and your horse is comfortable with the shafts, the weight and the feel of the drag while you drive him from behind—and you can trot him in it for short periods of time, without any nervousness—you can introduce him to the breeching, and then it's time to bring out the cart.

The Breeching
Your horse has been comfortable carrying the breeching, and he isn't bothered at all any more by the straps flapping around his hindquarters.

Before you can hitch him to the cart, however, he must accept the feel of the breeching going taut. Even though, as a foal, he may have first learned to walk forward on a lead rope with the pressure of a butt rope around his rump, we must now teach him to accept and even sit back into the breeching of the harness.

Ideally, you will have two helpers for this session. Have a helper stand on each side holding the breeching strap. Drive your horse forward, and ask your helpers to tighten the breeching against the horse's hindquarters while you practice stops from the walk. Begin with steady, gentle pressure, quietly applied, and work up to a fairly strong, intermittent, abrupt pull as the horse learns to accept it.

This requires good coordination between the three humans, to ensure that the breeching is tightened evenly and effectively. A sensitive horse will probably try to step forward again as soon as he feels the pressure of the breeching, and it will take repeated, careful work to explain to him that this is one time when we *don't* want him to move away from pressure. Most horses, however, learn quickly to accept this new demand.

• HITCHING UP FOR THE FIRST TIME •

The Training Cart

It is very difficult to find a suitable training cart for this beginning work. If the cart is lightweight, the seat is probably very low, and you won't be able to look over the top of your horse—which can be very dangerous, since you can't really see where you're going. If the cart lets you sit high enough to see over the horse, it's probably too heavy.

We came up with a workable solution by building up the seat on a standard training cart. The addition of a sturdy wooden box, plus a floor board built into the basket, allows the driver good vision without making the cart too heavy. This is the cart illustrated on pages 127–132.

We also exchanged the original light wheels for motorcycle wheels, because the original ones wore out and punctured too easily. The original shafts were too straight and would poke a horse in the neck in turns. The straight shafts would also occasionally get hung up on a fence or the wall of the indoor arena. To solve this, we constructed custom-made shaft ends that curve sharply out and down to give the green horse plenty of room to bend in his turns. The shafts are somewhat longer than average, also, so the driver and cart are in less danger from a kick. (The kicking strap will keep a horse from bucking or kicking high enough to get a hind foot over the shaft, but an energetic horse can still aim a direct kick backwards toward the cart itself. With the extra-long shafts, it's harder for him to connect and do damage.)

Unfortunately, this cart has no brake. The original design of this lightweight sulky-type cart meant that we couldn't find anyone to fit a brake to it. This training cart is used only in the ring on level footing—but we would still prefer to have a brake on it.

If we have a nervous, unpredictable horse to hitch for the first time, sometimes we'll hitch him to the road cart pictured in Chapters 11, 12 and 13—even though this is quite a bit heavier. The brake on the road cart provides a very important margin of safety, which can make all the difference in successful early driving lessons.

Hitching to the Cart for the First Time

It's a good idea to hitch your horse to the drag one last time before you introduce the cart. Have him pull the drag for a few minutes, asking him to turn and trot so you can assess his mood and remind him of his job.

You will need a helper; if your horse is the slightly nervous type, it's a good idea to have two helpers. Unhitch the horse from the drag and stand him in front of the training cart, facing it. Have your helper move the cart around a bit, raising and lowering the shafts and making all possible noises with it. Pull the cart in a circle around the horse a few times, then ground drive him while your helper pulls the cart along behind the horse.

When the horse shows you that he is completely untroubled by this, have him stand quietly and attach a lead line to the bit so your helper can hold him while you hitch him. (This is where you may want to use two lead lines and two helpers if you feel it is necessary.) Now, bring up the cart and hitch him.

You do not want to appear rushed or make him nervous, but do not waste any time while hitching. This is the most dangerous part of the driving process; there is nothing worse than a horse taking off when he's only half-attached to the cart. It's a good idea to fix both trace and breeching on one side, then cross to the other to do the trace and breeching on the other side. This minimizes the amount of time you spend crossing from one side of the horse to the other. If you then have to walk back around to make adjustments, at least the horse is completely hitched to the cart at this point.

The use of a kicking strap is highly recommended now. It's a simple bit of insurance that will inhibit thoughts of kicking or bucking. (Using a kicking strap on the drag wouldn't have prevented a horse from kicking or bucking,

Our young horse hitched to the cart for the first time, with two helpers leading him on loose lines and the driver walking behind the cart.

because of the drag's low profile and light weight; in fact, it would have made things more dangerous if the horse bucked or kicked, because then the kicking straps would have pulled the drag up off the ground with the force of the horse's movement.)

When he is hitched, take up the reins and place yourself either next to or behind the cart and ask your horse to walk forward. Your helper(s) will walk with the horse, keeping the lead loose and holding it at about the height of the horse's shoulder.

After you have walked for a few minutes, if the horse is calm and doing well, have him halt. Get into the cart and ask him to walk again, with your helper still holding the lead line. Finally, if all is going well, have him halt again while your helper removes the lead.

Now you are on your own.

If the horse is the calm, unflappable type and has accepted everything quietly, you can walk for a few minutes and then try a trot. If the trot makes him uneasy, come down to a walk, and try again a few minutes later. For a nervous horse, don't ask for anything more than a walk during the first few sessions. Encourage him to become thoroughly relaxed and confident before you attempt a trot. It's a good idea to bring your helpers back to jog with him on the lead lines when you do try the trot.

Keep your first driving sessions brief—no more than 15 minutes for a two-and-a-half-year-old horse. An older horse can take a little more, but

Here the driver is in the cart, but the helpers remain in case anything goes wrong.

don't push him too hard during these first lessons in the cart. The physical development will come gradually; the important thing to remember right now is that the horse must remain obedient, calm and willing.

How Should the Breeching Be Attached?

Run the breeching strap through the breeching fixture on the underside of the shaft and wrap it around the shaft at least once in front of the fixture. Guide the end of the strap back underneath the first wrap, and from there to the buckle. (If the breeching isn't long enough to wrap around the shaft, it's too short and you need to replace it with a longer one.) It is very important to keep the breeching strap in place and wrapped tightly around the shaft.

The trace should run through the loop created by the breeching strap. *Never* wrap the breeching strap around the trace, as this will inhibit the action of the singletree. If you forget to run the trace through the breeching strap loop, it isn't a terrible thing, but the trace may rub more against the horse, and if you are competing with this sort of arrangement you will be penalized for having improperly hitched your horse.

The breeching should be tight enough so that when the horse is in "pull," you can fit one fist between the breeching and his hindquarters. He should have total freedom and range of motion with his hind legs in any gait, without being restricted by the breeching. If the breeching is just a little too tight, especially in the walk and in the canter (where there's a definite back-and-forth movement in the horse's body), your horse will be bothered by the alternating action of first the collar bumping his chest as he pulls and then the breeching hitting his hindquarters as the cart comes forward.

On the other hand, even a slightly too-loose breeching will cause problems. The loose breeching may hit the horse hard and suddenly if he stops unexpectedly. Receiving a sudden and powerful yank on his haunches, he may jump forward again—and when you try to stop him, he'll be hit by the breeching again. This can be dangerous, especially with a nervous sort of horse. A brake will definitely help in this situation.

Your Training Area

Where you work your horse can have a great influence on the progress of your training. When you start a horse in driving, you must have the best footing possible on the most level ground available. It is nearly impossible for a weak or green horse to relax when he is constantly tripping or must pull hard simply to travel over the ground.

The best surfaces are smooth-mowed grass (almost lawnlike), packed sand or stone dust, or wood fiber footing. If the footing is too soft, the wheels of the cart will sink in and create extra drag. The footing should not be rock-hard, either; too-hard footing will place additional strain on your horse's legs, which will be stressed enough already with the new work and nearly constant turning he must do. Your training area should certainly not resemble a gravel pit, with loose rocks underfoot.

It does not matter if there is a *slight* slope to your training area, but it should be barely noticeable. It is very difficult for a horse to bend through a turn while traveling downhill, and constant changes in grade will cause him to be always trying to adjust to the differences between pulling and being pushed by the carriage. This will do nothing to help his balance and rhythm. Once he has progressed in his training and gained strength, he will be better able to deal with these factors, but any horse *always* deserves the best footing to work on.

The size and shape of your arena is also very important. The smallest place you should ever work a horse in harness is a 20-by-40 meter arena. Better is 20 by 60 meters, but the ideal size is 40 by 80 meters or 40 by 100 meters. If the arena is fenced, it should be a rectangular area, not an oval. Although you will drive it as an oval at first with your green horse, you will later want to use the corners to teach him to bend properly. Every corner should be as square as possible so that each corner will feel the same as you drive it.

You don't have to have such an ideal space to teach a horse his basics; you can drive and work in any open space. You will also be able to work on some of your exercises (developing longitudinal bend, performing smooth transitions) on the trails. A good training arena, however, makes everything a lot easier for both horse and driver. In a proper arena, everything is far more predictable. Your horse will soon understand where to go, and he will be able to relax and gain in confidence. You will also be able to judge whether the horse is performing correctly—if he is going where you have directed him, bending consistently through each corner and so on.

It is also a good idea to start your driving horse in a fenced area. A fence will increase security for both of you. He won't be able to undertake unwanted excursions into the surrounding countryside, and if he does get going too fast or you lose control, you'll know he can't run far or cause major disasters involving other horses, people or traffic.

Although it is not absolutely necessary to have dressage letter markers placed around the perimeter, it certainly helps to have some method of indicating certain points of the arena. You cannot accurately execute a transition at a specific point when you have no specific points to refer to. Using standard dressage letters will give you these reference points, and if you go on to showing in dressage competition, you will have learned where all the letters are located.

If you don't want to buy or make dressage letters, plastic buckets with rocks in them will do as markers, and so will old tires. Even if you never plan to compete in dressage, these will help you find your reference points for training. At a minimum, use four: place them at the middle of the two long and two short sides of your arena. Don't use cement blocks or stakes pounded into the ground (unless they topple easily). These could prove dangerous.

The Beginning, Not the End

All the pieces of your basic training should now be in place and working for you. Your horse accepts noises, he knows how to pull, he doesn't mind the feel of the shafts on his body, he trusts you and listens to your commands, and he is thoroughly voice trained to walk, trot, back and—especially—stop and stand. If your horse is comfortable trotting around the ring, relaxed and showing no apprehension toward the cart, you have done well.

Now the real work can begin. You will now begin to focus on the gymnastic development of the horse's body, as you work to change his natural

Our young horse is going in the frame he offers naturally. Note that he is bitted with a broken liverpool, since he can get strong at times. He has become thoroughly accustomed to this bit, as used here with the rein set in the ring, and also with the reins in the first slot. A double-jointed snaffle would definitely be preferable, but safety comes first. After a few weeks in this bit he understood his job well enough to change to the double-jointed snaffle.

Here the driver is asking the horse actively to stretch forward and downward.

After he has been encouraged to stretch, our young horse is now working with engaged hindquarters. He reached this Training Level frame very quickly (after only two weeks) because he is well built, and this is obviously the frame he is comfortable in. Compare this to what he offers on his own in the top illustration on page 131. For progress to continue, however, the driver must still ask him always to stretch and seek the bit, to ensure that the horse keeps reaching and doesn't just hold himself in this position.

balance to one that fully enables him to cope with the demands that your driving will put upon him. The photographs above will give you an idea of this process, which is described in detail in the next several chapters.

Along with the systematic development of his body, your driving horse will also need lots of mileage. He needs time and experience to grow into his job. Many people assume that if the horse accepts the cart, he's a driving horse. You must remember that getting the horse to accept the cart is only one step in his training. It's the beginning, not the end, and the next two years will show if you really have a driving horse or not. It will take you that long to really get to know a horse, to be always able to predict what he is going to do, and to build the mutual trust and understanding necessary for reliable driving—even if you know the horse well as a riding horse.

Don't even think of taking a horse driving in public or to a horse show when you aren't sure of him. It is always surprising at a show to see so many horses that have been driving for only a few months. (God bless the unsuspecting!)

Now, through progressive steps in the training process, we will move on to develop a truly fine driving horse.

CHAPTER
· 9 ·

HANDLING
THE REINS

Communication between you and your driving horse can only be effected through the reins, voice and whip. Although you begin your training with voice commands (and you will continue to use these throughout your driving), as your horse gains more experience and becomes more comfortable with the bit, the reins will become more and more the primary means of communication.

• THE IMPORTANCE OF CORRECT REIN HANDLING •

Handling the reins correctly is vital. Your hands telegraph your commands through the reins to the bit—and the bit is the goal toward which the horse is working. Your hands can communicate direction, reward, punishment or sympathy; give support, soothe a nervous horse or encourage a lazy horse. Every green horse needs a driver with educated hands; nothing ruins a good horse faster than incompetent or careless hands.

Although you have certainly been handling the reins with a degree of confidence (and competence) if you have been driving for any length of time, it is important to realize that there are many different methods of holding and handling the reins. For different competitions, also, different levels of finesse and rein-handling intricacy are required.

• ONE HAND OR TWO? •

There are different methods of holding the reins that are suitable for different types of driving.

The American Driving Society Rule Book leaves it up to the competitor (usually) to choose a method of holding the reins. The only exception is in

Advanced dressage tests, where the driver is required to drive two circles (one in each direction) with both reins held in one hand. This is considered a very difficult movement.

Unfortunately, many judges in pleasure driving classes like to see the reins held in only the left hand, while the right hand holds the whip and occasionally helps to direct the horse. This is supposed to be regarded as proof of an obedient, pleasurable horse. But how can you ask a horse to bend correctly around his turns when both your reins are held in one hand? It is not possible to accommodate him with a leading rein and a bending rein when both reins are in the same hand. (See Chapter 10, The Lateral Bend.)

If holding the reins in one hand while executing a circle is required only at the most advanced level in dressage, why do judges expect to see something similar in a pleasure class? Not even in ridden dressage—where we at least have the seat and legs to help the horse—is this required. It is not fair to the horse!

Even so, you should familiarize yourself with methods of holding the reins in one hand because there are times when you will need a hand free. When you are driving long, fairly straight distances on dirt roads or trails, you should practice holding both reins and whip in one hand so that you are comfortable with this in case you need to use your whip or if any emergency arises.

• HOW TO HOLD THE REINS •

The most common practice is to hold one rein in each hand. In ground driving, most trainers will hold the reins this way, carrying the whip also in the right hand. Whether the rein enters at the bottom of the hand below the pinky (or between the pinky and ring finger) and exits at the top, between thumb and forefinger, or enters at the top and exits at the bottom, is simply a matter of personal preference.

This is fine for general pleasure driving. Lengthening the reins is simply a matter of letting them slide evenly through the fingers; shortening the reins is accomplished by the same method used in riding, where you briefly hold both reins in one hand and slide the other hand forward to a shorter position, and then repeat this for the second rein. The whip, carried in the right hand, points half-left forward and upward. (If you think of the horse as being at "twelve o'clock," the whip should be pointing to ten o'clock, and held about halfway between the horizontal and vertical.)

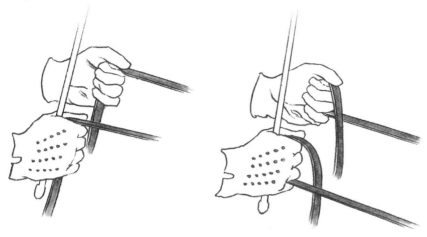

Common two-handed rein positions.

By holding the reins in both hands, you will be able to bend your horse correctly through his turns. It is not recommended, however, to hold the reins in this position while using the whip to signal your horse, because any movement of the whip will affect the rein held in the right hand. You will need, then, a one-handed position that you can easily move into if you want to use your whip or have your right hand free for any other reason.

●   THE ACHENBACH METHOD   ●

There is a method of rein handling developed many years ago by a German driver named Benno von Achenbach. Achenbach is regarded as the founder of the German art of driving, and he put a great deal of thought into developing the most sensible, efficient and safe method of handling the reins. The Achenbach method is thoroughly detailed in *The Art of Driving* by Max Pape.

We include here a summary of the most commonly used hand positions and the most important aspects of the Achenbach method.

1. The Basic Position ● Both reins are held in the left hand, running into the hand from above. The left rein runs between the thumb and index finger, while the right rein is held between the middle and ring finger. The reins are held firm by closing the middle, ring and pinky fingers around them; the index finger and thumb stay comparatively relaxed to avoid stiffening and tiring the muscles of the wrist and lower arm. The index finger and thumb can also accept the whip at any time.

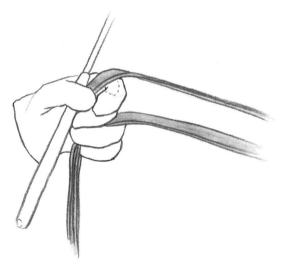

The Achenbach Method: The basic position.

This basic position should be used for driving with one hand, applying the whip or at any time the right hand needs to be freed for other purposes.

When the reins are held in one hand, you must be very careful to guard against the reins sliding through the fingers. Loosely held reins can be dropped or suddenly ripped out of your hand by an energetic, head-tossing horse.

Use your right hand to make adjustments in length, by pulling a rein longer or shorter through the fingers of the left hand.

2. The Dressage Position ● This is the preferred position for ring work, as it allows you full advantage of the rein aids, and it lets you change position quickly when you need to.

Begin with the basic position, outlined above. Hold the whip in your right hand, between the thumb and index finger. Then place all four fingers of your right hand into the right rein, from above. Close the lower three fingers of the right hand on the right rein, and pull some rein length out of the left hand.

Turn the right hand upright to resemble a riding fist, and hold it somewhat ahead of the left hand. The lower three fingers of the right hand are closed snugly on the right rein and the whip, while the thumb and index finger remain relaxed as described for the left hand (in the basic position, above).

The left rein passes through the left hand as in the basic position, but now the right rein passes first through the right hand and then through the left, making a short bridge of rein between the two hands.

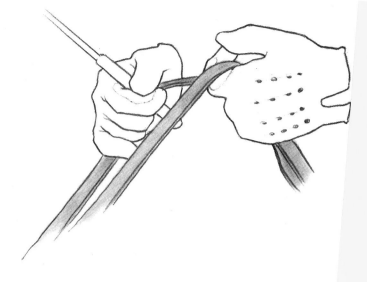

The Achenbach Method: The dressage position.

How much right rein length you pull from the left hand (and, therefore, how much of a bridge you have between the two hands) will depend entirely on the horse's level of training. Generally speaking, the more sensitive a horse is to rein commands, the less space you will need (about two inches is the minimum). A green horse can sometimes require up to a foot, because holding your hands farther apart seems to give him a certain degree of lateral stability, just as it does in riding.

If you are driving in dressage competition, you may be marked down if there is more than three or four inches between your hands.

When you need to free your right hand to use the whip, just push the bridged piece of right rein back into your left hand. While you are doing this, the bottom three fingers of the left hand must open, and you must temporarily grip the left rein between your left thumb and index finger, to avoid its slipping.

The great advantages of this position are:

- You always know how long each rein is in relation to the other;

- You don't change rein length when you take the right rein out of the left hand or return it to the left hand;

- Changing from two-handed to one-handed driving is very quick and simple, since the right rein is always in the left hand.

Also, this bridge between your hands actually mirrors the bit in the horse's mouth. You always know how much rein you are giving or taking, and it helps to steady one hand against the other.

The one disadvantage to the dressage position is that you do have to go temporarily into the next position to change your rein length.

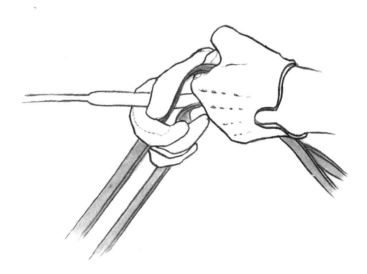

The Achenbach Method: The regular two-handed position.

3. The Regular Two-Handed Position • Begin with the left hand in basic position. Bringing the right hand down from above, grip the right rein with the middle, ring and pinky fingers of the right hand, and lay the thumb and index finger over the left rein. The whip is held by the thumb and index finger of the right hand. Both reins are now in both hands, which provides a lot of safety and a very firm hold if the horse becomes strong.

Either hand can now be removed from the reins if necessary.

You can lengthen the reins by pulling both reins through the left hand with the right, and then taking the right hand off the reins to return to basic position, or regain the dressage position.

To shorten the reins, the left hand leaves the reins and takes hold of them again in front of the right hand, and then the right hand returns to the dressage position, leaves the reins entirely or stays in the regular two-handed position.

A second method of shortening is to slide the right hand farther forward on the reins, and then follow with the left.

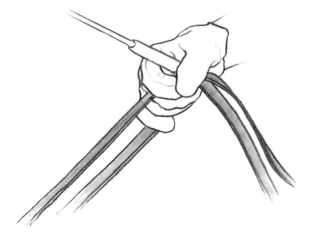

Holding the reins in the right hand, to free the left hand for another task.

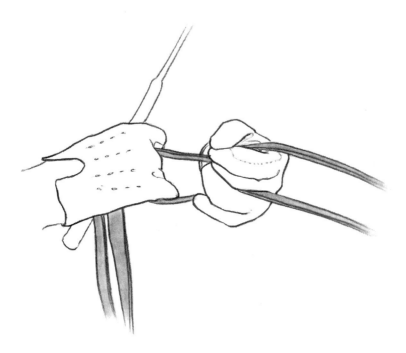

Shortening the reins.

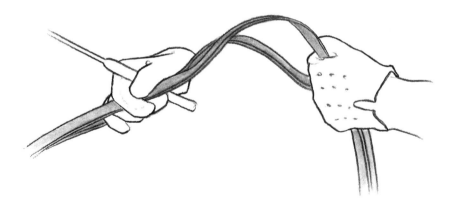

Temporary shortening of the reins.

If you need to shorten the reins only temporarily, as a brief correction, you can slide the right hand up the reins, correct the horse while both reins have some slack between the right and left hand and then let the right hand slide back to the left hand, gradually feeding the reins back to the horse until all the slack is used up. Your hands then return to your desired position.

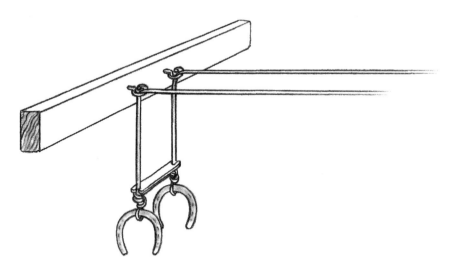

An easy-to-build simulator to practice the different rein positions of the Achenbach Method. The small piece of wood resembles the bit in the horse's mouth, and you can see very clearly whether this remains level when you change rein positions. You will easily be able to see how your movements affect the horse's mouth, and how effective your intended rein aids are.

Another advantage of this method of rein handling is that the whip cannot be held in any position except the correct one, which is half-left forward and upward. It is virtually impossible to hit a horse accidentally when you are using this method.

Of course, all this takes quite a bit of practice. Try fixing your reins to a post while you practice moving the hands, reins and whip from one position to another. You want to become so proficient at this that you won't have to think about fumbling with the reins while you are actually driving. Then you will be able to change hand positions, adjust rein lengths and make corrections without any hesitation.

• HOW DO YOU SIT? •

To handle your reins properly, it is very important to sit correctly in the carriage. This seems like a small matter—after all, your weight can't influence the horse, can it?—but it is vital.

Sit on the right side of the carriage with your body erect. If you ride, think of your tall, correct, evenly balanced riding position. Your shoulders should be comfortably back, not drawn upward, with your upper arms hanging at the sides of your body just a little ahead of the vertical.

Carry your hands relaxed, not artificially raised or pressed down. Don't break the wrists out, in or down. Your elbows should be bent at approximately a right angle; don't clamp them in, and don't stick them out to the sides.

As in riding, any stiffness in your upper body and arms will be transferred to the reins and along the reins to the horse's mouth, and you will block the flow of energy forward. Through the reins, your horse can feel how you are sitting. Don't slouch. Don't let nervousness become tension. Pay attention to your own position and balance if you want your horse to pay attention to his work.

You should feel tall, with your abdominal muscles holding you erect and your chest wide and open. Feel as if power and energy are streaming from your body. If that sounds strange, try this exercise: First, ask your horse to move forward at a trot while you concentrate on perfect position, with chest open and abdomen lifted. Then (without attempting to change rein position or give him any commands) see what happens if you slump, caving your chest and shoulders in and relaxing your abdominal muscles. Most horses will lengthen their stride much more readily when you open up your chest and raise your abdomen, and will shorten stride or slow down when you slouch or close up your body.

Sitting properly and handling your reins and whip correctly are vital if you hope to produce a good driving horse. The horse will be only as good as his trainer—and there's always room for improvement!

CHAPTER
· 10 ·

THE LATERAL BEND

The lateral bend is really the essence of dressage and distinguishes it from any other kind of training.

What exactly is the lateral bend?

· DEFINITION OF THE BEND ·

A horse is correctly bent laterally when his spine is conforming exactly to his line of travel, while his hind feet follow exactly in the path of his front feet. This means that he travels straight on a straight line, and follows the arc of the curve on a curved line. He does not lean through his corners like a motorcycle, but remains nearly vertical on a curving path. It is this that keeps the horse secure and balanced through his turns.

Straight vs. Crooked

We also use the term "straight" to describe a horse that bends correctly— and this can be confusing, unless you keep in mind that "straight" is the opposite of crooked.

To understand why, we first need to have an idea of how the horse's body naturally works and how a horse handles turns when he is by himself.

Nearly every horse is crooked, to a greater or lesser degree. (Whether the horse is born this way, or whether we make him this way from birth because of our own preference for physical one-sidedness, is open to debate.) Horses are never exactly the same on both sides; in nearly all cases, the horse's body is curved somewhat to the right, which means he is naturally shorter on his right side. This puts more weight onto his left shoulder, as illustrated below.

In addition, nearly all horses travel with their right hind legs somewhat outside their body, while the left hind leg tracks toward the right front leg. Thus, the horse is often carrying more of his weight on his left, making his left side the stronger side.

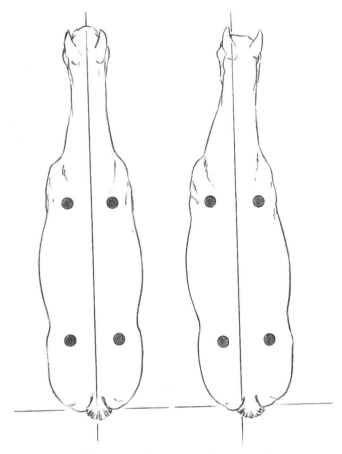

On the left: A straightened horse, with both sides of his body the same length and the hind feet tracking toward the front feet. On the right: A naturally crooked horse. His left side is longer, he is leaning over his left shoulder and his hind legs do not track correctly, with the left hind leg supporting more weight than the right one.

There are a very few horses who seem to be almost straight by nature, and there are probably some horses who are crooked in the opposite direction—though we haven't met one. The only horses who seem to be stronger on the right side and shorter on the left are those who are compensating for some unsoundness, or who are going through a stage in their training where they *seem* to be shorter on the left. (More about this later.)

Natural Crookedness
When a free horse negotiates turns on his own, he will always try to use his stronger left side. This means that, while turning to the left, he will swing his head and neck to the right and throw himself sharply onto his left

shoulder. The left hind leg, meanwhile, will help support his weight, while his right hind leg is to the outside of the turn.

On slippery footing, this can be dangerous, as his weight is not evenly distributed over his legs, and he can lose his balance easily.

Riders and drivers may sometimes feel that their very green horses may *turn* more easily to the left, because the left side is the stronger side—but this is turning, not bending.

In a turn to the right, the crooked horse may almost seem to bend, since he will still try to put weight onto his left shoulder—but his right hind leg still travels to the right of his body mass. The more naturally crooked a horse is, the harder it will be therefore to bend to the left, and the easier it appears for him to "bend" to the right. This is not a true bend, though, since his right hind leg is not supporting his weight.

If a green horse negotiates a right turn by looking to the left and throwing himself over the right shoulder, this is usually a good sign. It indicates that he is not very badly crooked naturally, or, because of some good training, his right side has learned to stretch sufficiently so that he prefers to travel over his right shoulder, instead of his left.

This may be difficult to understand initially.

Since a horse's left side is his stronger side and his left hind leg is accustomed to carrying more weight than the right hind, he will soon— through good training—bend more easily to the left than to the right. And that's a good sign, because it means he is accepting the reins properly. Once he accepts the support and direction of the reins, he won't fall over his left shoulder any more. As he learns to stretch his right side, he will prefer to fall over his right shoulder in a right-hand turn. (That needs correction, also, but is a strong indication that the horse's training is proceeding correctly.)

• CHANGES IN STRENGTH AND BALANCE •

We hear so many people say, "I don't know what I'm doing wrong. At first he could bend so nicely to the right and not at all to the left, and now he bends nicely to the left, but not to the right." That first "bending" to the right wasn't true bending, remember, and this progression appears to be the normal development through training. For most horses, once they reach this point, it will always be slightly harder to properly bend to the right, since their right side is naturally their weaker side, and stepping underneath their body mass with the right hind leg will always be more difficult for them.

This problem usually manifests itself in a stiffer right jaw. By leaning on the bit and going against the rein, the horse can keep shifting weight onto his shoulder, rather than carrying it on his right hind leg. Athletic horses with good natural balance usually don't have a big problem with this; when you are looking for a horse to buy, you should attach particular importance to how he handles himself in turns and circles to the right.

Traveling always over the shoulder (mostly the left shoulder), the horse is very difficult to manage in turns. Often, the driver will be unable to control the shape of the arc, since the horse throws himself into the turn. As a result, the wheels of the cart will describe a completely different path from that made by the feet of the horse—which can cause serious problems if you hope to clear any kind of obstacles.

The horse himself suffers, also. When he throws his weight over a shoulder, he is overloading his front legs in the turn. Horses that never learn to turn any other way are putting a lot of unnecessary stress (plus the weight of the cart) directly onto tendons, ligaments and supporting structures of the front legs.

Once the horse learns to bend correctly, the cart will follow exactly the track of the horse, the driver can control the arc of the turn by increasing or decreasing its radius, and the horse will be comfortably supporting the weight of the carriage and the stress of the turn on his hind legs.

Bending as the First Step Toward Collection

The only correct way to strengthen the horse's hind legs and back is through work with correct lateral bending. Without this, it will be impossible to reach our goal of converting pushing power into carrying power (and thereby obtain collection).

Through bending, we require the horse to contract one side of his body (on the inside of the turn) and to stretch the other side (on the outside of the turn). This helps to stretch the longissimus dorsi, one side at a time and far more than it can be stretched while the horse is traveling on a straight line. This lateral stretch really helps develop the horse's ability to stretch longitudinally. Bending also forces the inside hind leg to take up more weight, simply because the inside hind leg is now closer to the horse's own center of gravity on the turn.

Bending, then, is invaluable as a suppling and stretching exercise. We use it to strengthen first one hind leg and then the other; and we use it to stretch first one side of the body, then the other.

When the horse travels on a straight line, we cannot selectively increase the amount of weight either hind leg carries. We cannot straighten a crooked horse by traveling on a straight line, because we cannot stretch either side of him. He can easily escape into his natural crookedness without anyone noticing it.

In driving, especially, we have a unique opportunity to watch the whole horse, and to apply corrections. Riders must learn to feel for the action of the back and hindquarters, but in driving we can clearly *see* whether the horse's spine is actually following the arc of the turn. We can see it immediately, also, because our turn will not be round and smooth. And he can't escape us, because we can follow up immediately with the rein and whip to correct him.

How Do You Know if Your Horse Is Bending?

If you don't know whether your horse is bending correctly, you will need to develop a careful eye to follow his action. Watch many different horses, both from the ground and from the seat of a vehicle. Look for the following indicators:

1. The horse's spine is bent along its entire length to the arc of the turn. (See Chapter 5, page 68.)
2. The inside hind leg moves well under the horse's body, tracking precisely behind the inside front leg. (Allow for differences in comformation here; some horses are built wider behind than in front, and others are built wider in front than behind.)
3. In the trot, the hind foot should step down into the print left by the same-side front foot; in the walk, the hind foot should overtrack the front foot somewhat. (This will also vary, depending on the horse's conformation and level of training.)
4. The driver should feel that the horse is in total balance, not falling into the turn and not bulging to the outside. Both jaws should feel completely flexible, and a slight change in the amount of pressure on the outside rein will enlarge or decrease the size of the turn.

•   UNDERSTANDING THE DIAGONAL AIDS   •

To create a bend in the horse, we need to use what are called diagonal aids. It is easiest to understand the diagonal aids used in riding, and then see how we can apply these to driving.

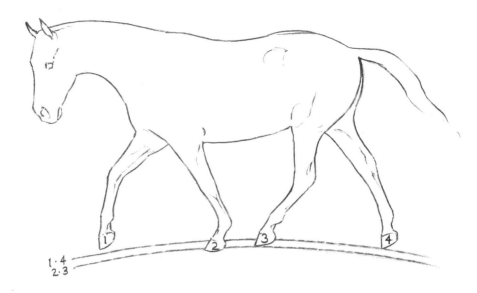

The horse truly bending around a turn. His hind feet follow exactly the path of his front feet.

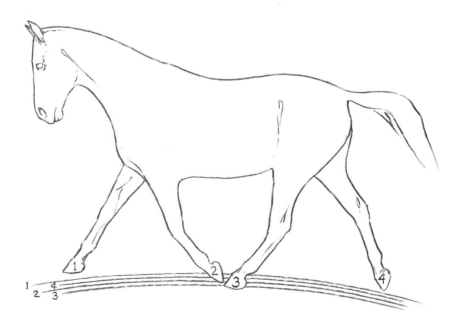

The horse not sufficiently bending around a turn. The hind legs do not track toward the front legs; this is clearly visible on the inside hind leg, which is held toward the inside of the turn. The horse moves on four tracks.

To bend something that is relatively straight—in this case, the horse's spine—we need three points of pressure: two on one side, some distance apart; and one on the other side, about midway between the first two points. Bend is created by pushing the middle pressure point against the other two, thus creating a curve in the straight horse's body.

The amount of the arc is determined by the amount of pressure, and any adjustments for crookedness or stiffness can be made by varying the amount of pressure at one or another of the three points.

In riding, these pressure points are represented by the rider's outside rein and outside leg on one side and the inside leg on the other side. The outside rein also acts as a "leading" rein, to determine the arc of the circle. By guiding the horse more to the outside of the turn with an opening rein while he remains bent to the inside, the rider enlarges the arc of the turn. By holding the outside rein closer to the horse's neck, the rider makes the arc smaller and the turn tighter.

The rider's inside leg works at all times, both to activate the horse's inside hind leg and make it work toward the outside rein, and to maintain the bend.

The inside rein asks the horse to look to the inside of the turn. The inside rein must always be as light as possible; if it applies too much pressure, it discourages the inside hind leg from moving forward. If the inside rein provides too much support, the horse can also lean against it—and shift weight down onto his shoulder again, taking the weight off the hind leg and destroying the bend.

If, however, the inside rein does not tell the horse to look to the inside, the horse may straighten his neck. In riding, a well-schooled horse will maintain the bend even without the action of the inside rein, because the trained horse is "locked in" between the outside rein and the inside leg.

Applying Diagonal Aids to Driving

In driving, of course, we don't have an inside leg *or* an outside leg.

We do, however, have an inside and an outside rein, a whip and an outside shaft. To bend the driving horse around a turn, you will make use of all of these elements.

The inside rein indicates that we want our horse to look to the inside. This must not be a fixed or pulling action, but a quiet give-and-take to keep his jaw supple; this is generally so subtle an action that an observer would not see the movement of the fingers on the rein.

The outside rein indicates and controls the size of the arc. If the outside rein is not doing anything as the inside rein is applied, the horse will make a very sharp turn to the inside—and in the most severe case, he may try to turn the carriage on the spot. Rein action must be a matter of degree, not an absolute on-or-off switch.

The greater the amount of outside rein pressure, the larger and more gradual the turn. Lighter pressure on the outside rein gives you a tighter turn. This means, basically, that turns are really driven on the outside rein. A well-trained driving horse will be controllable to the inch and will willingly go closer to the rail in a corner, responding to the direction of the outside rein without giving up the bend.

There is a continuous interaction between the inside and outside reins. In the beginning of a horse's training, this interaction may be very visible, as the driver must constantly adjust to the horse's unpredictable responses. Later, of course, the skilled driver and the skilled horse seem to be communicating without any perceptible rein movements—but the interplay between the reins is always present. This is not a see-saw action on the reins, but can best be described as having the outside rein say "Stay here," while the inside rein says "Bend." Negotiating a turn or circle is constant communication, with the reins saying "Stay here and bend," "Stay here and bend," as you direct the horse through the turn.

In the early stages of training, the horse may need quite a lot of inside rein to direct him into the turn, but, once he has learned to bend properly, this inside rein pressure should become a light, elastic contact.

It is vital to remember that neither rein is ever pulled hard or tight, because this would give the horse the chance to hang on it and stiffen. Don't confuse this, however, with a horse who offers a firm contact—perhaps with a considerable amount of weight in the rein, but always with a willing and giving jaw. Some horses, especially those with conformation problems, often need a very firm contact for quite a long period in their training. "Hanging" can happen with any amount of contact; by "hanging" we mean that the horse does not willingly yield to the bit, but opposes it with a stiff jaw.

•   DRIVING A PERFECT CIRCLE   •

What is a circle and why it is important?

Everyone knows what a circle is: a continuous, consistently curved line, ending at the point of origin. However, when people are asked to sit behind a horse and drive a circle, they often seem to forget what a circle is. Ovals, octagons, square or egg-shaped figures are often the result.

We use circles in our training to produce a consistent bend in the horse, and to refine and judge the horse's obedience to the aids.

To correctly drive any ring figure—especially circles—it's very helpful to have a rectangular ring that is exactly two or three times as long as it is wide. In a schooling area of this sort, it is fairly easy to determine where the path of the circle will be because your ring can be divided into two or three squares. It will also be very helpful to mark the midpoint of the short side of your ring, and the points along the long sides that are the same distance from the short side as the center of the short side is from the corner.

For example: If your arena is 40 meters wide by 80 meters long, you have two 40 by 40 meter squares in which you can drive two circles, each 40 meters in diameter. Your circle (in either square) touches the track in three places: at the midpoint of the short side (at letter A or C, if you have dressage markers) and at one point on each long side, exactly 20 meters away from the corner. (See below.) Your circle also touches the exact center of the arena, at X.

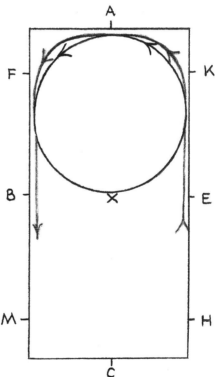

Driving a correct circle by making a distinct difference between circle line and corners.

If you do not have a fenced arena in the correct proportions with markers, find a large flat field and obtain a helper, some powdered limestone and 20 meters of baling twine. Use the baling twine to gauge the radius of the circle: one person stands at the center, while the other walks around him, keeping the twine taut and marking a circle with the limestone. Measure and mark two corners adjacent to the circle also (using 15 meters of twine, to form the radius of two 30-meter quarter-circles).

To drive an accurate circle, your horse will travel a path that touches the track in three places and crosses the centerline. To "touch the track" means that the horse steps onto the outside track of the arena for a step or two. He doesn't change his bend, and he doesn't remain on the track for any longer than two steps.

You must be sure you clearly indicate to the horse the difference between driving a circle and driving into the corners when you are following the outside track. In driving a corner, you approach the corner on a straight track, describe a quarter of a circle's arc, and straighten onto the track again when you have completed the corner. (The diameter of this corner arc depends on the level of the horse's training; when you can begin to think about driving circles with your green horse, you should be able to drive corners as parts of a 30-meter circle.)

To drive a 40-meter circle, you maintain the bend continuously throughout the figure—in this case, the bend will be less than that required to drive a corner. Don't go into the corners at all; simply focus on the arc of your circle, and look ahead to the next "contact point" on your track or on your centerline. If you begin the circle at A, you will end the circle at A, straighten, and then drive your corner, straightening again as you come to the long side of the arena.

If you don't have the room in your arena to drive 40-meter circles, but must begin with 30-meter circles, the horse's bend will be the same as when you drive through your corners, but you do not travel on a straight track anywhere until the circle is completed. As your horse's level of training progresses and he is able to bend correctly through smaller circles, the difference between driving a circle and driving through a corner will be even more pronounced.

Driving circles—especially with a green horse—can be a very humbling experience. It is often more difficult to drive an accurate 40-meter circle than a 20- or 30-meter circle because the larger figure seems so vast. It is easy to lose sight of your route, and the horse's bend on a 40-meter circle is really quite minimal (especially with a small horse). However, for the sake of your green horse, you should drive circles as large as possible in the beginning to avoid putting too much strain on him or asking him to do what he is not ready for.

Whether you intend to compete with your horse or not, these distinctions are very important. As with all of our training, it is vital to be very clear about what we ask the horse to do—and then have a way of determining whether he does what we ask. Correctly driven corners, circles and ring figures will help improve his steering as well as his suppleness and obedience.

•   CORRECTIONS   •

Most young horses, if they are brought along properly according to the program of ground training outlined earlier, will easily offer to bend through their turns. Ground driving with the reins run through the tugs, in particular, will teach the horse to bend well if it is done correctly.

Sometimes, however, this just isn't the case. Occasionally a horse will do fine in ground training, but once he must deal with the weight of the cart, he seems to lose the ability to bend.

If the horse has spent too long a period on the longe line, where he cannot be taught to bend—or if he developed problems because of earlier, improper training—it may be far more difficult to achieve the proper bend. He may actually be frightened of the turn, feeling that he cannot survive without throwing his weight over his inside shoulder and diving to the inside of the turn.

Using the Whip in Bending

If the horse refuses to listen to the reins, and does not bend at all through his body—perhaps bending in his neck, but not through his barrel—the whip can be useful, but only if he will accept it.

As you ask for the turn, apply the whip about where a rider's inside leg would lie. Most horses will learn to move away from the touch of the whip, yielding in their rib cage and allowing the inside hind leg to step toward the outside rein.

The outside shaft automatically helps to keep the horse's hindquarters in place, by limiting the amount the hindquarters can swing to the outside.

Some horses, of course, are just not impressed by the whip, and others—especially hot and nervous ones—only become frightened. You will have to judge for yourself if the whip is a help or a hindrance.

Training under Saddle

One fairly effective way to teach the driving horse to bend is to put him into good training under saddle. A skilled rider will definitely help the horse learn to bend, and, once he finds his balance under saddle, this training may transfer nicely back to driving.

A horse that bends well under saddle, however, may still not bend well when he is driven. And many people do not have the skill or the opportunity to school their horses under saddle.

If the bend is just not happening—or if it is happening in one direction, but not the other—it will help to remember what the priorities are when you negotiate turns with a carriage.

Control Begins with Steering

First and foremost, the horse must go where you want him to go. This is so basic that it can be forgotten, in all our concentration on bending and suppleness.

Usually, when the problem horse sees a turn coming up (and he knows it's coming, because he can see the fence or the wall ahead), he will stiffen his back. He seems to be thinking, "The only way I am going to be able to get this weight around this turn is to shove it over my inside shoulder. If I do it all quickly, I'll get it over with fast."

When the horse begins to stiffen like this and anticipate the turns, he will begin making the turns earlier and earlier—and soon you won't even be close to the corner when the horse takes you around the turn. This falling-over method of turning really frightens the horse, since he can't see where he is going, and he will probably become more and more nervous about it. The problem will worsen until he either rushes blindly through the turn, way before you actually reach the corner, or he stops altogether, refusing even to approach the spot where he must turn.

If, however, you insist that the horse goes where you want him to go—even if his back is hollow and his head is looking to the outside—he will begin to understand that you are going to direct him, no matter what. This can be a very difficult, sometimes physically exhausting task. You must work on turns at the walk for a long time, with constant interaction between the inside and outside rein to convince the horse to listen and stay with you. (Be sure to use a bit that does not hurt him, but that he respects.)

Remember also how effective sliding sidereins can be to give the horse lateral stability and invite him to stretch to the bit. This stretching is the next thing you will look for.

After Steering, Relaxation

When you have established the steering and you can place the horse where you want him, even though he is crooked and looking to the outside, the next step is to establish some level of relaxation and stretching. Work for relaxation before you ask for bending; the relaxation *must* come first.

Once your horse relaxes some and stretches forward, he will offer a softer rein contact and begin to negotiate turns straighter. You won't get bend yet, but you will get less crookedness. (See Chapter 11, The Longitudinal Bend.)

When the steering, the relaxation and the stretching are happening, you can begin to ask him to yield to the inside rein a little. Then the bend will start to happen.

One good technique also is to ask for turns when the horse is not anticipating them. If he can't anticipate, he can't worry himself with stiffening ahead of time.

Success Leads to Success

You will probably discover that once a real problem horse discovers the balance he can achieve through bending, he will learn quite quickly. After all, it's easier: He can see where he's going, his better balance makes him more comfortable, and he is finally pleasing you, gaining plenty of positive reinforcement.

With a horse that just doesn't seem to understand the bend at all, it may help for a few sessions to run the reins back through the tugs, rather than through the terrets on the saddle if there is enough space between the tugs and the shafts. Be careful of this, however, as there may be quite a bit of increased friction, or a rein may even get caught.

Some trainers believe that if your horse does not bend as well to one side as to the other, you must work him harder in his "problem" direction. However, the horse probably has a problem because he is weaker on one side. You can work him slightly more to that side than to the other, but be very careful of overdoing it, because overstressing this side can make him resist even more. When his muscles are made to hurt through overwork, he won't want to use them at all until they stop hurting. (Your horse is not interested in the "no pain, no gain" principle of conditioning.)

The best method for dealing with a weakness in bending to one side is to be sure that you change direction frequently in all your training sessions (every two to five minutes is good), and spend about the same amount of time in each direction.

Forgetting How to Bend

Once your horse bends beautifully at home, you decide to go to a show—and he won't bend at all. Why? First, the horse must cope with all sorts of mental distractions. Remember that when he is busy looking at everything around him, his head comes up, his back hollows and you've lost his attention. The horse can only bend when his topline is stretched. Mental anxiety causes him to tense his neck and back, and the lateral bend becomes impossible.

You may also be using a heavier carriage at the show than you normally do at home; or the footing may be deeper and more difficult. If he has to struggle to pull, he will be preoccupied with that, and it will be harder for him to balance the extra load on turns.

If this happens, chalk it up to experience. Don't blame the horse, but do your best to relax him while you're at the show, and when you're back home you can work a little harder to put him into better condition for the next show.

CHAPTER
· 11 ·

LONGITUDINAL BEND (DEVELOPMENT OF THE TOPLINE)

Correct training is correct training, whether your ultimate goal is to enjoy Sunday picnic drives or to strive for a national championship. Although it may seem that our training (especially as outlined here and in the next two chapters) is geared specifically toward "dressage" showing, this is not the case. Any horse trained properly and according to these principles, however, will perform respectably in dressage driving because it is this training that a dressage competition will test. We do not want anyone to read this far and then say, "Oh, this chapter involves dressage, and I'm not interested in that."

The principles of dressage training are valid because they work for all horses (including, by the way, mules) and can be adapted for all intended purposes. A correct training system, after all, is built on logic—and this logic revolves around the fundamental needs, instincts and physical abilities of the horse.

• "TEACHING TO AN OBJECTIVE" •

Anyone who has spent time learning to be a teacher of children understands the importance of "teaching to an objective." This means, simply, that before you can teach someone something you must determine four things:

1. What the student already knows ("Where are we right now?");
2. What we would like the student to learn ("What do I want to accomplish in this session?");
3. How we convey this ("How can I explain this most effectively?"); and,
4. How we gauge our progress ("Are we there yet?").

To answer these questions, you must have an objective in mind for each training session, and for each portion of the training session. Each time you bring your horse up from the paddock to "work" him, you should have a fairly clear idea of what you would like to accomplish. Your objective may be to introduce something new, to confirm something already learned or to correct a problem—but you must have an idea of what it is you want to do. Simply going out to drive around the field for an hour won't advance your horse's training very far. "Work" needs to be effective, and to be effective it must have direction and goals.

Of course, it doesn't always have to be just "work." Your objective may be very simple, perhaps just to have a thoroughly enjoyable pleasure drive. However, this still involves your careful attention to your horse's training. You may have all sorts of unforeseen problems to deal with: traffic and dogs and children and farm machinery, or a horse who needs encouragement to step through a stream or walk across a bridge. Each small part of the training fits into the whole, and you should be able to finish each "working" session or pleasure drive by noting exactly how your horse progressed.

The flip side of this is the need for flexibility. You may have to make drastic changes to your day's training objectives (especially with a young horse!). *You* may have begun your session with the objective of teaching your three-year-old to bend a little more smoothly through his corners, but your youngster spots a piece of plastic on the ground near the far corner under the trees—and suddenly the day's objective is to get him by that plastic without his snorting violently and scooting sideways. So much for the correct bend in that corner; now you're working on just getting him to steer and pay attention. But this is an important lesson, also, and it must be learned.

As we work our way through the training objectives outlined in this and the next two chapters, keep in mind how you will structure each training session to achieve a specific objective. Think also of how you might adapt each session to your particular horse—his needs, problems and preferences.

One vital aspect of training the horse for *any* task has to do with longitudinal bend. Our training will now work to develop this all-important goal.

•   WHAT IS THE LONGITUDINAL BEND?   •

The back-to-front stretching and bending of the horse's spine is called the longitudinal bend. (The relationship between longitudinal bending and the horse's body structure is discussed in Chapter 2.) The logic of muscular development dictates that there can be no lateral bend before longitudinal bend; we have chosen to discuss lateral bend (Chapter 10) first simply because it involves steering—and all trainers recognize the need for steering as a first priority.

The Relationship between Longitudinal and Lateral Bend

In reality, the longitudinal bend and the lateral bend cannot be separated from each other. For correct lateral bend to take place, the horse must be fully relaxed and stretched from back to front; but every training session (from ground driving onward) must include lateral bending, or we'd never get our horses around a corner properly.

When we speak of the horse taking on the "correct frame," we are really talking about longitudinal bend. As discussed in Chapter 2, we need to teach the horse to shift weight back onto his hindquarters to restore and improve his natural balance. This can only be done when the muscles of the belly and underline shorten (contract), the topline lengthens and the jaw flexes. This enables him to reach underneath himself with his hind legs. It is crucial that this development be accomplished gradually and systematically—never with force.

There is no progress toward collection without correct longitudinal flexion.

How, then, do we attain this very important objective?

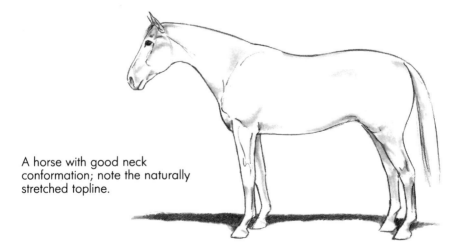

A horse with good neck conformation; note the naturally stretched topline.

The same horse, moving freely. This horse can balance and move in a higher frame than the ewe-necked horse, without having to use the muscles of the lower neck to compensate for a lack of topline.

The same horse, in harness, with a passive driver. Compare the topline to that of the horse on page 163.

Stretching comes easily for the horse with the well-constructed topline.

As he continues to strengthen the correct muscles, this horse will begin to balance in a higher frame; here he is moving in a Training Level frame . . .

. . . and finds it comfortable to reach a beginning Intermediate Level frame.

Eventually, an Advanced Level frame is possible for true collection.

•   THE SIX ELEMENTS OF DRESSAGE TRAINING   •

All "schools" of dressage agree upon the same principles in the horse's physical and mental education. There are six German words that perhaps best describe these principles and incorporate the goals and essence of dressage. All six are defined in terms of the development of the topline and the progressive change in the horse's balance and ability to pull or carry weight. These six goals are:

> *Takt*   Rhythm and evenness of the steps
> *Losgelassenheit*   "Letting go," submission, and relaxation
> *Anlehnung*   Seeking the bit and stretching to it
> *Schwung*   Impulsion
> *Geraderichten*   True straightness
> *Versammlung*   Collection

Here we discuss *Takt, Losgelassenheit* and *Anlehnung*; in Chapter 13 we address the more advanced goals of *Schwung, Geraderichten,* and *Versammlung.*

These first three goals are very closely interwoven, and it is difficult to look at each apart from the other two. A more complete definition of *Takt, Losgelassenheit,* and *Anlehnung,* however, helps us understand the importance of these elements acting in harmony.

This horse's "upside-down" or ewe neck, set low into the shoulders, makes it difficult for him to learn to balance and move his back muscles correctly.

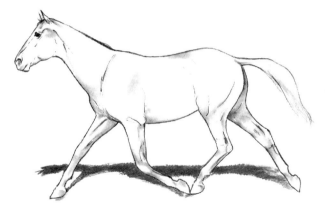

The same horse, moving freely. Notice the lack of muscling in the topline and the bulge at the bottom of the neck.

When the ewe-necked horse is put in harness, his problems magnify if the driver does not know how to teach him to stretch and become round.

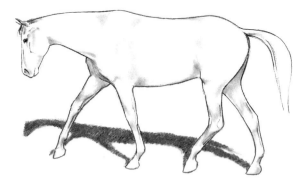

The same horse with a driver who is actively asking for the topline to be stretched downward and forward. Rebuilding the muscles of the topline is not an easy task! This is where sliding sidereins are especially beneficial.

The same horse working up to the bit, with some engagement. (See the top illustration on page 161.)

As the driver asks for more engagement, the horse can begin to move in a higher frame, and is now working at about Training or Preliminary Level.

This will be the limit of front elevation for this ewe-necked horse.

•   *TAKT*—RHYTHM AND EVENNESS OF THE STEPS   •

Takt means the clear, even and rhythmic sequence of beats in every gait: a four-beat walk (where each step occupies precisely the same interval of time); a regular, two-beat trot; and a clear, three-beat canter with a definite moment of suspension. If the horse cannot maintain an even rhythm in his gaits, he cannot learn anything else.

Most horses are born with a good natural rhythm, but when the demands of training are placed on them, they may suddenly begin to "run" at the walk, or offer a hasty, uneven trot or four-beat canter.

Good rhythm can usually be reinforced (or recaptured) through training on the longe line (or through long lining if you are very good at it), and this is one of the goals of groundwork: to make the horse steady, calm and even, at least at the walk and trot. The canter, because of its faster speed and inherent unevenness, can sometimes be very difficult to execute well if the horse is young, unmuscled or badly muscled. (Although it is desirable to teach a driving horse to canter quietly on the longe line, he should never be forced into it if he cannot find his balance easily. He might become frightened or fall and hurt himself. If your horse does not canter easily on the longe, continue to work calmly at the walk and trot only, and go back to the canter a few months later.)

Included in the definition of *Takt* is the necessity for a certain amount of energy in the horse's steps. For the rhythm to be maintained, there must be a strength and a freedom in moving forward. And although "ultimate straightness" is a later goal, the horse that is inherently very crooked will not demonstrate truly good *Takt* in both directions until his crookedness has been eased. (See Chapter 13, Impulsion, Straightness and Collection, and the discussion of crookedness under *"Geraderichten."*)

Why *Takt* (Rhythm) Must Come First— and What to Do if It Doesn't

Many horses show good natural rhythm on the longe line, but lose it when they are first hitched to a cart. If your horse begins to rush in the walk, shows signs of losing his forwardness, can't seem to find a consistent rhythm in the trot, jigs or generally just seems to be staggering around, you will have very little control over him until you have restored his rhythm.

Your goal is to establish an even, relaxed, forward and unconstrained stride.

With a nervous horse, this may be accomplished by doing something as simple as having a helper walk next to the horse for a while as he is driven.

It may also be useful to have another, very calm horse in the ring—perhaps being ridden instead of driven. It is very important to keep careful control of him, and tactful rein handling is vital. Your feel on the reins must be steady, secure and always right there to give him support—but you must not make him more nervous with too tight a rein contact. Do not make him go deep into the corners of the ring or ask him to bend; keep the track shaped like an oval. If he loses his forwardness and becomes upset, the rhythm will deteriorate further.

You must also be sure you tell him where to go and (tactfully) hold him to it. If you don't, he may be very insecure about his path; he may also lose his balance, begin to throw himself around turns and become even more upset. This must be corrected before anything else, because knowing where to go will give the horse more peace of mind and will help him to relax.

You may have to put him on a fairly firm rein contact at first, especially if he is rushing. It may also help to put the sliding sidereins on, to give him some guidance and support. You will have to decide what will work best, but no matter what approach you take, your first objective is to gain control, and your second objective is to reestablish a steady, relaxed rhythm at both the walk and trot.

The lazy horse will require a good deal of encouragement in the form of voice and possibly whip. Loss of forwardness causes a loss of rhythm, but encouraging a lazy horse is generally much simpler than calming a nervous horse.

When good *Takt* is achieved, it leads naturally to a lengthened topline, with the horse stretched forward and downward—and this is your goal, because once the horse reaches the point where he *stays* stretched, he is calm and relaxed and rhythmic.

Rein Handling: Creating Good Rhythm and Stretch

A horse may stretch for one stride, and then raise his head and hollow his back on the next stride. How can you tactfully ask him to put his head down, become stretched and round, and *stay there*?

Your hands must work on his mouth tactfully, but with some horses also quite firmly.

However, make sure that your arms stay relaxed, your wrists are soft, and that you don't feel any stiffness in the joints of your arms or hands. Beginning with a steady, comfortable rein contact (and with your hands following the neck-telescoping gesture when he is walking), work the bit gently from side to side in his mouth, tightening the fingers of first one hand and then the other to slightly increase rein pressure, left-right-left-right, not necessarily in rhythm with the horse's steps, but as he needs it. For some horses, the motion must be very, very subtle. Others may require a firmer rein action, but you must never make the horse appear to have his head pulled from one side to the other. Think of "massaging" the horse's mouth.

This motion must be constant, gentle, slow, peaceful and friendly. It should become second nature to you, because you will always be carrying on a dialogue with the horse in this manner. Quick, jerky motions will annoy or upset the horse. The contact with the horse's mouth is never lost; it is not an "on-off" pressure, but a "slightly-more, slightly-less" feeling.

Keep the bit contact and the massaging motion constant no matter where the horse puts his head. However, when your horse raises his head, try to make it more uncomfortable for him. When he makes any attempt to lower the head and neck, lighten your contact by following him with your hands and reward him—even if the head lowering occurs as he obnoxiously rips the reins down. You must yield with the hands and praise him with your voice. Sooner or later, he will begin to look for the place where things are most comfortable for him. Examples of this are shown on the bottom of pages 131, 160 and 163, and the top of page 201.

It is crucial that your reins do not work backwards on the horse. You do not want to restrict or discourage forward movement. This may sound impossible, since every rein action seems to be restrictive. Remember, however, that when your horse was first longed in sliding sidereins he learned that a certain pressure on his mouth is not supposed to hold him back, but rather help him to become supple and even more forward.

Your rein action should be telling the horse: "Look, you have to give in to the reins, you must soften your jaw, but you can always make your neck as long as possible and you can keep moving. Just try it." How to convey this feeling (instead of a restriction) to the horse is a matter of practice, feel and mental attitude. It can cause great frustration on the part of both horse and driver if it is not done properly, and you can upset the horse to the point where he might do something dangerous, like rear or bolt. If you feel that your own rein action is not helping the horse, put the sliding sidereins back on and let them help the horse find his balance and rhythm. As the horse learns this, you will learn the correct feel of his mouth, because the sliding sidereins provide the right "massaging" action as the horse steps forward in each stride.

Some trainers recommend that the horse should be given his head as much as possible in this early stage. They feel that if the horse is "interfered with" as little as possible, he will find his own rhythm and eventually begin to stretch on his own. This just doesn't work. For one thing, it is dangerous, because the driver has virtually no control over the horse. Furthermore, some horses never will discover how to move correctly on their own, as illustrated on page 163. Most horses, when left to figure things out on their own, will go through a great deal of uncertainty about what they should do with their bodies. They learn bad habits and develop the wrong muscles—and then it's a real chore to reeducate them. (The photograph below shows a very clear example of this.)

Any horse can learn from the very first day of training which muscles to use (and how to use them correctly) to remain balanced and comfortable. Although he won't be able to perform perfectly at the beginning, with the proper training program he will learn—without undue force, stress or pain.

Here is a horse with a very strongly developed bottom line, indicated by the bulge in the lower neck and in the throat. Also, the throatlatch is definitely too tight, but the curved breast collar does help by accommodating the windpipe. The joints of the bit appear loose and may pinch his lips; it could be improved by wrapping the joints with latex. (And the curbchain should be made to lie flat.)

The same horse as in the photograph opposite, giving an indication that he could have a lovely neck. The neck is actually set high onto the shoulders, despite the overdeveloped bottom line. He proves that he can easily tuck the bottom-neck muscles away and stretch through the topline. His conformation is actually very good, and with correct work he could have a nice topline with his neck running smoothly into his withers. Two additional notes on the harness: the strap of the neck collar sits a little too far back, and the breeching hangs too low.

Structuring Your Lessons

No ring figures (circles, serpentines or tight turns) should be attempted while you are working to restore or improve *Takt*. Simply drive in as large an oval as possible, and be sure there are no obstacles to negotiate or unnecessary distractions to worry about. Of course, you do have to change direction every few minutes, but try to do this in such a way that you maintain a smooth line, making large, gentle turns so that you don't interrupt the horse's rhythm.

Work a great deal in a *forward* walk. You may want to work only at the walk for a few sessions, especially if your horse has problems settling down in the walk. The walk must have a definite marching rhythm. Even if you find your throat is sore from encouraging him to "Walk on," you have to insist on the maximum walk all the time. This is very important in all stages of training.

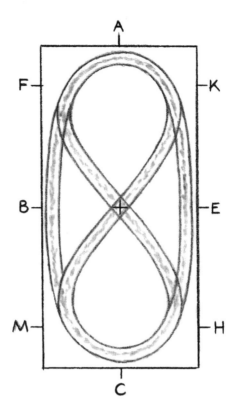

Developing *Takt*. The track is an oval, with no well-defined corners. The diagonals to change direction develop out of very generous and gradual turns.

If your horse has a very poor natural walk, however, you may be better off concentrating at first on the rhythm of the trot, returning to work on the walk after his condition and confidence have improved.

Don't worry about how the horse executes the transitions from one gait to another. *Do* remember to use your voice commands, and try to use your reins as little as possible to bring him from the trot back to the walk. Any rein contact working backwards at this stage will interrupt the rhythm.

Begin in the walk, and then alternate walk and trot. Change direction and gait every few minutes, and keep your sessions short: no more than 20 to 25 minutes for a young, weak or green horse, and about 30 to 35 minutes with a horse that has been accustomed to other kinds of work previously.

Keep asking for the downward stretch and the regular, steady rhythm you established earlier on the longe line. A horse that offers large, even and forward steps must be in a relaxed state of mind, and this will help us achieve our next goal.

• *LOSGELASSENHEIT*—"LETTING GO," OR RELAXATION •

As soon as *Takt* is established, we can concentrate on creating more suppleness. *Takt* is not possible without a certain degree of suppleness, but once the horse is calm or motivated enough to move forward in even and rhythmic steps, we can start to secure this suppleness. We do this by making the horse move forward more energetically and at the same time asking for more secure contact through the reins. As we do this, we will also begin to lead the horse more securely onto our intended lines, making our steering and control more precise.

Our focus will now be on *Losgelassenheit,* which means that the horse thoroughly relaxes and "lets go" of the stiffnesses in his body. He does not need to be stiff because he does not need stiffness as a defense; he submits his mind and his body to the job at hand.

In *Losgelassenheit,* we see the complete stretching of the topline. The ligaments that run from poll to withers and from withers to tail are fully stretched, and we can actually see the muscles along the horse's vertebrae begin to work. Our main concern now is simply to keep him stretched, moving forward and accepting our guiding rein aids with calmness and confidence. He should carry his neck stretched forward and downward; he still can and should poke his nose out some, but he also needs to have soft jaws, showing that he is accepting the guidance and control of the reins. We aren't looking yet for perfect understanding of the bit; nor are we looking for a "frame."

We can begin now to ask the horse to look to the inside when we go through turns. Both longitudinal stretch and lateral bend are integral components of the suppleness and "letting go," and our training sessions now will include ring figures to increase the horse's ability to bend. (Refer to Chapter 10, The Lateral Bend.)

As you make your turns, you will support him with the reins, leading into the turn with the outside rein and asking him to look to the inside with the inside rein. If the early attempts at bending are not successful, do not worry. Be sure first that your horse goes where you want him to go, willingly and without changing his rhythm. As his strength increases, so will his ability to bend.

It is essential that this beginning bending work not be introduced too abruptly. As your horse gains confidence in his balance, he will trust you (and your aids) more, and gradually he will let go with his body and give it to you. If, however, you scare him with unreasonable demands—too-tight turns, rough rein aids, abrupt transitions—he will stay suspicious, concerned and tense.

What promotes *Losgelassenheit*? The horse's total attention to his job; his comfort and confidence in his physical strength; the trust, communication, and understanding between the horse and his trainer.

What can block *Losgelassenheit*? Fear, discomfort, distrust, tiredness, exciting distractions, youthful exuberance or anything else that causes the horse to halt the free forward flow of energy.

Training to Promote *Losgelassenheit*

In your first training sessions, you and your horse described a large oval in your field or ring. Now you will try to drive with two long straight sides to your training track. (Whether you can also drive with two short straight sides at either end of the arena will depend on the size of your training area.)

The only figures you should use now should be large circles, smooth large corners and straight diagonals to change direction. The transitions should still be gradual. If your horse seems balanced enough, you can work on smoothness or a quicker response, but do not worry if he puts his head up during a transition. Your horse must gain balance and confidence before he can make good transitions, and if you press for this too early, you will only upset him.

The gaits are: a free, unconstrained walk with light rein contact (or, with a very obedient horse who will stretch on his own, a loose rein); a forward trot in good rhythm (*not* a quick or fast trot); and maybe a quiet canter if the horse likes to do it. (Attempt the canter only when the horse steers well and is easy to control in his forwardness.)

You can also work on obedient halts, but do not press for perfectly straight or square halts. If your horse is calm, responsive and willing, you can also begin to work on the 180-degree turn and a few steps of reinback. (See Chapter 14, Driving for Pleasure and Competition, for a full explanation of teaching the reinback.) If he can't handle these exercises without getting upset, don't push him. It means he's not ready, physically or mentally.

Try to drive each corner as if it were a quarter of a 30-meter circle. As you begin to incorporate circle work into your training, keep the circles large, a minimum of 20 meters in diameter—30 to 40 meters, if you have room. Accuracy is not very important yet, but it *is* important that all turns and figures are executed smoothly. Be very concerned about your horse's fragile balance, and avoid everything that may upset it. Do not sacrifice smoothness and balance for accuracy. As long as your horse doesn't begin to cut corners, drift out badly on his turns, or generally disobey you, don't worry about correcting the shape of the figures.

Remember to let your horse truly stretch forward and down. It is very important to give him full freedom of his neck whenever he asks for it, and while he is stretching you must maintain a constant but extremely pleasant contact with the bit. When he raises his head again, the contact must also be there; now, however, it should be a little stronger and firmer to encourage him to stretch down again. Constant contact is crucial. He must not learn that there is a place where he can avoid contact with the bit. If he learns that he can avoid the bit by putting his head in a particular place, he may spend his time looking for that place instead of listening to you.

Sliding sidereins can help a great deal to promote *Losgelassenheit*. They show the horse the way to stretch down and forward, lengthening his topline.

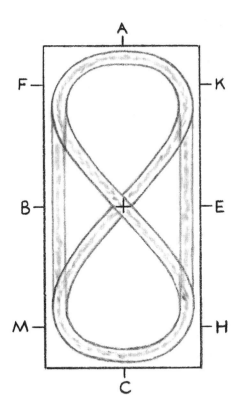

Developing *Losgelassenheit.* Corners are driven as part of a 30-meter circle. There are definite straight lines on the long sides, and the diagonals have become a little longer due to a slightly tighter turn after the corner.

The lower he stretches his head and neck, the better—unless he actually hangs down on the reins. If this happens, he may need a little jerk on the rein to remind him that he must respect the bit.

A typical training session at this stage might look like this:

- 3 to 5 minutes: Free, forward walk with very light rein contact, changing direction often, with no circles and only minimal bending through corners, encouraging the horse to stretch.

- 10 minutes: Trot on a fairly long rein, changing direction frequently. Be concerned about having the horse go where you want him to and maintaining rhythm and suppleness; incorporate a large circle or two into your pattern.

- 2 to 5 minutes: Walk again, asking for a little more rein contact, working to bend a little more through the corners, maybe driving a few circles.

- 8 to 10 minutes: Trot on a slightly shorter rein, trying for the best possible bend in your turns and adding more circles. Remember to change direction frequently. More talented horses may be asked to trot on a little stronger at times along the long side or across the diagonal of the ring.

Further work to develop *Losgelassenheit*. Forty-meter circles are introduced, with three different locations available for circles.

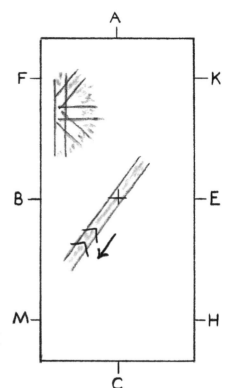

First attempts at 90- and 180-degree turns can be made; also, reinback for one or two steps may be introduced.

Give him a short break with a walk on a loose rein or a long rein (still in contact), and then you can finish up with practicing 180-degree turns or a few steps of reinback, if you feel he's ready for this. Keep these additional requests very moderate in the beginning.

Note: Each time you have to take a shorter rein contact to get the effect you desire—in any exercise—it is important to then reward the horse with a longer rein length as soon as you can, yielding with both hands without losing the contact. Reward him also each time he does something very well by walking and giving him the rein. This will depend on the situation and the horse's temperament, but in one session you should probably do this five to ten times.

A Training Level dressage test would be possible at the latter part of this stage, but you could not expect your horse to perform it perfectly.

Once *Losgelassenheit* is established, we're well on the way to the next training goal: *Anlehnung,* or accepting and reaching for the bit.

• ANLEHNUNG—SEEKING THE BIT •

This is a difficult term to translate. "Reaching for the bit" and "accepting the bridle" are elements of *Anlehnung,* but don't convey its complete meaning. When a horse has achieved *Anlehnung,* he looks for the bit, stretches towards it, and takes a secure contact on it—but he does not lean or pull against the driver's hands. (See illustrations on pages 161 and 164; these show the gradual development of increased *Anlehnung.*) He accepts and trusts the bit as a comforting support for his balance. His obedience also improves, and the lateral bend gets easier for him.

As the horse reaches for this security, sometimes the weight of the rein contact will increase quite dramatically in the driver's hands. As long as he does not hang on your hands and stiffen his jaws, it would be a mistake to deny him this strong rein contact. It has grown out of his trust, submission to the bit and willingness to do what the bit tells him to. He is taking this very firm contact because he has begun to push energetically, without restraint or evasions, toward the bit—but he is not strong enough yet in his hindquarters to take weight off his forehand. This will be especially true of energetic horses that love to go, but are physically not built to flex well in the haunches and "sit back." (These horses tend to have a straight croup and straight hind legs.)

If the contact must be constantly established and reestablished by the trainer's hands, instead of by the horse reaching for it, then the horse is simply being held together by the trainer. There is no *Anlehnung,* and tension is created instead.

With the horse that is demonstrating correct contact, however, we can do a great deal. This is where we can begin to concentrate on "gymnasticizing" the horse's body and mind. Since we have him so securely on the bit, we can begin to work on precise turns and figures, observing the correct bend and proper engagement of the inside hind leg. We can continue to improve his responsiveness by frequent changes of direction, and by beginning to drive large figure eights. This way, he will gain strength and become lighter in the hand through the gymnastics of the figures.

It is also important to remember that turns and circles, and the application of the diagonal aids that we use to create the lateral bend, can help us restore a shaky longitudinal bend. However, if the horse consistently holds his head above the bit and has entirely lost the longitudinal bend, lateral bend won't be possible—and turns and circles won't help. The longitudinal bend (and stretching of the topline) *must* come first, at least to some degree. If your horse has trouble bending on his circles he may not have the longitudinal bend sufficiently established.

Once your horse has developed rhythm, relaxation and stretching toward the bit in his ringwork, you'll definitely want to go out on the trails. (With a well-behaved horse or a horse that has been ridden before he began his driving career, you are probably already driving on the trails.) Work in the ring, after all, can become boring, and nothing can replace the good work your horse must do on hills. Pulling up hills—as long as you don't overstress your horse before he's fit—will dramatically increase a horse's hind leg and back muscles, once he's learned to do this correctly. ("Correctly" means by rounding his back and lowering his neck when he's pulling.) And hill work makes the horse work harder without putting excess lateral strain on the ligaments and joints of his legs.

Working outside the ring will also help the horse to learn how to lengthen his stride at the trot—or, at least, to put more power into it. (See Chapter 12, Transitions, for a full discussion of lengthening stride in the trot.)

Training Sessions to Focus on *Anlehnung*
The gaits available now are a true working trot in a secure rein contact, some lengthening in the trot, a free forward working canter (again, canter is optional), a free walk on a long rein, and a working walk on a comfortable contact. Your horse should also halt pretty much "on the bit," and be able to perform smooth transitions in which the head stays on or close to the vertical. Downward transitions should now be taken on the horse's hind legs. This means he glides down into the lower gait without falling on his forehand.

Figures and exercises will include corners driven as a quarter of a 20-meter circle, plenty of 20-meter (or slightly larger) circles at the walk and trot, frequent transitions through all the gaits, and a correct reinback of three to four steps. "Correct" means that he remains straight while stepping back in a two-beat, diagonal footfall, remaining on the bit without any resistance in the jaws.

Accuracy becomes more important now as the horse advances in his training, but smoothness and relaxation are still crucial. If, for instance, you intend to execute a transition at a particular place but the horse doesn't feel quite ready for it, you will wait a few steps and ask for the transition only when he feels right.

You should be able to drive a very good Training Level dressage test, and a Preliminary Level test should be within your horse's capabilities, also.

A typical training session at this stage of your horse's development might look like this:

- Begin working at the walk on a very long rein for a few minutes, changing direction frequently. Be sure your horse moves freely forward and stretches for the bit in a very long frame.

- Gradually shorten the reins and trot the horse on into the bit in a free, forward working trot, keeping a long low frame. Drive corners generously, asking for bend but not insisting on a tight bend. Incorporate lots of large circles and changes of direction into your trot work; the changes of direction can be driven as straight lines or as half of a figure eight. Depending on the horse's disposition and conformation, this warmup may take from five to 15 minutes. A well-built, calm horse may need less of this, while a nervous, energetic horse may require a longer time to relax and settle down.

- Make a smooth transition into the walk, gradually giving the horse all the rein and letting him stretch all the way out and down for a few minutes. Then take up a shorter contact, and ask the horse to walk forward in a working walk, interspersed with periods of free walk on the long rein on the long sides or across the diagonals of your arena. Try to truly lengthen the horse's steps. You might spend about five minutes on this, or more if you feel your horse is ready for it.

- Going back to the trot, this time you will ask for a shorter rein contact and begin to work on correct corners, circles and figure eights. You might try turning onto and traveling straight along the quarter lines or the center line. (You will be surprised how difficult it is to drive a straight line without the guidance of a fence, wall, or path.) Incorporate walk-trot and trot-halt transitions into this work, practice your reinbacks and 180-degree turns, and include some lengthenings at the trot. If your horse canters well, practice your trot-canter transitions and do some cantering both on large circles and straight lines. This portion of your lesson may last for 20 or 30 minutes, depending on the horse.

  Each time you feel the horse does something especially well, give him his reward by yielding the reins (but still keeping the contact) for a few steps. You can do this at the gait you're in, or you can give him a larger reward by coming down to the walk.

- Finish with a few minutes of walk on a long or loose rein, again changing direction several times.

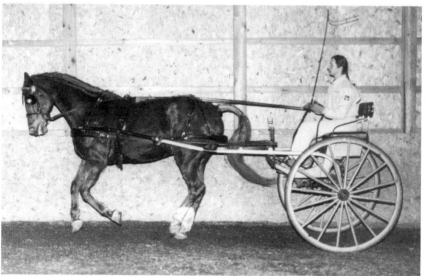

These two pictures illustrate the benefit of canter work in relaxing the horse's back and engaging the hindquarters. Although this fellow is going too strong against the bit and coming too much behind the vertical, we can clearly see the coiling and stretching of the back that can only be achieved through the canter. No other gait will give us this range of use of the back muscles.

Of course, you don't have to do everything mentioned above in one session—and certainly not every time you drive! You may just want to concentrate on walk-trot transitions, or polish your well-executed turns.

Work in the ring should never last longer than an hour. A 45- to 50-minute session is better, unless you are doing a lot of walking.

Remember that each training session repeats the steps for the whole training program. This means that during your warmup you will focus on the horse's rhythm (*Takt*) and relaxation (*Losgelassenheit*) to be sure that these are established before you move on to exercises designed to increase suppleness and reaching for the bit (*Anlehnung*). If the rhythm and relaxation aren't there, you can't go any farther until you reestablish these first two goals. There will be days when—because of the weather, or your horse's mood, or unexpected distractions—you will not be able to do as much as you would like. Although you should approach each training session with an idea of what you hope to accomplish for that day, sometimes you may have to set that day's program aside and simply concentrate on the earlier, more basic goals.

Even when your horse is able to eventually work on collection, you will begin each training session by examining and establishing first his *Takt,* then *Losgelassenheit,* then *Anlehnung,* and so on. This is the basis of all progressive training.

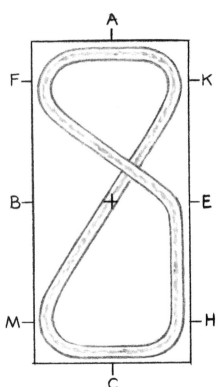

Developing *Anlehnung*. The corners are parts of a 20- to 25-meter circle and the short diagonal can now be driven. There are definite, straight lines now also on the short sides, as the corners become more defined.

Additional figures can be driven, including figure eights of 40- and 30-meter circles . . .

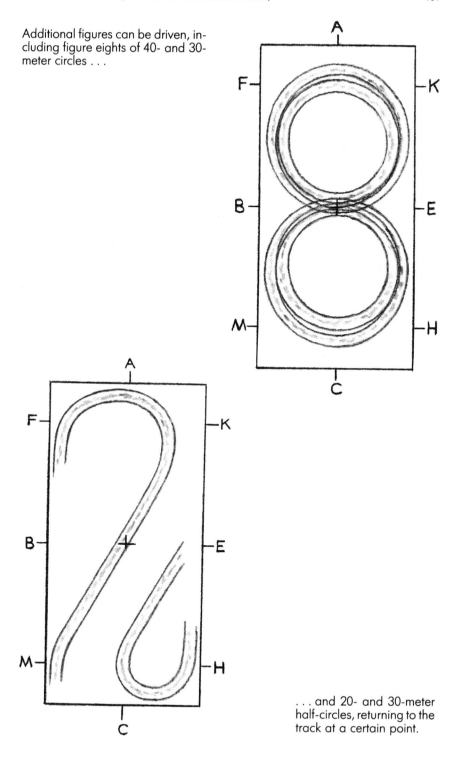

. . . and 20- and 30-meter half-circles, returning to the track at a certain point.

Further training for *Anlehnung* can include 20- and 25-meter circles, in almost any location . . .

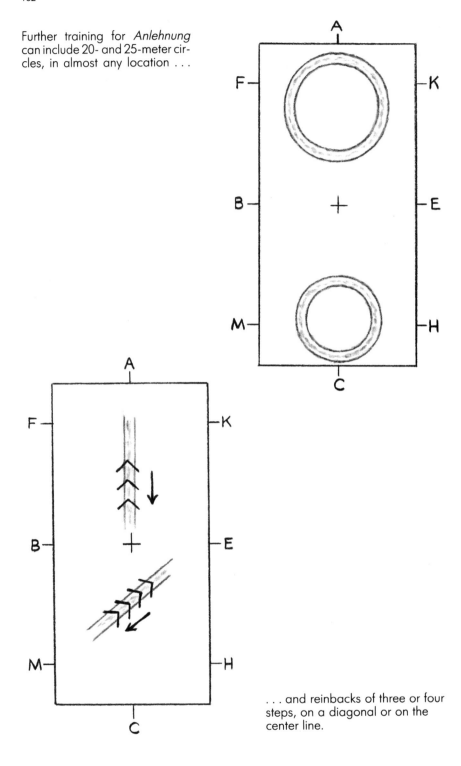

. . . and reinbacks of three or four steps, on a diagonal or on the center line.

Turning onto and off of quarterlines
is also an excellent exercise . . .

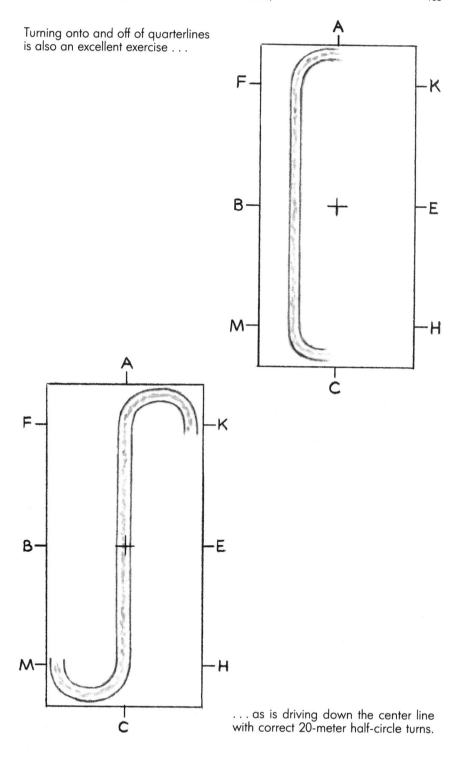

. . . as is driving down the center line
with correct 20-meter half-circle turns.

Work to develop *Anlehnung* can also
include tight turns of 180 and 360 degrees; possibly "on the spot," without letting the horse step forward.

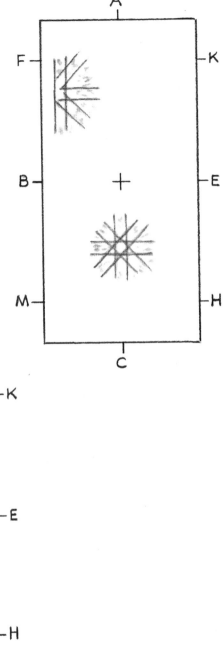

Another good exercise is a
three-loop serpentine.

The Interrelationship

These first three training goals are closely interwoven. A horse cannot be rhythmic when he does not let go, and a horse that has not learned the basics about rhythm and reaching for the bit in a long, low frame will not be able to let go into relaxation.

Expect to spend a long time working to perfectly establish these three basic goals—a year, or perhaps two years, depending on the horse and the trainer's abilities. The longe line helped you to introduce these three goals; ground driving gave both of you a chance to learn a feel for each other. Through driving, you are further developing the rhythm, the relaxation, the stretching and reaching for the bit.

Before we take our training further, it's a good idea to review some of the problems that might occur.

Watching for Problems

This early training will not always go smoothly. Green horses tend to be quite fussy in the mouth as they learn to find their new balance with the cart. Bobbing and tossing the head, opening the mouth, stiffening the jaws, lugging down on the reins or shoving the head down so violently he nearly pulls the reins out of your hands—all these things are normal in a green horse, and often just have to be waited out.

If any such problem gets worse instead of better, however—or if the problem persists longer than a few weeks—check for ill-fitting equipment or possible soreness in the horse's mouth, legs or body. And if your horse has been progressing nicely, but suddenly begins to exhibit some of the behavior mentioned above, look very carefully for physical problems.

Be sure that you are not asking him for work that he can't yet handle. A young, green horse may develop problems as a result of:

- Pulling a too-heavy cart he can't balance well;

- Going on an over-long drive before he's conditioned for it;

- Tackling too many hills before his balance and muscles are ready;

- Being asked to turn too tightly before he can bend well.

If you are sure that you are asking only for things he should be able to handle, and nothing is wrong physically, you may want to put your sliding sidereins back on, or—if you are already using them—shorten them a little for a few sessions until the horse is stabilized better.

The Question of Being "On the Forehand"

It is important that the horse moves forward and accepts being pushed forward by the driver. This does not mean that the horse rushes along in quick steps, but that he does step energetically and powerfully toward the bit.

At the very beginning of driving work, not much of this "push" directed by the driver will come back to the horse as energy he can use to carry himself. He will have to use all of it to move his load and himself forward in big energetic strides, and his front end will probably appear lower than his hind end. Many trainers think that when this happens, the horse is working on the forehand. However, this is the only way a green driving horse can work at this stage of his training, and the only way he can manage to reach with his hind legs well underneath his body.

As long as the power is being generated and the reaching of the hind legs is occurring—along with the correct lateral and longitudinal bending—the horse is doing well, even if he appears to be "on the forehand." (See illustrations on pages 20, 131 and 201.) Since the hind legs are being placed correctly under the horse's center of gravity, they will gradually become accustomed to carrying more weight, and the horse will—over time—be able to elevate himself in front by lowering his hindquarters. This doesn't happen overnight, however. The hind legs must be strengthened gradually, with the full flexion of all the joints in the hindquarters.

The Nervous Horse

With the nervous, energetic horse this can be a real challenge. You must first get him to relax so he doesn't try to rush, but you must also preserve the forward energy. Once the nervous horse is relaxed to the point where you must encourage him slightly to move on, he will be working well. (As long as you didn't have to wear him out completely to get him to that point!)

Nervous horses often become upset, are easily and frequently distracted—and when this happens, they become tense. When a horse is tense, good work doesn't happen. These horses can try your patience, but usually, once they do learn to relax and listen, they are a great deal of fun to drive because they like to work and put a great deal of energy into their movements. They are far more eager about their jobs than their more laid-back stablemates.

• WHERE DO YOU GO FROM HERE? •

Once you have achieved rhythm, relaxation and a true stretching toward the bit in your horse, you will find that he is a real pleasure to drive. He definitely should be ready now to go onto the trails and roads, even if he is a difficult or nervous horse, because he is listening well to your commands and is physically strong enough to have confidence in his work.

If all you intend to do is to enjoy driving in the countryside, your horse's formal education can stop here. Just return to your training area once in a while to refresh his reaching, bending and turning abilities, and to correct any problems that may develop. If you are content with your horse's level of training and you feel that you have created a safe, responsive, pleasurable driving horse, congratulations. You don't *have* to concern yourself with attaining the last three goals—increased *Schwung* (impulsion), *Geraderichten* (true straightness), and *Versammlung* (collection)—although a horse trained through these will be even more enjoyable and responsive, no matter what your demands.

If, however, one of your goals is to compete with your horse in pleasure driving, dressage or combined driving events, you cannot be content with this stage of training. There is more to be done. Before we move on to a discussion of impulsion, straightness and collection, we need to examine the question of transitions.

TRANSITIONS

A transition is a change in gait (as from a walk to a trot) or a change in the length of stride within a gait (as from a working trot to a lengthened trot). Transitions require:

1. Obedience and "mental agreement" from the horse; and
2. An increase or decrease in speed, and the horse's ability to change the longitudinal balance.

Transitions are very important for three reasons:

1. When done correctly, transitions increase a horse's suppleness and longitudinal balance;
2. Transitions increase the strength of the horse's hindquarters; and
3. The quality of the transitions is a very useful indicator of the horse's ability, stage and correctness of training.

• HOW TRANSITIONS OCCUR •

Unencumbered and on his own, the horse will normally deal with a change in gait by lunging, with his head up, into an "up" transition, and falling abruptly onto his forehand in a "down" transition—again usually by raising his head. This may serve him well enough when he has no burdens to pull or carry, but it is not the most effective way for him to deal with a cart and driver.

How would we like him to execute a transition? He should calmly and energetically move forward into the faster gait by fully accepting the bit and stepping into it, bringing his hind legs well under his body, and thus giving us full control of his motion and power from the very first step—all without rushing.

In a downward transition, we want him again to fully accept the bit, smoothly take up his weight on his hind legs without weighting his forehand, and instantly assume the lower gait—without any unbalanced steps and without losing his forwardness. "Dying in a downward transition" is a very common judge's comment in dressage tests at Training Level, and indicates that more work is needed in this basic training.

As we can see, there is a very big difference between what a horse will offer naturally in a transition and what we require of him when he is hitched to a vehicle. (Not surprisingly, owners often say that a well-schooled dressage horse will also become noticeably more agile in his free, unencumbered balance.) It is clear that only correct longitudinal development will lead to our goal of balanced transitions—and it is for this reason that transitions are such an effective gauge of a horse's training.

This is also the reason why we cannot work on accurate transitions until *after* we have established a secure longitudinal bend. And this is why we have to be very patient with the horse during his early training in harness. Until the correct longitudinal bend exists, we can use transitions *only* to change from one gait to another, and we cannot demand truly correct transitions.

The green horse's transitions will be wobbly, uncertain, hesitant and unbalanced. He must never be punished for this, or he will learn to fear transitions. We can ask him to come down to a walk when we want him to, and he should begin to respond to that command as soon as we give it, but it may take him several steps to comply. This is perfectly all right. It is far better to make your transitions gradual and pleasant at first, and wait for the balance and accuracy to come later, than to become impatient and pull harshly on the reins when he is doing his best.

Patience is needed also in upward transitions. For quite a while, your green horse will put his head up when you ask him to trot on. He will probably be unstable, rush a little or lack forwardness in the transitions. Again, this is perfectly all right at this stage. (See page 223 as an example of this.)

If, however, your horse overdoes the rushing and you feel he is simply being naughty, you must correct this. Don't go to war with him, however. The easiest and kindest way to do this is to put the sliding sidereins back on for a few sessions so he learns that he is not supposed to throw his head around. The sidereins won't force him to do anything he can't do, but he will give himself a jerk in the mouth when he's being naughty, and soon he will discover that it is easier and more pleasant to behave. Raising his head slightly in the up transition is okay, and this he can do in the sliding sidereins.

• TRANSITIONS TO INCREASE SUPPLENESS •

We often hear that transitions are useful in suppling a horse, and this is true—once the horse is relaxed and confirmed in his *Takt* and *Losgelassenheit.* So often, however, we see people working on transitions when their horses are very stiff or tense. (Stiffness is physical; tenseness is mental.) Insisting on accurate transitions when a horse is stiff only creates a stiffer horse, who then becomes frustrated and possibly angered by the impossible demand. For transitions to work as suppling exercises, they must be done correctly—and any stiffness precludes this.

When the horse *is* longitudinally bent—or at least relaxed—then the transitions, executed smoothly and correctly, will help supple, strengthen and collect the horse. Transitions executed with force will destroy any longitudinal bend, and only teach the horse to use his front legs as a brake.

Transitions that have a suppling benefit are all those that ask the horse to change from one gait to the next gait up or down: walk-trot-walk, walk-halt-walk, trot-canter-trot. Strengthening and collecting benefits are gained from the transitions that require him to move to a gait that is two or more stages up or down: trot-halt-trot, canter-walk-canter, and trot-halt-reinback-trot. These require the horse to flex his haunches more energetically.

In general, transitions also improve a horse's attentiveness to the aids and to the job at hand.

Too many transitions, however, can annoy or frustrate a horse, especially when the footing is deep or the cart fairly heavy. When you are asking for frequent transitions, watch the horse's attitude carefully. A few good transitions are worth far more than many mediocre ones.

• HOW TO PROPERLY EXECUTE A TRANSITION •

Every transition requires more effort than the gait you are in. Therefore, the gait you are in must be as perfect as possible. At the walk, this means the stride must be big, calm and forward, with the horse willingly stretching to the bit. The trot must be forward, engaged, free and rhythmic, with the horse again working towards soft jaws. If this is not happening, the execution of the transition is guaranteed to be poor.

If the gait you are in is lacking, restore it by pushing the horse a little more firmly towards the bit and check the softness of his jaws by moving the bit softly through his mouth. You should have the feeling of "loading the spring," as you quietly push the hindquarters forward and contain the energy in your hands.

When you feel ready, give your verbal command. It's always a good idea to say a word or two to your horse before you give him the actual command, something like "And now . . . trot." This is a sort of verbal half halt and gives the horse the chance to ready himself. (See "The Half Halt" later in this chapter.)

As soon as the horse responds, receive him in your hands. To do this, you will hold him through the transition if his longitudinal bend is a little shaky, or yield slightly with the hands if he stretches nicely and works into the bit. Remember that when you give your verbal commands, they must be consistent and make sense to the horse. In other words, a command for an up transition should be spoken firmly and with encouragement, perhaps even loudly; if you want him to come back to a walk, you should say this in a low, soothing, somewhat drawn-out voice.

Prepare for your up and down transitions in exactly the same way. This may not seem logical at first, since in order to slow down it would seem that the horse has to decrease his energy. But this is not the case. It actually requires more strength for the horse to execute a good downward transition, because we are asking him to take all this forward energy and his own weight onto his hind legs. We want him to literally "sit down" and absorb the forward momentum, gliding down into the lower gait without any sign of "braking" with his front legs.

This is where having a brake on your cart helps a great deal. It facilitates your horse's work, especially when he is first learning to handle this shift in weight during downward transitions.

As you work on your transitions, it is important to remember that the horse's body is naturally shorter in the trot than in the walk, and shorter in the canter than in the trot. You must make allowances, therefore, for the length of his frame in every transition. This means, for instance, that when you are coming down from the trot into the walk, plenty of rein freedom must be given to the horse as soon as he takes his first step of walk. This is even more necessary when you are coming down from the canter to the walk. When you ask for a walk out of the halt, you need to provide him with more length of rein than when you are moving from a halt to a trot.

In contrast, when you go from the walk to the trot, you will have to shorten the reins. (Remember that the rein length has more to do with the horse's length of frame than with his speed.)

•   TEACHING THE LENGTHENED STRIDE IN THE TROT   •

Lengthening stride within a gait is a more subtle form of transition, but many of the same considerations apply. "Lengthening" means to increase the distance covered by the horse at each stride, without a change in rhythm. To lengthen the stride, the horse must increase the forward energy, or impulsion.

A good place to introduce the lengthened trot is on the trails, on a level, straight stretch of field or dirt road with smooth footing. A lazy horse will be more willing to lengthen for you if he is heading toward home; with an energetic horse, you may want to ask for lengthenings first while heading away from home. And if he's *very* energetic, put him on a slight uphill stretch to increase the load he must handle.

If you don't have a suitable place on the trails, you can work on this in the ring, but your horse won't have quite the same incentive to lengthen stride on his own. Your ring will be okay, as long as you have a fairly long straightaway or diagonal to work on.

Before you ask him to "Trot on," establish a steady, regular trot, being sure that you keep him stretched through the poll and on a steady rein contact. If you are working in a ring, keep him well bent and engaged through the corner before you ask him to move out on the diagonal or long side. Be sure he is in good balance, working towards the bit. The working trot has to feel as if there is so much energy being built up towards the bit that all you have to do is yield slightly with the reins, and he will trot on stronger. If you don't have this feeling in the reins during the working trot, the chances for a lengthening are very slim.

If the trot is energetic and forward before you ask for the lengthening, he should lengthen willingly. You will yield the rein contact slightly, but *do not* throw the reins away. Your horse should feel as if his frame and his steps are becoming longer, and he is stretching forward even more into the bit.

Once the horse responds to your request and pushes off with his hind legs more energetically without making his steps quicker, be happy with a few good strides, and don't be discouraged if it doesn't seem perfect. He might come off the bit, get a little quick or travel wide behind. These are all very natural reactions. Patient, progressive training (and stronger muscles) will improve and eventually eliminate these problems.

The Horse with Natural Talent

Horses that possess a natural ability to lengthen will find it fairly easy, and moderate lengthenings can be attempted fairly early in the training (see Chapter 7). Although the weight of the cart may inhibit his ability to lengthen when a horse with this natural aptitude is first driven, he will regain this ability after he gains some strength and learns to reach for the bit while remaining in contact. This type of horse will naturally offer a lengthened trot any time you ask him to move forward more strongly. (As an example of this, see illustrations on page 224.) Although he does not fully stretch the topline, it is easy for this horse to exhibit power and a lengthened stride.

Correcting Problems • If you know that your horse can lengthen his trot easily, but he goes into a canter instead of increasing the trot when you ask for it—especially if he becomes upset and worried about your request—it may be helpful to go back to work on the longe line.

Put your sliding sidereins on and ask the horse to trot energetically forward on the large longe line circle. As he approaches the wall of your training area, or at a point where you have a long straight stretch ahead, you must move forward with him so that he moves straight ahead for several strides. Ask him to trot on as you do this. (See illustration on page 104.)

If he canters, pull him immediately back into the longe circle and insist on a trot. It is important that he respects the command and realizes that he must trot, not canter. Repeat this until he offers you a lengthened trot, instead of the canter. When he does lengthen the trot correctly, even if only for a few steps, you will guide him quietly back into his working trot and longe circle. Usually, you can establish this longer trot stride in one or two longe sessions, and then you can go back to driving.

The Less-Talented Horse

Some horses, of course, cannot offer a natural lengthening because of the way they are built. For these horses, learning to lengthen can be very difficult. Often, a lack of natural lengthening can be traced to a lack of freedom in the shoulder. A straight shoulder doesn't allow the horse to suspend his front legs long enough to stay out of the way of the pushing hind legs. To avoid stepping on himself, he must move the front legs out of the way quickly. Instead of lengthening, he quickens. We see this quite often in the pony breeds.

The horse with a neck that is set on very low will also have quite a hard time. In this case, the front end is just so heavy that it is very hard for the horse to keep it off the ground long enough to produce a lengthened stride, especially when he is pulling a carriage.

The most common reason for problems with lengthenings, however, has to do with the engine. To lengthen, the horse must be strong enough and his hindquarters must be built well, not only to push but also to carry weight on his hind legs for a moment during each stride, to maintain his balance. This is very difficult for horses with weak hindquarters (see illustrations on pages 200–201), and also for horses that have been bred to trot fast, such as Standardbreds and Morgans. These horses have been bred for push only, not for carrying themselves. Thoroughbreds, also, have been bred for racing, and often exhibit similar problems.

There are, of course, wonderfully built Standardbreds, Morgans, Thoroughbreds and ponies who make excellent driving horses and do very well in lengthenings—but these are exceptions, not the rule.

•   DEVELOPING GOOD LENGTHENINGS   •

For the horse that does not naturally offer to lengthen, but goes faster instead, correct muscling and absolute obedience to the aids will help overcome this problem (in most cases). Once these horses are strong enough not only to push but also to carry themselves in beginning collection, they can be asked to trot on stronger to produce a lengthened stride. This strength will have to be created through work on hills and lots of energetic working trot, frequent transitions (especially trot-halt-trot transitions), canter, many correctly executed turns and reinbacks.

Reinback is a collecting exercise; it also improves the flexibility of the haunches. It must, of course, be executed correctly: the horse must not evade sideways, step "wide" behind, drag his feet, stiffen his back, rush or fight in any way. If your horse does not back well with the weight of the carriage, return to practicing reinbacks in ground driving. Once he does it perfectly, willingly and easily in ground driving, you can ask him to reinback when hitched to a cart. (See the sections on backing in Chapter 7, Basic Ground Training, and in Chapter 14, Driving for Pleasure and Competition.)

Good riding can also help strengthen the horse's hindquarters, especially through well-executed shoulder-in, plenty of canter work and frequent transitions (trot-halt and canter-walk).

It is important to remember that a secure rein contact must be maintained to keep your horse from falling on the forehand. Some horses almost require being held together with the reins for a while until they understand the demand. For horses that seem to have a problem learning to lengthen while pulling a carriage, this work can be introduced on the longe line and/or in ground driving. (See the longe exercise explained above.) Another good exercise is to work over groundrails on the longe, asking the horse to make larger steps by gradually increasing the distance between the poles. Work your way up from three to six poles.

If your horse double-longes or ground drives really well and goes exactly where you tell him to, you can do this exercise on a circle. If not, you will want to put the poles along a straight stretch of track, and you will have to run along with him as he travels straight out of his circle and over the ground poles.

This sort of work will give him the idea of what you want, and it will show both of you that he can do it. To produce a trot lengthening when you are driving, your horse must gain strength and balance in the work described above (hillwork, energetic trot work, transitions and bending).

Teaching lengthening to a horse who has no natural inclination can sometimes take years, and some horses may not learn it at all. They can still be wonderful driving horses, of course, and you can still compete if that is your goal. Lengthening at the trot is required in dressage tests above Training Level, but when the judge asks for a "trot on" in a pleasure driving class, it isn't usually marked down if a horse gets quicker instead of lengthening, as long as he shows a definite effort. Even in the dressage tests, lengthening is just a small part of the test (in lower levels, it only counts for one or two scores). Your horse can still be competitive if he is otherwise willing and obedient and bends well.

• THE HALF HALT •

Probably no other term is more often used or more often misunderstood in training than "half halt." There is a great deal of confusion about what it is, what it means and what it is supposed to do.

The full halt brings a horse to a stop. In contrast, the half halt interrupts for a very short moment whatever the horse is doing at that moment. It creates more energy, helps him to rebalance himself and tells him to pay attention to some new demand or command. A half halt is executed by the coordinated application of all the aids—preferably with as little rein action as possible.

In riding, this is relatively easy to do, since we have our seat and legs as well as our hands to support and direct the horse. In driving, however, the reins provide our only continuous physical contact with the horse, and we will have to rely mostly on the reins, assisted by the whip and voice. The whip can help with the demand for forward and lateral attention without a lot of rein, while the voice will enable us to execute up and down transitions, as well as reinbacks. Once the horse has learned to fully submit to the reins and maintain a continuous longitudinal bend without the driver having to constantly correct and reestablish it, very little amount of rein action should be necessary to execute half halts; however, rein actions still may be very frequent.

Trainers often recommend that you perform a half halt just before you turn a corner, before you ask for a transition or before you change the engagement or length of stride in a gait. It often sounds as if a half halt is something isolated—something that is to be applied once, and then it is over with.

Actually, driving a horse in an arena requires a nearly continuous application of half halts, varying in degree as required. The *only time* we do not correct (half halt) a horse is when he is doing exactly what we want him to do. Then we can afford to simply hold the reins passively, and we do not have to be concerned about pushing him into them. When these rare moments do happen, it is an absolute thrill, and worth all the time spent on good training. However, those moments do not last long: a new turn requires our help, some distraction has come along, the horse loses his balance and so on.

So while working on precision work in a ring, you will more or less have to half halt the horse all the time. It is a never-ending communication, as you tell him with all your aids to pay attention, or push him with your voice or whip into the bit. These constant half halts may be very subtle—just a light rein correction, perhaps, when a little stiffness creeps into his jaw—or they may be very severe, as when you must take a very firm hold on the reins and push the horse strongly toward the bit to keep him from throwing his head up, shying or disobeying.

• ADJUSTING YOUR DEMANDS TO • THE HORSE'S RESPONSES

Every new command, every transition, and every change in lateral flexion requires careful preparation.

For instance, let's pretend you are coming down the long side of your arena in a good working trot. Even though your horse is doing well on the straight side, before you come into the corner you must check with him to see if he is still soft in the jaws and ready for the change in direction and bend. Your reins have to tell him now that soon you will guide him more onto the outside rein, and your inside rein will soon ask for a change into the lateral bend. You don't actually bend him before you get to the corner, but a few strides out from the corner you will subtly ask if he will accept this when you do get there.

If you feel some resistance, you still have a few strides in which to correct this before you actually get to the corner, to prepare him before he must deal with the changes in his body and balance demanded by the bend.

If your horse did not feel right as you came down the long side—if he was not accepting the bit well and traveling in good rhythm—then you know the next corner is going to be very difficult. In this case, you must try to soften his jaws and bend him more longitudinally before the corner, and then keep demanding his attention all the way into and out of it.

This means you are half halting nearly all the time. This will be the rule for most horses, most of the time. If your reins stop talking to him, he will either give up the bend and try to proceed straight through the corner, or he will come off the aids. It is this need for constant communication and correction that makes driving in the arena so different from driving on the trails. In the ring, we want every step of the horse under total control; in return, the horse can expect continuous help and direction. This is what makes the horse—eventually—so supple and obedient: being told always what to do and how to do it, and always receiving constant help from the aids so that he can accomplish these demands.

IMPULSION,
STRAIGHTNESS AND
COLLECTION

Different trainers will work toward different goals with their horses, and not everyone will aspire to the higher levels of dressage driving and competition. The basics of training are the same for all driving horses, however, and if you have now created a safe, reliable, responsive driving horse, you have done well.

But if you do aim for competition (or you just want to have fun training your horse to his very best), after you have laid a solid foundation of basic training, what next?

Once the first three elements of *Takt* (rhythm), *Losgelassenheit* (relaxing and stretching) and *Anlehnung* (reaching for the bit) are confirmed, you can concentrate on the next three goals of dressage: *Schwung* (impulsion), *Geraderichten* (straightness) and finally *Versammlung* (collection).

PROGRESS TOWARD THE ULTIMATE GOAL:
COLLECTION

Most training mistakes occur at this stage of training, after the horse has become somewhat experienced and fairly reliable as a driving horse. Often, the trainer will now expect the horse to progress rapidly to "collection." This is the time, however, when the horse is still learning to pull well and needs to concentrate on reaching underneath himself with his hind legs, gaining strength and learning to bend correctly through his turns.

Many trainers just haven't driven a horse that is truly reaching for the bit. If you haven't felt what this is like, you probably won't realize how much attention must be paid to this vital stage of training, which forms the basis of all progress to come and lays the foundation for true collection. Try to develop a really observant eye as you watch other drivers work their horses, and ask a friend to work with you as you learn what looks and feels right or wrong with your own horse. (A video camera can be an enormous help as a training tool, to help you correlate your horse's good performance with the right "feel" as you drive him. Watching tapes of other drivers can help you develop that critical eye, also.)

Once you've got your horse comfortable in harness and steering fairly well, you may think: "Now I must shift weight back onto his hind legs by elevating his front end with the reins. Then the horse must work harder with the hind legs, and he'll get stronger this way."

No. This is not the way it works.

Only the continuous reaching for the bit will enable the horse to stretch his topline, and *this* will increase the reach and the strength of his hind legs, as explained in Chapter 2. If, instead, you forcibly pull the horse into some semblance of "collection" with the reins, he will fight. Fighting the bit will cause tension and a locked back, and no true collection can occur.

The horse will then be forced into something that may *look* like collection because the neck and head are higher; however, the withers will be pushed down, the back will be hollowed, the hind end cannot reach underneath the body any more and the haunches lose their flexibility. *In this position, the horse is actually working on his forehand—even though the head and neck are higher than the hindquarters.* (This false collection is called "absolute elevation"; in true collection, there is "relative elevation," because the forequarters are raised as a result of the hindquarters being lowered. This can only happen when the horse's topline is stretched and the bottomline is shortened.)

In a forced, absolute elevation (as in illustrations on pages 15 and 225), the horse usually also exhibits unyielding jaws, resistance to the bit and very obvious attitude problems like bucking, leaping, stalling, rearing and general disobedience to the driver's commands. These horses usually look angry, frightened, frustrated or confused. Their mouths are either working like crazy or they have lost all movement in the mouth as a result of the pain. When the horse resorts to this kind of behavior, the trainers who have put them into this position usually resort to a more severe bit.

It is best to completely discard this notion of achieving "collection," and look instead at the next goal of classical training: impulsion. Impulsion and straightness must be confirmed before we can expect to attain true collection.

•   *SCHWUNG* (IMPULSION)   •

Impulsion is an increase in the energy and power of the horse's push-off from the ground. It does not mean an increase of speed for the sake of speed; instead, it means an increase of energy in every step. We want the horse to make "stronger" steps. (Of course, this will also increase the rate at which the horse travels over the ground, but this is *not* accomplished through moving in a quicker rhythm.)

How often dressage judges complain about a lack of impulsion! And competitors become paranoid about it, because they do not know how to get more out of the horse. Driver and horse are both working as hard as they can, but the impulsion doesn't seem to happen. In most cases, the cause of this is either a lack of readiness in the horse or some hidden resistance in his body. In the latter case, the resistance must be identified and handled through careful, correct driving and beneficial exercises.

Here we have a horse with a naturally well-developed topline. Unfortunately, she is sickle-hocked and does not have quite enough bone in her hocks and hind cannons to compensate for the weakness. Because of this, there will be a definite limit to the development of her hind-end power. However, due to her honest and very willing disposition she gives everything she has. This picture shows her in an engaged working trot on a light bit contact.

This picture shows her in a moment of relaxation and reaching to the bit in a long low frame. Note how much less power is produced behind and how much more front-heavy her body appears. However, if she were just beginning in driving, this would be all we could ask from her.

Here the mare is making a good attempt at lengthening her stride. Note the lowering of the croup, the increased push-off behind, the greater reach of her front legs, and the lowered and lengthened frame.

How Impulsion Is Created

Impulsion can occur only when *Takt* (rhythm), *Losgelassenheit* (relaxation and letting go) and *Anlehnung* (reaching for the bit) are firmly established. As soon as one of these first three basics disappears, there is no impulsion possible because any stiffness or resistance will prohibit the flow of power through the horse.

Working on this goal (and the next two) is really a matter of continuing and repeating the work of the previous goals, with more emphasis on refining the acceptance of the aids and increasing the horse's energy.

We will work the horse through all the previous exercises, transitions and figures, but now we will ask for more engagement. We will ask the horse to work more energetically towards the bit. This doesn't mean he will get heavier in the hand, but rather lighter—because he will begin to push himself off the bit and let the excess energy flow back into his body.

This may not make much sense at first glance. After all, when we push the horse more into the bit, we have to hold the bit more strongly against the driving aids, and this automatically increases the amount of pressure in the hand, especially since we still expect the horse to stretch himself to the bit.

So how can we expect him to get lighter in the hand?

If the horse is ready and truly strong enough to work on impulsion, he is also capable of flexing and compressing his haunches to a certain degree. This, after all, is the only way he can produce more power—and this is already the beginning of true collection. When we ask him now to increase his energy while having him in a secure rein contact, he will compress his hindquarters more and put more energy towards the bit. Since we have asked for more energy than he needs for merely traveling along, the excess energy will be sent back by the bit into his body—which will help him take the weight off his forehand. He can now arch his neck more and carry it a bit higher than he did previously. (Compare illustrations on pages 200–201.)

To imagine what is happening, think of our leaf spring analogy. If you fix one end of the leaf spring, and push from the other end, the increase in potential energy will make it pop up. When you hold the front of the horse through the bit, and push the rear forward, he "pops up" through his back, coiling his loins.

He will still stretch to the bit, but it is not so much of a forward *downward* stretch anymore; instead, you have the feeling that he is "wrapping himself around the bit." He will still put pressure onto the bit, but by being able to carry himself more from behind he will flex more easily in the jaws and will give a lighter feel in the reins.

If, however, the horse has not been properly brought along, and he does not have the strength to compress his haunches to produce this extra energy but rather starts going more quickly—or if he is not stretching his topline properly—his back will "pop down," the underside of his neck will lengthen and bulge, the jaws will stiffen and he will increase the weight on his forehand. (See illustrations on pages 15 and 225.) Then one of the following will happen: If he carries his head fairly low, he will become heavier in the rein; if he carries his head high, he will give up or fight the rein contact. In any case, there is no true impulsion created because the energy in the steps does not increase.

Often, when a horse is first learning to increase his energy, he may get heavier in your hand for a while. It may take him a little time to learn that he can move in this different way. If, however, after a few sessions of attempts to increase impulsion, your horse does not show progress—or even becomes worse instead of better—you will know that he is just not ready yet, and you will have to spend more time concentrating on the previous goals.

At this stage of training, the horse will still carry more weight on his forehand; although we can say that the horse is working *towards* collection, he is *not* collected yet. Any shifting of weight from the front to the back is a step in the process.

How do we develop increased impulsion in our good driving horse?

Training to Develop Impulsion

It is important, as always, to ask for very little in the beginning, to monitor progress carefully, and to back off when the horse becomes nervous. Forcing him or asking too soon for lengthening, especially, can result in a multitude of problems. The horse often takes quick steps, rushing off on the forehand and spreading his hind legs in an attempt to take the load and the work away from his hindquarters, which may not be strong enough yet to make the correct effort.

A typical training session at this stage might include:

- Fifteen to 20 minutes of warmup, using exercises outlined earlier to develop *Takt, Losgelassenheit,* and *Anlehnung.* (Remember that in each training session you should reestablish all the previous goals before you concentrate on the current one.)

- Once you feel that your horse is rhythmic, relaxed and stretched through his topline, you can begin to ask for a more energetic working trot. Think of "loading the leaf spring" as you begin to drive figures such as circles, half circles and figure eights—all designed to increase the engagement of the inside hind leg and create more overall suppleness. Your corners are now deeper and more forward; you should be driving them as parts of a 15-meter circle. Ask for frequent transitions (described under the training program for *Anlehnung* in Chapter 11, and in Chapter 12, Transitions) and incorporate lengthenings into your work.

● If your horse is already showing some talent in his lengthenings, you can ask him for a bit more polish: Require that he remain steadily on the bit during his lengthened trot, exhibit more power in the push-off, sustain the lengthened trot for an entire long side of the arena and be able to give you good lengthenings several times in a row.

● Lengthenings are important exercises to develop impulsion. Some horses, however, do not exhibit a lot of natural talent for lengthenings, and with these horses you may have to increase impulsion substantially before you *get* any lengthening. If your horse hasn't shown a natural talent for lengthening his stride, but you feel he is ready for increased impulsion, try this exercise:

Drive on a 20-meter circle at a forward working trot, making sure he is bending perfectly and accepting the aids fully. "Load him up" as much as you can by pushing him up into the bridle without allowing him to get quick, upset or too heavy in the hand. Then send him onto a straightaway and ask him to "trot on." If he does not increase the length of the stride—or only manages a very slight lengthening—it doesn't matter, as long as he shows an increased effort. Reward any success, no matter how slight.

If, after several sessions of asking for lengthenings, he doesn't seem to be making any progress, put him back on the longe line or long lines to work on lengthenings. (See page 104.) Try him again later in the cart when he fully understands what you are asking for on the ground.

● When you are concentrating on increasing impulsion (during all this increased-energy work, not just in the lengthenings), be sure you do not overdo it. Ask for the "loaded spring" for only a few minutes at a time, and for a total of perhaps only 10 or 15 minutes during a training session. (A very strong horse may be able to give you a total of 30 minutes—though not all at one time, of course.) Intersperse the concentrated work with many short periods of walk on the long rein, or occasionally trot on a long rein.

This work is very taxing on a horse's joints, and it is *not* beneficial when it is overdone.

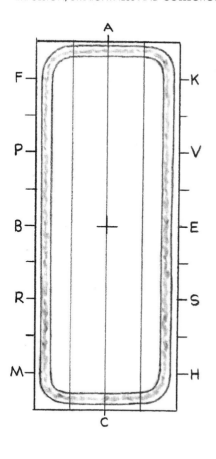

Developing *Schwung*. The corners are now driven as part of a 15-meter circle.

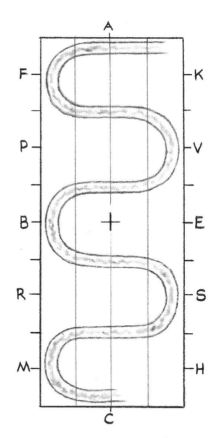

Additional figures can include a five-loop serpentine . . .

- This is also the time to work on a lengthened walk stride with the horse moving up into the bit. Until now, we have worked only on free walk on a long rein, or a working walk on a relatively shorter rein. Now we can

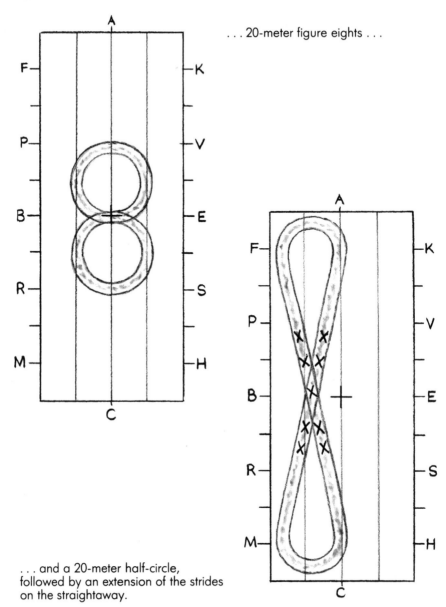

. . . 20-meter figure eights . . .

. . . and a 20-meter half-circle,
followed by an extension of the strides
on the straightaway.

begin to ask the horse to step more energetically into the bit by maintaining a secure contact and lengthening the steps. If the horse's conformation allows for it at all, you should see a clear overstep of the front prints by the hind feet.

Begin at the working walk, and ask your horse to step more energetically into the bit without hurrying. Search for the feel of the "loaded spring" at the walk, and then ask him to "walk on." You do have to make an allowance for the length of his neck—his entire frame will be longer in a lengthened walk than in the working walk—but your reins will not be as long as they are in the free walk. Again, keep these sessions brief, and reward him for all good attempts at lengthening.

- Conclude your training sessions as you always do, with a few minutes' walk on a very long or loose rein to allow the horse to fully stretch his topline.

If dressage competition is your interest, you should now be able to drive a very successful Preliminary Level test, and an Intermediate test should also go quite well, although the required collection will still be lacking.

•   •   •

Many of the horses shown in dressage driving have been especially bred for natural *Schwung* and extensions, which makes work a lot easier for them and for their drivers; but many of these horses are not performing at their full potential, because even these horses must be brought along slowly and carefully. The fact that they have natural talents doesn't mean their trainers can skip any steps in their education. The naturally talented horse may be able to progress more quickly than his less able stablemate, but a danger exists: Many talented horses have been asked for too much, too soon, simply because they offer so much on their own. It is easy for the driver to overlook the importance of gradual strengthening, and this results in overwork, resistance and unsoundness.

•   *GERADERICHTEN* (TRUE STRAIGHTNESS)   •

Since all horses are naturally crooked to varying degrees (see the discussion of crookedness in Chapter 10, The Lateral Bend), our training has, from the beginning, concentrated on stretching and strengthening the "hollow" side of each horse (usually the right side). Straightening the green horse was one of our earliest goals, but we had no means of working on it specifically, because the horse was not accomplished enough to accept our support through the aids. We have worked to achieve straightness all through our training—this is, after all, one of the essential tasks of dressage.

By now, however, if the horse has been brought along properly, he has enough strength to work with his hindquarters truly underneath himself, and what we call the *Geraderichtende Biergearbeit* (literally, "straightening-bending work") is a major part of this stage of training.

How do we know our horse has reached this stage and is ready to concentrate on this goal of absolute straightness?

Stretching and bending have helped the horse to reduce his natural crookedness, but now the horse understands the reins well enough to pay attention to our more subtle signals. He is strong enough now to truly engage himself and work up into the bit, into the outside rein, while maintaining a very light contact on the inside rein.

It is time now to ask for really precise turns and bends, expecting the horse to go still deeper into his corners (driving corners as parts of 13- to 14-meter circles with a single horse) and perform multiple serpentine loops across the width of the arena. We can also ask for total straightness on straight lines.

In riding, we use lateral exercises such as shoulder-in, travers and renvers to bend—and thereby stretch and straighten—the horse. In driving, however, we are generally limited by the shafts to working the horse on a single track. (It *is* possible for an expert driver with a talented horse to perform a shoulder-in while driving, but this is not recommended. It can prove very difficult to correct when done wrong; it may simply teach the horse to go crooked on a straight line. The hazards generally outweigh any potential benefits of the movement in driving.)

One effective way to increase your horse's straightness is to use progressively smaller turns and circles (correctly executed), and to change the bend frequently through ring figures such as serpentines. This work not only improves straightness by increasing the horse's responsiveness, but also increases impulsion, thus creating an additional amount of engagement necessary for future collected work.

Bending the horse is no longer only a means of dealing with turns; we use it now as a tool to refine our training. Since bending helps stretch the outside of the horse, the more evenly we are able to bend a horse to each side, the more equal his body development will become on each side—thus straightening the horse more and more. This is how we overcome his natural crookedness.

Since our horse is strong enough by now to properly use his inside hind leg, we can ask for absolutely precise turns, and he is responsive enough now to listen to our slightest rein corrections. By "precise," we mean two things: that he can perform movements with great accuracy, and that he is absolutely correct in the use of his body. There are no more slightly stiff jaws, no more keeping one hind leg a little to the inside, no more trying to anticipate turns.

His mouth should now feel completely soft and light on both sides, and each ever-so-subtle change in your rein contact will mean something to him. It is like sensitive power steering in a car.

Training for *Geraderichten*

For the first 15 or 20 minutes of a lesson, work through your first four goals. Of course, if your horse is truly at this stage, you should be able to establish *Anlehnung* almost instantly at the beginning of each training session. Make sure to begin, nevertheless, in a long and relaxed frame, shortening the frame as the horse's body warms up.

Let the horse tell you when he is ready for the more advanced work. An energetic, athletic, powerful horse will probably let you know that he'd like to get down to work immediately, as he seems to say, "Don't fool around,

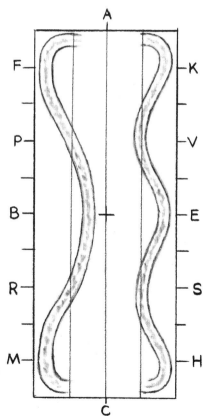

Developing *Geraderichten*. Suggested exercises include a single serpentine with a 15-meter deviation from the track, and a double serpentine with a 10-meter deviation.

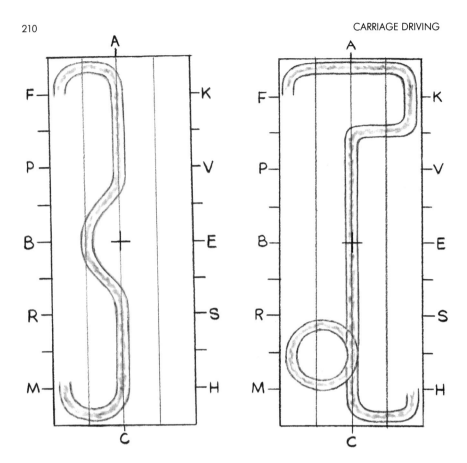

let's go do something. Give me a challenge." A laid-back, older or less perfectly built horse may say to you, "Give me some time to adjust my body again to the work ahead."

In the warmup, your figures will still always be of generous size, your transitions will be only from one gait to the next higher or lower and you may use cantering as a very beneficial exercise to loosen the back muscles. Although you are asking for correct bend and accuracy in your warmup, you keep your actual demands simple until his body is ready. You may have to make a few compromises in the warmup, waiting until he is ready to give his best.

After the warmup, you can begin working specifically on the precise execution of tighter turns and circles (but no smaller than 15 meters). Serpentines, half circles, lengthenings and all the exercises mentioned previously should now be fully incorporated into your work, and you can create your own "fantasy" patterns of figures. Just be sure you plan ahead, and try to execute a transition or a figure exactly where you have determined it should be.

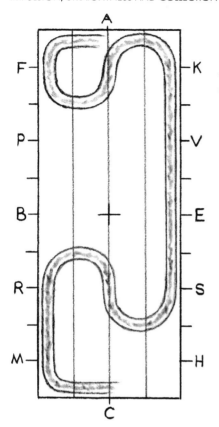

Drive your own "fantasy" figures (combining elements of other standard ring figures). These can be designed to promote straightening and help develop collection.

It is important to remember in all of these exercises that the horse must always step into the outside rein by softly accepting and yielding to the inside rein. Your horse must never lean into a turn; his body must remain vertical, perpendicular to the line on which he is traveling.

You should be constantly aware of how your horse is moving:

- Is his spine (from poll to tail) truly bent on the arc of a turn, and straight on a straight line?

- Does his inside hind leg really track toward his inside front leg at all times, as shown on pages 68 and 148?

- Are his ears at the same height? (If not, he's falling over a shoulder or tilting his head.)

Practice perfectly smooth transitions into and from the halt, straight reinbacks of several strides, and lengthenings that show real power. A talented horse with excellent lengthenings can work on an extended trot, while the less-advantaged horse should be asked for true lengthenings of greater duration and frequency.

In an extended trot, the horse tries for his "maximum" trot, and it will seem to be directed more "uphill," as he works with greater shoulder freedom and more flexion in the haunches. (See page 220 for a good example of this.) The poll-to-tail length is actually shorter in the extended trot than in the lengthened trot, because of an arched neck and coiled loins, but the whole frame for an extension is still clearly longer than that of a working trot.

If your horse canters, you can also practice many canter-trot and canter-walk transitions, canter lengthenings and circles. Of course, you also need to continue working on the free, forward and unconstrained walk, and on lengthenings in the walk. Conclude your sessions with some relaxed working trot on a long rein and walk on a long rein. With a talented horse, you can work on extended walk, which will show even more pushoff and greater length of stride than the lengthened walk. Horses with a naturally poor walk may never be able to execute an extended walk.

And you must never forget to reward your horse's good responses with a yielding hand; several times during the lesson, you should present him with a totally giving hand—or at least a very long rein—so he can stretch his hard-working muscles and joints.

If you compete in dressage, he should be able to give you a very good Intermediate Level test, and an absolutely perfect Preliminary test.

All this work will continuously strengthen your horse's hind legs, and will lead you to your last goal.

• VERSAMMLUNG (COLLECTION) •

Collection is not an isolated goal, and it is not something that happens suddenly after you've worked through all the other related steps. If your training has been correct, you have been working on collection from the first day you put a harness on your young horse. Basic collection work began very early, with all your efforts to encourage the hind legs to step under the body.

However, we now have all the necessary tools and required strength in the horse's back and hindquarters to shift weight truly backwards to the lowered haunches. If the horse has been worked correctly through the previous five goals, he should (depending on conformation and athletic ability) now be carrying about as much of his own weight behind as in front.

Before we can ask him to shift his balance even further back to his hindquarters, we need to understand what collection really is, what it means to the horse and to what degree pulling a carriage will affect this goal of collection.

What Is Collection?

In establishing the goal of collection, we are asking the horse to use his power to travel in an "uphill" manner (See illustrations on pages 22, and 220–221.) By placing more weight on his hindquarters, he gains great freedom and mobility in his shoulders, and he executes all movements with ease and agility. (See Chapter 2 and the discussion of shoulders.)

When he is truly collected, he carries more weight on his hind legs than on his front legs. His steps are shorter, which means that he covers less ground with each step, yet the rhythm of the steps does not slow or quicken. This happens because, as the haunches compress more, each foot remains in contact with the ground slightly longer than when the horse is in a working or lengthened frame—but, while the foot stays longer on the ground, the leg is compressed more and is "loaded" with more power and thrust.

A horse that exhibits false collection may slow down the rhythm of his steps when he is asked to shorten them; he may shorten the steps with a *loss,* rather than an increase, of power; or he may increase the time his feet are off the ground, rather seeming to float above it. See pages 15 and 225 for what can happen when this loss of power occurs. (Suspension has no part in any of the collected gaits or movements performed in driving; it is only correct in the extended gaits.)

All of this means that the horse has to produce maximum pushing power, forward and upward, continuously working towards the bit—and the bit is no longer a support for him, but merely a guidance. What we are really asking him to do is to offer, all by himself, to work as hard as possible and keep shifting his balance backward with every stride.

This is where we run into our first problem. Why should our horse want to work as hard as possible, all without any assistance except for our voice and whip? It would be so much easier, from his point of view, to just slacken off a little and lean on the bit. Not surprisingly, this is often the case!

Obtaining collection in riding is fairly easy, at least for a skilled rider on a properly trained horse. The rider has the seat and body to encourage the horse. If this isn't quite enough, spurs and a whip can be added. Through all these aids—natural and artificial—it is not difficult to maintain a light mouth and enough impulsion to generate good collection.

In driving, the skilled handling of the reins alone will help create and maintain collection. Of course we can encourage our horse with the whip and voice, but not at every step as a rider's seat can; and the slight differences in the way we drive our horse against the bit will be really the only thing that tells him if we want a working trot or a collected trot.

Why Collection Is So Difficult in Driving

It is quite true that many classical dressage trainers (including those at the Spanish Riding School) prove that horses can perform in perfect collection in the long reins. Many people would say there is little difference between performing in the long reins and driving. They forget, however, to consider the cart.

If you put your well-trained driving horse to a light jog cart and work him only on excellent footing, you can certainly expect your horse to be able to give you true collection.

If, however, you put a heavier carriage behind him and ask him to pull on a slope or in deep, bumpy footing, everything changes.

A rider can constantly correct his own center of gravity—and that of his horse—to balance them both. The driving horse never has this assistance; instead, he must constantly adjust his own center of gravity to the weight of the cart.

As long as he has to pull, the mass of the carriage is really always in front of him, transmitted through the collar; he must always try to catch up with it. In the early stages of his training, he leaned his weight into the carriage and used the weight of the vehicle almost as a fifth leg, taking some support from it as he pulled. (See page 217 for an example of this.) With correct training and increased strength—and assuming the weight of the vehicle hasn't increased—he no longer needs to lean against the carriage's weight because he can now move it with greater ease from his hindquarters. (In the illustrations on pages 218, 220 and 221, the same horse moves without leaning into the collar.)

However, if the weight of the vehicle is increased (either because a different vehicle is used or because the footing changes), this will change dramatically for him. He must compensate for variations in the load weight, and some of these variations occur extremely rapidly. He must adjust his balance to this new load—permanently if it is simply a case of a heavier vehicle, or temporarily if the footing has changed from smooth to deep or uneven. The changes in balance can come frequently and rapidly: From step to step, his situation may change from feeling no weight from the carriage, to a steady normal weight, to a sudden excessive weight. On unlevel footing, the carriage can actually travel alone, and the horse may have to shift his balance quickly, moving from pulling a heavy weight to braking against it.

In addition, the harness (*any* harness) is always restricting his shoulder freedom somewhat. (See the discussion of harnesses and shoulder action in Chapter 2.)

As long as we ask him to keep his weight evenly distributed and therefore moderately collected (approximately half over his hindquarters and half over his forequarters), a well-conditioned horse will be able to make the necessary adjustments. He will be moving his own mass horizontally, in alignment with the moving direction of the carriage. The illustrations on the tops of pages 218 and 219 show the horse moving horizontally, with the direction of the carriage.

But as soon as we ask him to shift *more than* half of his own weight back, we take away from him the weight in front that he had used against the load. Suddenly he must create more power from the hindquarters for his own body carriage, and, since we made pulling harder for him by taking his thrust (produced by weight) and some of the speed away (which helps make moving a load easier), he must also work harder to move the load.

In effect, we are asking him to work forward and upward, but the carriage still needs to be moved only forward—because we cannot alter the center of gravity of a vehicle as we can with a rider. When the horse attempts collection, his work load actually increases.

This is where the problems arise. The horse feels suddenly restricted in his necessary forward movement by the firmer rein contact. The rein contact is meant to tell him to sit back and collect himself, but if he is not capable of doing it (because of a lack of strength or education) he will get upset, angry and frustrated. (See illustration page 225.)

This is why we see so much resistance to collection in driving horses competing at the Advanced level in shows. Show carriages are always fairly heavy, ground conditions are rarely optimal and only very athletic horses with several years of proper strengthening are able to produce a degree of true collection in a heavy carriage.

The people who have created the requirements for driven dressage are obviously very aware of this problem, since even an Advanced test does not ask for long stretches of collected trot—and the collected trot work is interspersed with quite a bit of working trot. This is very different from ridden tests, where collected trot is required beginning at Second level. Once a ridden horse progresses beyond Second level, working trot is no longer included in the tests. Driving horses, then, in our opinion, are really only required to show a light degree of collection (as compared with ridden horses), and the lowering of the haunches is fairly minimal.

However, many judges do not acknowledge collection unless the horse's head and neck are carried very high, as would be appropriate in a highly collected horse. This is unfortunate, because many Advanced-level horses are therefore required to elevate the head and neck artificially. When too much front-end elevation is demanded, without the haunches being lowered, the result is a locked back. (This is illustrated clearly on pages 15 and 225.) Then the foundation of true collection—the stretch of the topline—has been destroyed, and the horse is really on his forehand. He is thus enabled again to thrust his weight against the carriage—but he is no longer in collection.

Many people think high collection is quite possible for the driving horse, since they misinterpret collection and judge it only by the height of the head and neck.

Also, many judges do not seem to be aware that collection is developed gradually—and some like to see Preliminary Level competitors traveling in Advanced Level frames. This confuses trainers, drivers and spectators alike, and most people feel pressured to put unreasonable demands on the horses who are not ready for advanced collection. And often, no regard is taken of the individual horse's conformation when his frame is compared to that of the "ideal." (See illustrations pages 159–161 and 162–164.)

On the other hand, more and more judges are complaining about "the loss of the basic principles" in the higher levels, which results—logically enough—in inharmonious and badly performed tests.

So, is the goal of collection at all justified in driving?

Yes, since work to develop collection really should be considered simply another level of gymnasticizing the horse and building his strength. However, especially in the beginning stages, it should be done only in a light cart on excellent footing to give the horse a fair chance to execute it properly. When we put him then in a heavier cart or ask him to work on difficult footing, we will have to make allowances for him.

A truly collected horse will have fun in his work. He will make it look easy and effortless, will submit to the lightest aids, and will always give the impression of moving "uphill." His entire topline will be stretched to the utmost, and he will resemble our loaded leaf spring.

A horse exhibiting proper collection is fully *durchlaessig,* or "permeable." That means that all of the produced energy flows totally unobstructed to the bit, and goes from there back into the horse's body, where it is fully under the command of the driver. In Germany, we use the term *vom Gebiss abstossen,* which translates as "pushing himself off the bit." This doesn't mean that he is "off the bit" as opposed to "on the bit," but that the horse gives the feeling of "wrapping himself around the bit," and is in self-carriage. (See the section under *"Schwung* [Impulsion]" earlier in this chapter.)

The pushing power that the horse has gained from his impulsion and true straightness will now (together with the carrying power) produce the shorter but stronger, higher and more energetic steps of true collection. (These shorter steps of collection must never be confused with the short, tense steps of a nervous horse, which can sometimes look more "animated" and impressive than true collection, especially to the unknowing observer.)

If, on the other hand, a horse is being "held together" by strong driving aids and strong rein aids, we know that the six goals of dressage training have not been accomplished. The horse has been pushed too fast, or his training has not been correct, and we see it in his resistances: tilted head, gaping mouth, pinned ears, clamped or flagging tail and a stiff neck or hollow back.

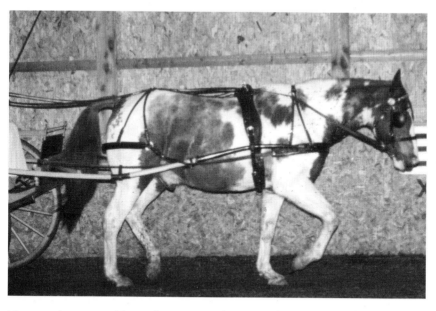

Here we have a gelding who is somewhat rump-high and whose neck is not attached or shaped naturally as well as the mare in the previous illustrations. Although he does have sufficient bone and good angles in his hind legs, his hamstrings do not tie in as low as we would like; being rump-high and quite lazy, he has no great interest in exerting himself. This picture shows him in his favorite gait, a totally disengaged trot on the forehand.

Here the same horse is showing a well-engaged working trot. His rump is slightly lowered and his topline is nicely stretched.

When asked for increased impulsion before lengthening his stride, he again stretches nicely through the topline and noticeably lowers his quarters, thus enabling his forehand to lighten and come up off the ground easily. This is a good example of "loading the spring."

Here he is also producing an increased effort from behind; however, he has come considerably behind the vertical. Note that the croup is not lowered. The forehand appears weighted, and the horse does not give an impression of moving uphill. The energy seems to vanish into the ground in front of him. (Compare this to the preceding illustration.)

A good lengthened trot with well-engaged hindquarters.

A beautifully engaged extended trot. Note that his frame is yet longer and his quarters are lowered even more, as compared to the preceding illustration. Due to the increased lowering of the hindquarters, the root of his neck has elevated further and his shoulder freedom has greatly increased.

Here he is asked to collect his stride. The created energy is caught by the bit and is now turned into the shorter, more elevated strides of the collected trot. His frame and stride length are markedly shorter, but again his quarters are definitely lowered. Note the increased compression of the hind limb. (Compare this picture to the illustration on page 217, and notice the dramatic changes created by correct work.)

A different phase of a collected trot stride. Here he is beginning to bend through a turn, which gives his neck a slightly different look as compared to the preceding illustration. Note how he shortens and raises his lower neck as he balances for the turn. In the bottom photograph on page 218, all the power is directed into forward, ground-covering movement; here, the power is recycled into a more condensed and agile stride.

Here he destroys our attempts at collecting him by simply cocking his left jaw. This is all it takes to block the necessary energy flow. The root of his neck has lowered, and his hindquarters are up—he is our "rump-high" horse again.

How Long Does It Take to Develop Collection?

The time frame depends on your skill as a trainer, the frequency and consistency of the work program, your horse's athletic ability and—most important—his mental attitude and disposition. Assuming that you begin his harness training as a two-year-old, and all factors are favorable, your horse will not be able to exhibit any true collection before the age of six. It will take at least until age four for him to find his balance in harness and develop enough strength for real *Anlehnung.* Another year of correct work must be devoted to *Schwung,* and yet another year will be needed to develop true *Versammlung* through *Geraderichten.*

This, of course, is if all factors are ideal. Layoffs caused by injury, bad weather, winter vacations or anything else will slow the process down considerably.

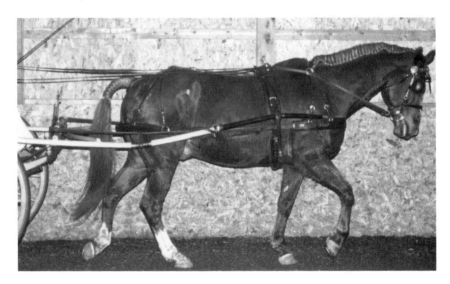

Here we have another very interesting horse.

He is an older gelding, very energetic and powerful, but with a history of bad training and only three months' worth of correct work. This picture shows his conformation very well. His withers are higher than his croup, his neck is of good length but clearly shows a dip in front of the withers and does not have the natural short-and-upward curve along its bottom line that we would like. It is not a ewe neck, but is often referred to as a straight neck. He appears hammer-headed here, but he is not; he just puts a near-constant pressure against the bit because all he wants to do is go fast; since he also has a clean throatlatch, he quite often brings his head behind the vertical. He possesses a wonderfully short, broad, strong back, a deep hip and very powerful hindquarters. His hind legs are a little straight, but he has excellent bone and his hamstrings tie in all the way down to the hock and give him tremendous power. He shows a relaxed walk here, but his head should not be behind the vertical.

When we ask for the trot, he becomes clearly above the bit and somewhat out of control. This is a typical reaction to an upward transition at his stage of training.

This is a little better. If he would be less resistant in his jaws, and if he would lengthen and lower his neck a little, his front legs would be allowed free movement and we would have a very nice engaged working trot, as his hindquarters are very active and well underneath his body.

Here he shows us a very nice, relaxed—yet very powerful—attempt to lengthen his stride. Note how he has elevated the root of his neck; his topline is stretched and nicely relaxed. His head is just in front of the vertical, and his front legs move freely. He puts less weight onto the reins, and even his face has a happy and relaxed impression. However, at this stage of training we would like to see his whole frame a little longer and lower.

In this picture he exhibits even more power. If he did not have the small resistance visible in his lower neck, we could call it a perfect extended trot.

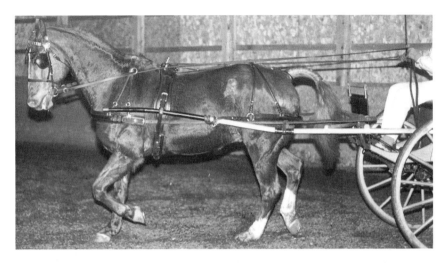

Here he shows us what false collection is all about. His head and neck seem to be in the perfect position, and he certainly appears quite impressive. But look at the tightness in the neck, the bulge on the bottom of the neck and the dip in front of the withers. Note that the hindquarters are not lowered at all and his stride is very short and tense.

Training for Collection

Once your horse is completely confirmed in the first five goals, your training sessions can concentrate on fully developing *Versammlung*.

Skillful long lining and ground driving can definitely help develop the horse's concept and his collection. *If* you are expert in teaching piaffe on the long lines, this can help improve his strength—but if you don't really know what you are doing in this area, you will do better to continue with driving exercises. Misapplied groundwork can make horses very upset, and may teach more fear and tension than anything else. Skilled long lining is an art in itself, and beyond the scope of this book to properly discuss.

A training session at this advanced stage might consist of the following:

- As always, you will warm up your horse by working him through all the previous goals, incorporating all (or many) of the previously described exercises and movements.

- To prepare him for more collected work, you should spend time working your horse through all of the collecting transitions: Trot-halt-back-trot; extended trot-halt-extended trot; canter-walk-canter. Include changes of stride length within a gait; the lengthened trot should be increased now to a true extended trot.

Of course, you will do quite a bit of bending, alternating this with extended work. If you have taught him piaffe from the ground, you can also ask for this, a few steps at a time. All of these collecting exercises will bring the horse to the point where asking with the reins for a little bit more weight to be shifted backward (while you encourage him with the voice and/or whip) will not be a problem for him. Collected canter will be quite easy for the horse now—easier than collected trot, since the canter has more natural thrust and automatically requires the loin to coil. Transitions from collected to extended canter and back to collected canter will also help improve his collected trot.

- Keep the truly concentrated collected work very brief at first, perhaps only 30 seconds at a time, requested several times during the session. You can build this up to two to three minutes of concentrated collection, and ask for it three to four times during a training session. The moment you feel that the horse is giving you a loss of power instead of an increase in power, you must stop attempting to collect him and ask him to move freely forward again.

  Eventually you may be able to work up to five minutes of collection (collected trot or canter) at a stretch, and ask for it three or four times during your lesson. Many horses, however, will never be able to give you this much, no matter how correct and careful the training has been. They will always be limited simply by a lack of physical ability.

- Remember to finish all training sessions with some forward working trot and a walk on a long or loose rein.

Bad training will be very obvious now, since an incorrectly trained horse will just not be able to lower his hindquarters. If this is the case, severe resistance will arise. Lowering of the haunches cannot be achieved by harsh rein action or any cruel, rough aids. Collection is the result of all the previous training, and should come easily for the horse when he is ready for it. If it does not, then the horse is simply not ready, and the training emphasis has to remain with the previous goals.

Regarding the Use of the Curb Bit

Remember that a curb bit is *not* a tool to obtain more collection or a certain frame from a horse. A horse driven in a curb bit should at any time be able to perform the same movements in a snaffle bit. The basic idea of the curb was, and still should be, this: The respect the horse has for this more severe bit should allow the driver an even lighter contact. The curb reminds the horse of its presence; in no case should the driver's hands ever pull the curb bit beyond a 45-degree angle.

A horse that puts a lot of weight against the bit—against *any* bit—while traveling in a "collected" frame is not truly collected or in self-carriage. It indicates that the horse has been asked to do more than he can handle, and it points to a problem of some sort: unsoundness, lack of strength, poor conformation or a lack of proper training.

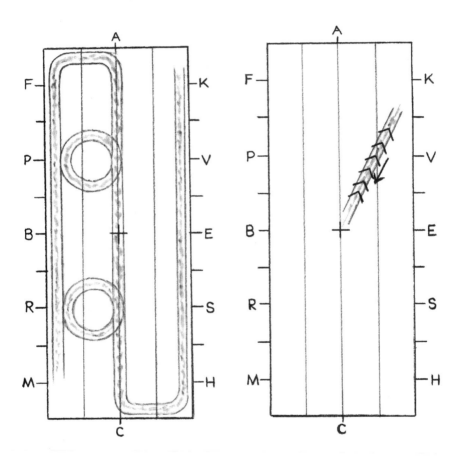

Developing *Versammlung*. In addition to all the figures of *Schwung* and *Gerade-richten*, add lots of small circles and reinbacks of six to eight steps.

DRIVING FOR PLEASURE
AND COMPETITION

Driving, after all, is supposed to be fun—for you and for your horse. Even the most seasoned show-ring competitor still enjoys the pleasures of quiet country driving. For some drivers, pleasure driving is merely an occasional diversion, but for many people, it is the ultimate goal and perhaps the only reason they have taken up driving.

One of the nicest things about having a carriage and a reliable country driving horse is that other people can share your activities. You can bring along a couple of children or a nonhorsey friend, without having to provide extra horses or trying to teach everyone to ride well enough to manage a trail ride. Pleasure driving can also be enjoyed by people who lack the abilities to tackle the greater physical demands of riding.

• FROM THE HORSE'S POINT OF VIEW •

A great many horses seem to genuinely enjoy driving on the trails. Many horses very clearly indicate that they prefer driving over riding—there's no rider bumping and shifting around on top, no misapplied leg aids to deal with—and nearly every horse will prefer being on the trails to working in the ring. Even though most people drive a heavier carriage on the trails than they do in the ring, your horse will find it less tiring to travel on the trails because he will make fewer turns. The straight-ahead nature of most country driving is far less taxing on his legs.

Your horse may become very bored by ring work. You'll want to spend time on the roads and trails as soon as you can, both to relieve the tedium of training sessions and to use hills to improve the muscles in his back and hindquarters.

The lazy horse, in particular, will find trail work a lot more fun than ring work; it will also help motivate him to go more forward without your constantly pushing him. Many horses who plod unhappily in the ring are delighted to find themselves on new and interesting trails, and actually "going somewhere."

The nervous horse, on the other hand, may be uncomfortable when he's outside the security of the ring's known territory. If your horse's nervousness translates into a head-high, back-hollow way of going, work on hills will *not* necessarily create correct muscle development. You must spend more time in the ring with this fellow, and make your forays into the countryside brief and well planned, following the same route for quite some time to provide him with reassurance. (Remember that sliding sidereins are also handy for reestablishing correct balance, and can be used quite comfortably in most road and trail work.)

• YOU KNOW YOU AND YOUR HORSE •
ARE READY WHEN . . .

Before you drive on the roads and trails in your area, your horse should be familiar with them already through ponying, ground driving and perhaps riding. Then, taking the carriage out on the trails shouldn't be a terribly traumatic move for him. You do need to review a few things first, however, to be sure you're both ready.

If your horse is by nature willing, obedient, and very easy to control, you can consider going out onto the trails sooner than with a horse who is headstrong or has a relatively insensitive mouth. If he is nervous or spooky, especially, you had better make sure you've established the following conditions before you venture out of the ring.

Before you leave the relative safety of your enclosed training area, your horse should be able to pass eight tests.

1. Ground Driving on the Trails
He should ground drive willingly and calmly on the intended route, and be able to accept the hazards of this particular trail or road (dogs, shadows, traffic). Riding and ponying will also help familiarize your horse with the trails, but there's no substitute for ground driving, because you are more closely simulating the actual control you will have over your horse when he's pulling a cart.

2. Secure Steering
He should steer well and safely. He doesn't have to be perfect yet, but when you tell him to turn right, he must turn to the right—not only with his

head, but with the rest of his body following. If you tell him to turn right, and he turns his head right but continues to travel straight ahead (or, worse, turns left and falls over the left shoulder), he is most certainly *not* ready for driving out of the ring.

3. Acceptance of the Bit

Your horse should accept the bit willingly. This means he must flex at the poll and yield in the jaws when bit pressure is applied, and he must submit to the command of the bit without fighting it, pulling against it or becoming upset with it. If a young or green horse seems otherwise ready, but still has some problems with accepting the bit, you can drive him on the trails for a few times with the sliding sidereins.

Trail work should always be fun for the horse, and it should give him a break from the continuous demands of ring work. In the ring, he must keep his head and neck in the right place and pay constant attention to the reins; on the trails, it is pleasant for him if you can safely drive with only a light rein contact—but the emphasis must be on safety, and he does have to accept your commands to come onto the bit readily when it is required. Some horses find everything so interesting out on the trails that they forget all about listening to the driver, and begin to consider your rein aids as nothing but pure nuisance. The sidereins will help remind them that they still have to listen.

4. Obedience to Commands

He should obey *all* your commands willingly, especially the command to halt. He should halt when you tell him to, and should remain standing quietly for as long as you want him to—even if he's heading toward home.

5. Negotiating Tight Turns

He should be able to negotiate fairly tight turns to either side, being able to turn around on a narrow road if necessary. Ideally, your horse will already know how to do a 180-degree turn, more or less on the spot.

This last requirement can be a very valuable safety maneuver. On more than one occasion, we've gotten out of a tight spot simply because our still-green horse had learned this skill. Once, we met up with a dogsled team rushing toward us. The sled driver yelled that he didn't think he could control his dogs and was afraid they might attack. Another time, a loose herd of cows moved our way. How nice it was to be able to quickly and calmly turn on the spot and trot away from danger!

How can you teach your horse to turn this tightly?

This attempt at a 180-degree turn was made too early! He's obviously confused, is overbending his neck severely to the left, and is in great danger of hitting the wall with the right shaft in his next steps.

As soon as your horse is going forward willingly in the ring or field, and he understands bending through the actions of the inside and outside rein, you can attempt a tighter turn of about 90 degrees. Begin by slowing the walk almost to a halt, and then take up the inside rein very firmly. Your outside rein yields, and remains passive in a light contact, unless your horse tries to move forward rather than sideways.

The objective is to pivot the cart, keeping the inside wheel pretty much on the spot, while the horse is crossing over with both front and hind legs on a small arc, looking in the direction he's moving, but without stepping either forward or backwards.

As you begin to teach your horse this tight turn, it is okay if he steps forward a little at first, but he must never step backwards unless you specifically ask him to do so. If he steps backwards while you are trying to turn sharply, he can injure himself—and he can also back you into danger. Move him forward briskly if he starts to creep back.

If he moves forward more than sideways, use both reins to reestablish the near halt, and begin the turn again. Be very sure not to pull his head too far to one side, because then you will lose control of his body. The horse will fall over his outside shoulder and can then pretty much do what he chooses, perhaps moving straight ahead or going in the other direction. He may also hit his head or neck on the inside shaft (especially if the shafts are straight rather than curved). If he hits the shaft hard, he may become very upset about this uncomfortable restriction. If this happens, drive forward to straighten him and try to turn again a little later. See page 231 for an illustration of this problem.

Your horse may not understand what you are asking for at first. You can try touching him with the whip, fairly low on the outside barrel (on his right side if you are turning left) to encourage the sideways movement—but you should try this only if he is comfortable with the touch of the whip.

Some horses just do not understand what you are asking for, and become very confused. If your horse responds with nothing but confusion and frustration, postpone further lessons for a few weeks until his ring work is more confirmed.

You may also want to enlist the aid of a knowledgeable helper. Have your horse halt and then, while you are pulling gently on the inside rein, have your helper push the horse's barrel and the shaft sideways, a step or two at a time.

Be pleased with even a step or two to the side during your first attempts, and be sure you praise your horse for any correct attempts. It is very important that you never pull hard and long on the reins, even if the horse is slow in responding or does not respond at all. All rein action must be give-and-take. If a horse is forced into tight turns too early, he can become very frightened and begin to rear, balk, back up, leap forward or try to bolt. Any sign of one of these problems is a signal for you to ease off. Either your horse doesn't understand what you're asking, or he's just not ready to deal with this maneuver.

Generally, the more advanced a horse is in his understanding of the rein commands, the easier it will be to teach him tight turning. Horses that have been ridden extensively (and well) before they begin to drive will usually have no problems with this at all. See page 65 for a good example of a horse beginning a tight turn.

6. Backing Up

Your horse must be able to step backward on command at least two or three steps, and he must *quit* backing when you tell him to. He doesn't have to back perfectly yet in harness, but he should be willing and able to back a few steps, fairly straight.

Before you ask him to reinback when he is hitched, your horse must first be able to back willingly, straight and for the required number of steps in ground driving. You should not be using the reins to *pull* the horse backwards in ground driving; rather, he should step back willingly as a result of your voice and light rein commands.

Before he can push a cart backwards, he must also be willing to step back into the pressure of the breeching. The first few times you ask him to back when he's hitched, be sure the cart is a light one. Lighten it even more by getting out to stand beside it, or ask a helper to assist the horse with the weight of the cart as he steps back.

The first few times you give the command to back up, ask only for a few steps—and don't repeat the command too often, no more than approximately five times during a training session. Keep him calm and responsive, and don't ask him to hurry backwards. Always let the horse walk or trot forward between practice for the reinback, and *don't ask him to back every time you halt.* It is very important that the horse *not* anticipate the command to back. Anticipating or rushing backwards is dangerous, and should never be allowed.

If your horse does step back too quickly, too far or when you have not asked him to, use your voice immediately and strongly, and add a touch of the whip if necessary.

Once he has learned to move a few steps back in the light cart, you can add some weight to it, change to a heavier cart and eventually ask him to back up a slight slope. (And, if your horse is balky about a reinback in the cart, try asking for it on a slight downward slope at first so that gravity helps him. Then you can move to level ground when he is comfortable with this.) You may find yourself relying quite a bit on this skill when you go out on the trails.

7. Strength and Condition

Your horse must be in good physical shape. If your cart is very heavy or the terrain very steep, the horse must be in good condition or he may stall on you halfway up a hill, which can be quite dangerous. Pulling a heavy cart up a steep hill is difficult work, and a young or unmuscled horse can experience serious problems. Many horses will not automatically have the desire to pull harder or put more energy into climbing a hill—this is something that has to be taught. If they are also out of shape, they will be very reluctant to work at the limits of their physical strength.

Some horses, however, do seem born with the desire to tackle hills and hard work, and these are the horses that will put on condition more quickly once you do get out onto the trails. Any horse who shows an eagerness to climb a hill—within reason!—can be an absolute pleasure to drive. The ones who almost have to be pushed up hills never seem to be willing to work harder than their drivers.

A few months of regular ring work should strengthen your horse sufficiently for the trails, but you must also pay attention to the condition of the ground. Pulling a heavy cart through deep mud can be much harder than being ridden or ponied through the same mud. If the weather and ground conditions make driving especially difficult, you may have to put the cart aside for a while and resume your ponying, riding or ground driving along the trails until conditions are better.

8. Acceptance of the Whip
Your horse should accept and understand signals from the whip. (See Chapter 6.)

Once you feel you and your horse are ready to enjoy the great outdoors, you need to consider the following factors:

1. Plan the first route carefully. Don't drive through the center of town or along a busy highway the first time out, if you can possibly avoid it!

2. Choose the best time of day, and wait for good weather. Go at a time of day when you will meet the least commotion. The less your horse has to distract him for the first few outings, the better. Don't choose a cold, breezy, stormy day for your trail drive, but wait instead for a calm day with nothing blowing around.

3. Look ahead of time for a suitable spot to turn around, if this is the only way to get back home again.

4. Make sure the person coming with you knows horses, is agile and courageous—and won't sue you if anything goes wrong. This sounds drastic, but "better safe than sorry." Of course, you would *never* go alone on your first outing.

5. Check your cart and brake to be sure everything is in good operating condition.

6. Check your "spare parts" and tool kit. In your carriage you should have: a halter and leadrope, sharp knife, pliers, hammer, hoofpick, spare trace, spare rein, hole punch, and plenty of strong cord or wire. You should be ready to repair anything that breaks or malfunctions.

7. If you feel your horse may need a stronger bit for trail work than he usually does in the ring, make sure he's accustomed to it *before* you go out on the trails.

8. You may want to ground drive your horse along the route, then return to the barn to hitch him and repeat the same route, if you aren't completely sure of his reliability.

9. Drive your horse at home, in your ring or work area, for a few minutes first. You want to make sure everything works well and your horse is in a good, relaxed mood before you leave for the trails.

10. Be calm. Don't make the horse nervous with quick, erratic moves of your own. This is probably the hardest of all to do! It can be very exciting to take your horse out for the first time, but you do not want that excitement to be communicated to him.

•   COMPETITION   •

You may not aspire to the highest levels of formal showing, but many drivers are tempted by some form of competition. Aside from satisfying your competitive spirit, showing can be a useful training experience. Your horse will learn to handle himself calmly in unfamiliar surroundings with strange horses around him. You can use competition to measure your own progress. In dressage, especially, you can gain valuable information about how an expert (the judge) feels your horse is doing.

Of course, you may not be immediately successful in showing. You may disagree with a judge's decision, or your horse may not perform as well at a show as he does at home. Competing in shows can be stressful for you and your horse, and serious showing involves a serious financial outlay.

If you do plan to show, it's a good idea to learn what the competitions consist of and what is expected in each one.

Driving competitions in the United States are governed by the American Driving Society (ADS), which was formed in 1975 to promote driving and to establish criteria for judging in various competitions. Anyone seriously interested in driving should join the ADS. (The address is listed in the Bibliography and References section.) If you plan to show, you should—at the very least—obtain a copy of the ADS Handbook, which contains the rules for all driving competitions recognized by that organization.

Types of Competitions
There are four major types of driving competitions recognized by the American Driving Society:

1. Pleasure Competition
2. Coaching Competition
3. Dressage
4. Combined Driving

There is also a fifth category, endurance driving, which is fairly new and not yet regulated by the ADS.

Besides these, nearly every breed registry has its own list of driving classes for its shows. The American Horse Shows Association recognizes several other types of competition (such as fine harness and roadster), and there are also all sorts of rallies, which are organized by local driving clubs to serve as fun gatherings of their members.

Pleasure Competition • In a pleasure class, horses are shown in groups together and required to execute different gaits and transitions, in both directions and at the command of the judge. Competitors may also be asked to perform individual tests such as circles or figure eights. Horses are expected to stand quietly in the line-up and back readily. They are judged on performance, way of going, manners, condition, the fit and appropriateness of the harness and vehicle, the neatness and appropriateness of the driver's attire and the overall impression.

There are many variations on the basic pleasure class, and there may be combination classes such as "ride and drive" or "combination hunter" competitions.

The required gaits in a pleasure class are walk, slow trot, working trot, and strong trot ("trot on"). In the slow trot (formerly called the collected trot), the horse should move with slower and shorter strides than in the working trot, but without a loss of impulsion.

The ADS defines the working trot as a "pace between the strong and the slow trot and more round than the strong trot. The horse goes forward freely and straight, engaging the hind legs with good hock action, on a taut but light rein." The strong trot requires the horse to show both a "clear but not excessive increase in speed and lengthening of stride while remaining well balanced and showing appropriate lateral flexion on turns; light contact to be maintained. Excessive speed will be penalized."

From the description of the required gaits, it would appear that a horse trained in dressage would do very well in pleasure classes. However, checkreins *are* allowed in these classes, and there are very great differences of opinion among judges as to exactly what a pleasure horse should look like.

Obstacles classes also fall into the pleasure category. Obstacles are usually created from rubber traffic cones with tennis balls balanced on top, and you are judged both on the time it takes to complete a course and on the number of penalties (if any) you incur by knocking over the cones and/or balls. The cones are set in pairs at measured distances; the width between cones depends upon the width of the vehicles in the class.

Pleasure marathons are judged, timed drives held over a prescribed course, which may include up to four obstacles. Many people who have obedient, reliable—but not "flashy"—driving horses find these very enjoyable.

Coaching ● Coaching classes are limited to horse or pony four-in-hand teams, put to a road coach, private coach or park drag. Competition rules are based on old coaching traditions.

Dressage ● Dressage competitions are run as one phase of a combined driving event, or as separate classes offered at a pleasure show. As the interest in driving dressage increases, we can also expect to see "dressage only" driving shows.

In dressage competition, each driver is required to drive a dressage test, alone and under the critical eye of one or more judges. The judge gives each horse a score (between 0 and 10, with 10 being "Excellent") for the different gaits and movements, and adds written comments. Each entry also receives "collective marks" for gaits, impulsion, submission and the driver's correct use of the aids. The score sheet is tabulated by the show personnel, and is returned to you later after the class is pinned.

Both the scores and the judge's comments can be a valuable training tool, because they give you a yardstick to measure your progress by. Sample copies of all the dressage tests are available from the ADS.

Combined Driving

This has grown out of the Olympic sport of combined training, or eventing. In driving, the three phases are dressage, marathon and obstacle driving. Penalty points accumulated in each phase are totaled to produce a final score, and the turnout with the lowest penalty score is the winner.

Divisions are separated for singles, pairs and four-in-hands. There are four levels of competition: Training, Preliminary, Intermediate and Advanced.

Dressage tests are judged as described above. The marathon is the driving equivalent of a ridden cross-country phase, and tests the fitness and stamina of the horses, and the driver's judgment of pace and horsemastership over distance and through designated hazards. The obstacles phase is similar to an obstacles class in a pleasure competition.

Attire

In almost every type of show ring competition, each driver is required to wear a driving apron, hat and gloves, and carry a whip. The driver should be dressed "conservatively."

Ring Etiquette

When you are driving in the ring, do not shout at your horse, unless it is necessary to prevent an accident. Clicking with the tongue is discouraged. Excessive use of the whip is inappropriate, but judges do like to see the whip used as an appropriate aid.

As to styles of handling the reins, the ADS encourages "that all reins be held in the left hand with most of the direction done by the right hand, which also holds the whip. However, except for the use of hand holds, which is prohibited, a person's method of driving is optional."

To get a good idea of what is involved in any form of driving competition, you should attend a few shows and watch several tests. It also helps to join a local driving club and ask lots of questions!

•   THE SAFETY CHECKLIST   •

Always . . .

1. When you are hitching a green horse outside in the yard, point him toward a wall or fence. Let him face any activity or commotion so he can clearly see it, and have a knowledgeable person head him, standing right in front of him. Holding a horse from the side can result in the horse spinning around and hitting the handler with the shaft.
2. Get your green horse accustomed to having a rein caught under his tail before you hitch him for the first time.
3. Be sure he is used to all the sights and noises you may encounter on your drive (lawnmowers, dirt bikes, air brakes, gunfire, horns, etc.).
4. If you have to drive on busy roads, have a slow-moving-vehicle triangle on the back of your cart. Think also of carrying a red flag with you, and a flashlight in case you are caught after dark. Reflectors on your vehicle and reflective tape for your horse's browband and collar are also a good idea.
5. Be sure your horse is shod properly for the task at hand, using studs when necessary.

6. Your harness and cart must be in good repair. Be sure the brakes work correctly and evenly.

7. Carry your spares kit, and make sure it is complete.

8. Know and observe traffic rules!

9. Have yourself and your turnout insured with a homeowner's or renter's liability policy.

10. If you go alone on a drive, tell somebody where you are going and when you expect to be back.

11. Wear protective headgear, and recommend that your passengers do also.

Never . . .

1. Remove the horse's bridle while he is still hitched.

2. Have anyone in the carriage when the driver is not in it.

3. Ask a horse to do anything while hitched that you have not already asked him to do in his groundwork (backing, cantering, turning).

4. Approach a blindered horse from behind without talking to him first.

5. Have a child or nonhorsey person attend to your horse when you have to leave the turnout.

6. Leave a horse hitched to a cart without supervision.

7. Go on a drive without a spares kit.

8. Go on a drive without a last check of your equipment.

9. Set off for a drive on the road or trails alone if you are not absolutely confident of your horse's obedience.

10. Participate in a group drive if your horse isn't used to driving in company with other turnouts or riders.

PAIR DRIVING

Driving a pair is a lot of fun and a great challenge. Before you attempt pair driving, however, you should be very confident about your ability to manage a single horse while anticipating and avoiding problems. Although many of the same principles apply, there are some marked differences between single and pair driving, mostly due to the differences in equipment.

There are really two types of pair driving. The first consists simply of hitching together any two horses that you happen to own, and enjoying your drives on the trails. If the horses are somewhat matched in size and temperament, trained properly and hitched safely, you can have some wonderful drives. The second sort of pair driving, which is far more complex, involves the careful matching of two horses to make a "real" pair: horses that look alike, move alike and work together in harmony. This is the pair you'll want to take to shows.

We will focus mainly on the second type, although many of the following considerations will apply to any two horses who are hitched to one vehicle.

• MATCHING THE HORSES—WHAT TO CONSIDER •

These are the factors that will influence your success in choosing horses for a pair.

Size, Movement and Conformation

Ideally, the two animals would be of the same size, weight and body length. Allowances can be made, however, if the horses are similar in other important aspects. Differences of up to three inches in height, several inches in body length and up to 200 pounds in weight can be almost unnoticeable if the horses carry themselves in a similar fashion, with the same length of stride and way of moving.

NORMAN HAPGOOD

This photo shows two horses of different size. The off horse is three inches shorter in height and quite a bit shorter in overall body length. He also weighs several hundred pounds less. However, he possesses the same type of build, body carriage and length of stride. Although not an ideal pair, they worked well in performance. Note the blinders, which give plenty of space to their eyes; also note the breeching connected to the breast collar. The carriage is an all-purpose vehicle, here equipped with the wider yoke and singletrees. The lamps are removed for marathon driving.

Horses that are closely matched in size and build but do not exhibit the same movement may eventually learn to move more alike. Usually, the shorter-strided horse will try to catch up with his partner.

Temperament

Temperament is a key factor. Two horses may look and move like twins in the pasture, but if one is lazy and the other nervous when they are in harness, chances are very slim that they will work together. One will always seem to be dragging behind, carrying his head lower in a relaxed stride, while the other will seem always a little ahead, traveling against the bit with high head and short, tense steps.

Trying to correct this with the reins can make matters even worse. If you try to restrain the nervous horse, he will become even tenser because he feels held back. If you try to push the lazy horse, the nervous horse will certainly notice, and become even more agitated.

The only solution is to school both horses in single harness, working to calm the nervous one and energize the quiet one. This can be a long-term, frustrating task. It's far easier to begin with two horses of similar temperament.

Color and Markings

Color is another factor to consider. In pleasure and turnout classes, identical color and markings may help to compensate for differences in size, conformation or movement. However, if you are competing in dressage or combined driving, the performance aspects are much more important.

Age

If both horses are experienced driving horses, age differences aren't important. Putting two young, green horses together as a pair, however,

This drawing is a copy of a 1918 photo with the caption "M. H. borrowed his brothers' horses to take his girlfriend on a date." Note how high those poor animals are checked up, and the neck collars are not even close to touching their chests. Note the tremendous pull exerted by the yoke on the horses' necks, necessary in this hitching arrangement to hold up such a long pole. It's hard to believe that there was such ignorance at a time when the horse was an everyday means of transportation.

can be dangerous. It's much better if you can start a green horse with an older, quiet, more experienced partner. Remember also that even though your older horse can train and compete at a higher level, you must adjust your pair-driving demands to the abilities of the greener horse. Your pair will have to compete at a lower level at first, until they are more equal in education and experience.

•   SELECTING A VEHICLE   •

Many of the considerations discussed in Chapter 6, Auxiliary Reins and the Whip, apply to a pair carriage. There is one vital difference between vehicles for pairs and singles, however, and this is the manner of hitching the horses. With pair driving, you will be using a pole instead of shafts. There are three different pole arrangements, and three different ways of hitching the horse to the carriage.

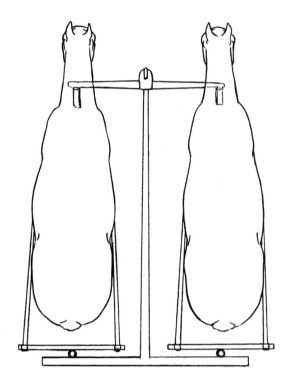

A pair hooked to single-trees with a yoke arrangement. The length of the yoke determines how far away from the pole the horses are placed. The horses do not feel pulled toward the pole at all. The yoke is kept as close as possible to the horses' chests, thus keeping the downward pressure on their necks vertical and as light as possible.

Pole Arrangements

Drop Pole • On carriages that do not have a fifth wheel, the drop pole is attached through a clip-on mechanism to either side of the front axle. The horses hold the pole off the ground by a yoke, which is attached to the horses' collars with leather straps that run through a hardware loop on either end of the yoke. The center of the yoke attaches to a leather holder that fits over the pole. The end of the pole protrudes four to six inches from the holder. This holder comes off the pole very easily. If the traces are too long or a trace breaks, the holder can detach from the pole while you are driving and cause a disaster, because the carriage can then move forward and hit the horses in the hind legs. If you use a drop pole, you must have a safety device attached to the end of the pole to keep the holder secure. Fasten a small leather strap or place a cotter pin in a hole drilled through the end of the pole to keep the holder in place.

Make sure that the yoke is snug on the pole when the horses are in pull (traces and collars are tight). The yoke should not be pushing forward on the pole, but it also should apply no excessive resistance. If the collars are not set firmly on the horses when they are in pull, but instead are being pulled off their chests, the traces are too short. The horses will then be pulling not with the collars but with other parts of the harness. The horses cannot pull properly, and the harness may break from improper stress.

At a show, we once saw a pair that clearly had no collar contact. After a few classes, the horses quit pulling–right in the middle of an obstacle course. They had to be unhitched and walked off the course. Deeply embarrassed, the owner said that his horses had never quit before. Unfortunately, none of the judges said anything to the owner; he may never have learned that his horses quit because they could not pull properly.

The drop pole has one disadvantage: The reins can get caught easily around the tip of the pole and on either end of the yoke if the pole is close to the horses. And if the yoke is kept farther out front so that catching a rein is not a risk, the horses will find the pole much harder to hold up. Although the pole is not very heavy, it will apply a constant forward and downward pressure onto the top of the horses' necks if the yoke is too far forward.

To avoid having the reins hang up, we keep the yoke and the tip of the pole as close as possible to the horses, so their heads are always ahead of it. Hitched this way, they can easily hold up the pole, and a rein gets caught only rarely. We like the drop pole and yoke arrangement. Its great advantage is that no jolts or movements of the carriage are transmitted directly to the horse, as happens with a stiff pole, and the yoke attachment is a lot friendlier to the horse than the pole-strap attachment. (See the discussion of these attachments in the following section.) The drop pole keeps the horses both connected to and away from the pole much more efficiently than the other two types of hitching, and this is very helpful in dressage driving, where correct lateral bending is so important.

Stiff or Standing Pole • The stiff pole is seen on fifth-wheel carriages. It is connected to the fifth wheel so the tip of the pole is at the height of the horses' shoulders. The pole is connected to the horses' collars by a pole-strap or chain, at an angle of about 45 degrees.

The pole must be at least long enough to be even with the horses' noses, so each horse can be tightly connected to it by the pole-strap. If the pole is too short, the horses cannot be connected snugly enough and they will be in danger of getting hit by the carriage. As with the drop pole, when the traces are tight, the collars must fully rest on the horse and the pole connection must also be very secure. If the pole-strap is not tight, the jolting of the carriage will cause the pole to swing around, bumping the horses on their shoulders or faces, especially in turns.

The advantage of a stiff pole is that the horses don't have to hold up the weight of the pole. The disadvantage, however, is that the stiff pole transmits all of the up-and-down jolting and sideways movements of the carriage directly to the horses. The pole will also move drastically up or down when driving up or down hill.

Hitched snugly at a 45-degree angle to a stiff pole, the horses also have a hard time remaining straight. They will feel that they are being pulled toward the pole, and their lateral freedom is greatly restricted.

By contrast, the drop pole and yoke attachment allows you to hitch the horses at any desired distance away from the pole. A longer yoke will place them farther apart, as in the figure on page 243; a shorter yoke will bring them closer to each other and to the pole. Also, the yoke can swivel back and forth in front of the horses like an evener, and this helps to accommodate them in turns.

Can a yoke be used with a stiff pole? No. The stiff pole must move up or down with the carriage, so the horses must be connected by a fixed strap. The yoke, however, must always be carried at the same height. On a stiff pole, a yoke would tug constantly and forcefully on the horses as it moved up and down, and it would quickly destroy the fifth wheel of the carriage.

Spring-Loaded Pole • The spring-loaded pole is a recent and welcome development. It was invented specifically for marathon carriages to solve all the drawbacks of both drop and stiff poles.

The spring-loaded pole is similar to a stiff pole, but instead of connecting directly to the fifth wheel, it rests on a powerful shock absorber

A spring-loaded, standing-pole attachment connected to a shock absorber. A leather sleeve has been wrapped around it to make it less obvious. Note also the fifth wheel on this carriage.

that allows it to move easily up and down. When the carriage and team are on level ground, the pole remains at the height of the horses' shoulders.

Because this pole has the advantages of both the drop pole and the stiff pole, it can be hitched with either a pole-strap or yoke attachment. (We prefer the yoke, for the reasons noted earlier.) The spring-loaded poles can be made of aluminum, so the yoke can be attached with a swivel bolt, which eliminates any protrusion at the tip of the pole. Reins do not catch on the tip, but the yoke still has full horizontal and vertical freedom of movement. (See the figure on page 241.)

Of course, these shock absorbers do not look very stylish and they certainly aren't traditional. If you want to use a carriage with a spring-loaded pole for dressage or pleasure competition, you may want to make it less noticeable by covering it with a dark leather sleeve. (See the figure on this page.)

Although the spring-loaded pole was originally designed for the newer, narrow-track marathon vehicles, you can also have this pole arrangement custom-built or retrofitted into some very stylish-looking carriages. We had a carriage built in Indiana to our specifications and are very happy with it. The spring-loaded pole looks like an old-fashioned stiff pole, but with a yoke attached–so it looks like a drop pole in front. We chose a wooden pole for this vehicle, but an aluminum pole would also have been an option.

A pair hitched to roller bolts with a pole-chain connection. Because of the angle of the chain, the horses will always be pulled toward the pole.

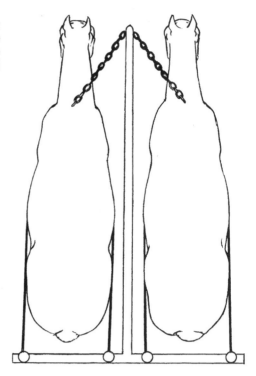

Methods of Hitching the Traces

There are three arrangements for hitching the traces to a pairs vehicle.

Evener • The two singletrees are attached to one evener, and this evener is attached to the center front of the carriage below the pole. This type of hitching is now rarely used in pleasure driving. Its origin is in work horse driving, and its purpose is to keep both horses always in the same degree of draft, even if one horse is lagging behind his partner.

The advantage of using an evener is that you don't have to be constantly checking to see if both horses are working equally. The disadvantage is that there can be quite a lot of back and forth movement of the two horses, and one horse can manage to hang back off the bit without your being able to do much about it, except to constantly get after him with voice and whip. Using an evener also gives the whole hookup a very "loose" feeling. Most drop pole attachments have a limited evener movement, which is kept to a minimum by the construction of the evener and its hardware. This prevents excessive back-and-forth movement between the two horses, but it still ensures—at least to a degree—that both horses must pull the same weight. For long pleasure drives on the trails, this is a very useful arrangement.

An evener with full range of movement. Note the metal dees on the evener; they are used to fasten the evener to the axle or frame if a limited movement is desired.

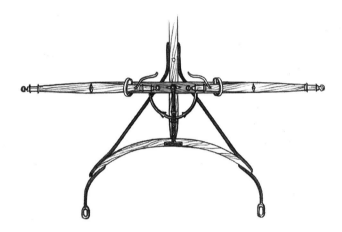

This is a drop pole with a limited-movement evener.

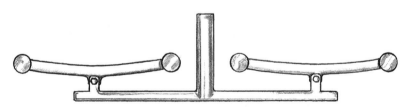

A singletrees attachment, with curved singletrees, which allow for a greater range of movement.

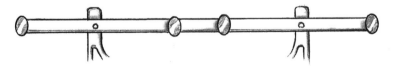

A rigid roller-bolt arrangement.

If the two horses do not work well together, however, the movement of the evener can cause problems. If your pair doesn't pull off simultaneously, the horse that does pull promptly will make the collar slap onto the chest of the horse that doesn't. A young or inexperienced horse may find this upsetting enough to become discouraged from pulling.

One solution is to block the movement of the evener entirely by connecting each end of the evener (with a strap or rope) to the axle.

Singletree • With this common arrangement, the horses are connected to the carriage through singletrees, which are fixed to the splinter bar. The advantages are that you do not need to worry whether both horses pull on at exactly the same time, and you will not get the "loose" feeling created by an evener.

The disadvantage is that you cannot always determine if both horses are working the same. One horse in a pair of ours was always quite good at making us think he was working; he would keep his traces almost (but not quite!) as tight as those of his partner. When he was told by voice and whip that he must not cheat, he would become very upset and leap forward for a step or two, then settle back again into his sneaky way of pulling.

Roller Bolts • With this hitch, the traces are connected directly to round, spool-like fixtures mounted on the splinter bar. This arrangement is seen very often on heavy coaches and on many stylish carriages used in competitions.

The roller-bolt attachment has no advantages whatsoever, and it makes the horses' job very hard. Because there is no give-and-take with the fixed roller bolts, this type of hitch prevents the horses from moving their shoulders freely, and it greatly increases the strain on their shoulder muscles. Remember that during a few inches of each step, the horse must move the entire weight of the carriage by his shoulder muscles alone. (See Chapter 2, Equine Mechanics.) This is particularly hard for him to do at the walk, because the load has no momentum to speak of. Why would anyone hitch heavy carriages onto their competition horses with unyielding roller bolts, when we know that draft horses can best pull their very difficult loads with an evener? Singletrees or eveners make far more sense from the horses' point of view.

THE IMPACT OF HITCHING ARRANGEMENTS
ON THE LATERAL BEND

Our equipment must be designed to allow lateral bending. As we explained in Chapter 9, Handling the Reins, bending a single horse in shafts is impossible if the shafts are too narrow or the singletree has too little movement. In pair driving, we have a similar problem. Since the pole doesn't bend through turns, the horses must be able to adjust their positions to it.

The less room the horses have next to the pole, and the less movement their singletrees have, the more difficult it will be for them to bend. This problem is especially apparent with the inside horse on any turn, since he will have to move his front end away from the pole. The outside horse, on the other hand, can move toward the pole in the turn.

To encourage good balance and lateral bending, be sure your singletrees are wide enough and are set far enough away from the pole so each horse can bend freely through his turns. The yoke should be long enough to reach from the middle of one horse's chest to the middle of the other horse's chest when they are correctly hitched. A long yoke gives them the freedom to move away from the pole and bend correctly; a shorter yoke will tighten the turnout for obstacle driving, but it will also pull them toward each other and toward the pole, restricting their lateral movement.

Comparing Pole and Hitch Combinations

In our worst-case scenario, we are driving a large pair of horses hooked directly to roller bolts. They are wearing neck collars and are connected by a pole-strap to a stiff pole. Remember that to be hitched properly there should be absolutely no slack in the traces when the pole-strap is taut. (Note: Breast collars must never be used with roller bolts. A breast collar requires a trace attachment that has some flexibility to it, because the breast collar sits lower on the horse's chest than a neck collar does. Using a breast collar with roller bolts will cause the collar to rub constantly across the horse's chest.)

Although the horses' use of their shoulder muscles is restricted at every step–because of the total lack of any "give" in the roller bolt attachment–they will still be able to move on a straight line. However, in the turns, the outside of each horse's body must become longer; and there is absolutely no way this can happen with this arrangement. The fixed hookup to the roller bolts allows for absolutely no lengthening of the outside trace; the pole-strap allows for no movement of either

The restrictions of roller-bolt hitches. This is the maximum "bend" horses can show on roller-bolt and pole-strap hookups. Only well-trained and very willing horses will be able to do this at all.

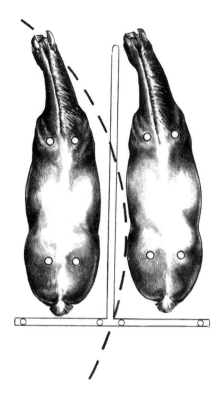

horse away from the pole in front; and, although the neck collar can give an inch or two by twisting to the outside, it will destroy the horses' shoulder movement. It may make them look (and be!) lame, and they may try to get out of this by breaking into a canter. Also, because of where the roller bolts are usually fixed on the splinter bar, they place the horses very close to the pole. Not enough room is allowed for the barrel and hindquarters to move as the horses try to bend; and the pole-strap won't allow the front end to bend, anyway.

In their best efforts, a pair hitched by this arrangement can turn their heads slightly in the turn, or remain straight–but this requires very well trained, honest horses. (See the figure on this page.) They will have to step sideways rather than forward; they may even have to cross their legs through the turns. Most horses, when confronted with this unreasonable demand, will throw themselves over the inside shoulder and scramble around the turn. (See the figures on pages 252–253.) This is the most apparent with the inside horse, who should show a greater degree of bend since he is traveling on the inside track and describing a narrower turn or smaller circle.

Common problems: This is what usually happens with roller bolts and a pole-strap connection. Looking to the outside, the inside horse falls badly over his inside shoulder, while the outside horse stays more or less straight; however, in order to negotiate the turn, here the outside horse is also falling over his inside shoulder. Not what we want!

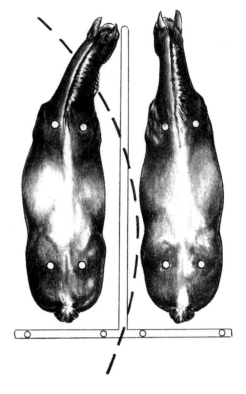

Now let's consider a much better combination of pole and hitch. We will drive the same pair with breast collars (which allow for more slippage across the chest, and can thus help lengthen the outside trace without putting restrictive pressure on the shoulders), singletrees of a good width set a few inches away from the pole and a pole-strap attachment.

Our horses can now move their barrels and haunches as needed through the turn. But the pole-strap is still a fixed restriction in front, especially for the inside horse, who must always travel somewhat in advance of the outside horse in a turn. The movement of the breast collar helps, but the inside horse still can't advance enough or move away from the pole in front–so he still must throw himself over his inside shoulder to negotiate the turn. The pole-strap with its diagonal pull always gives the inside horse the feeling that he is being pulled toward the pole and away from the direction of the turn. The solution to this last problem is found in a yoke attachment. The yoke can swivel on the pole, thus advancing with the inside horse, and the yoke strap itself allows for the sideways movement that is very much needed in tighter

This unbalanced, uncomfortable pair demonstrates what we usually see in the lower levels: Both horses are looking to the outside and falling badly over the inside shoulder.

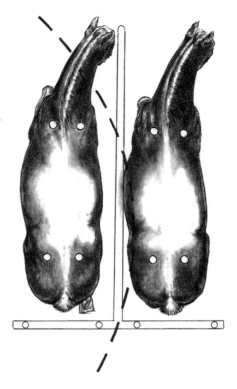

turns. The yoke also allows the inside horse to move farther away from the pole so he will be more comfortable. (See the figure on page 254.)

To summarize, your worst combination of equipment would be roller bolts set tight and close to the pole with a pole-strap attachment and neck collars. The larger the horses, the more restrictive this hitch is. Small horses are better able to maneuver in any hitch, but for all horses, your best combination of equipment is wide singletrees with good swivel movement, a correctly sized yoke attachment and breast collars. (Neck collars will work well also, if the singletrees and yoke attachment are correct.)

Why not use an evener? You might think that a limited evener arrangement would work even better than the singletrees-and-yoke combination described above. From the horses' point of view, this is true because an evener gives horses a chance to bend even better through their turns; however, it is far more difficult for the driver to keep a steady rein contact with both horses in an evener. In dressage competition, especially, the frequent changes of direction and pace are

A much better hitch. True bending exhibited by both horses,
made possible with a yoke
arrangement and appropriate
singletrees set far enough out
from the pole.

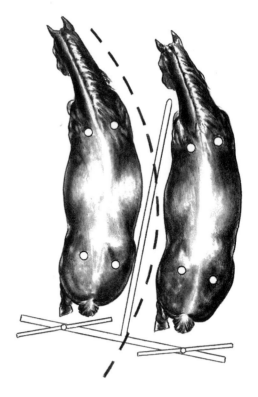

difficult to execute smoothly with an evener, since a constant bit connection with both horses is difficult to maintain.

Pair Carriages for Combined Driving

Many people who compete in combined driving events at the lower
levels use one carriage for all three phases. To be truly competitive in
the marathon, however, you need your entire turnout to travel on a
narrow track. Giving the horses some distance from each other with
wide singletrees and a wide yoke works very nicely in dressage, but
when you negotiate the very tight spaces of marathon hazards, you
can't have wide singletrees that increase the overall width of your vehicle. Your pair needs to be able to tuck snugly together to bring you
through clean.

You don't have to buy a separate vehicle just for the marathon, at
least not at the lower levels. But having a closer hitch will be to your
advantage. To solve this dilemma, we had two sets of singletrees made,

one wide and one fairly narrow. The narrow ones are short enough to be flush with the carriage for the marathon, and the wide ones are each four inches longer. The manufacturer attached a second set of fixtures to the splinter bar five inches out from the original fixtures for the shorter singletrees. We also had two yokes made, of different lengths, to correspond to the width of the singletrees. One carriage can easily be adapted this way–without great expense–to suit the demands of the different phases.

• HARNESSING THE PAIR •

The same basic principles apply when you are hitching a pair as when you are hitching a single horse, with a few exceptions. In pair harnesses a short, adjustable "cross" rein connects the left side of the off horse's bit to the left (full-length) rein of the near horse. And the near horse's right rein is connected by a cross rein to the off horse's full-length right rein. The driver, therefore, holds only a single pair of reins to control both horses.

Also, because the carriage has a single pole instead of a pair of shafts, the breeching must be different.

Adjusting the Cross Reins

The outside reins are full-length, and the inside reins are the short cross reins that are attached and adjusted by buckles to the outside reins. The cross reins allow us to influence both horses at the same time with only one rein. That's the advantage; the disadvantage is that the rein action will not be absolutely precise, especially on the cross reins.

The action of the cross rein will feel quite different to the horse. It is no longer a straight backward pressure, but is now a sideways/backward pressure. The horses need to become used to this different feel; in the beginning, a green horse may move his head closer to the pole to comply with this unusual sideways pressure.

Also, it is very easy for a horse to evade the pole-side rein by simply sucking back a little and turning his head toward the pole. Especially in turns, the outside horse will be looser on his (cross) inside rein because the inside horse is advancing more and shortening his inside (full-length) rein. This is why driving dressage with a roller-bolt attachment is still popular. You can certainly keep both horses locked into the reins all the time; but the sacrifices aren't worth the gain, because the horses are physically incapable of bending with a roller-bolt hitch.

Each inner cross rein has a buckle attachment to connect it to the outer rein, and a number of holes that allow you to change the length of the inner reins. There are different styles of pair reins, but the best are Achenbach reins. These offer 11 holes, spaced four centimeters apart, which allow for very fine rein-length adjustments. With the Achenbach reins, a good starting point is hole number six for narrow horses, number seven for medium horses, and number eight for larger horses.

Handling the Reins

The horses should be kept straight and parallel to the pole, with their heads showing a slight tendency towards the outside. If the horses then do not work equally into the reins when you are traveling straight, you can begin to adjust the reins to compensate for their differences. (For a full discussion of the Achenbach rein-handling method, read *The Art of Driving* by Max Pape.)

In general, you want to make adjustments in the rein lengths so that both horses give you an equal feel in the reins and remain straight in their bodies. If you have one energetic horse and one laggard, it will generally not work well to shorten the reins of the more energetic horse, even if you are using a very soft bit. Usually, the energetic horse is moving a little ahead of his lazier partner because he's already shortening his neck and going more strongly against the bit. If you try to take him back more with the reins, you may be able to keep him from pulling as hard, but he will probably become agitated and will shorten his neck even more, which will lead to tenseness.

As mentioned earlier, this is a difficult problem to solve. The best thing is to train both horses singly, calming the energetic one and energizing the lazy one.

Also, be sure to teach each horse his name. As you drive them singly, use the name frequently so each horse learns it well. (Be sure the names do not sound alike!) When you drive them as a pair, you will then be able to speak to each horse individually.

The Breeching

Much pair driving is done entirely without breeching, especially in Europe. Pair breeching is not really necessary if you have a smoothly functioning vehicle brake and use it properly. However, breeching is strongly recommended for safety whenever you drive on the trails or in a marathon. It also makes a reinback much easier for the horses.

Most people don't use breeching in dressage or pleasure competition because of the appearance. The less leather on a horse, the more elegant he looks. This is largely a matter of preference. However, if you expect your horses to give you an engaged, straight and even reinback in a dressage test, your chances of success will be far greater if you use breeching. Pair carriages are difficult to move backward; if the horses have to reinback with their necks alone while the false martingales are pulling the bellygirths toward their elbows, they won't be especially happy about it.

There are two types of pair breeching:

1. Martingale attachment. This type has side straps running from the breeching to the false martingale under the horse's belly. This doesn't seem very comfortable for the horse because if it is short enough to function correctly, it exerts a constant pressure on the false martingale, causing it to cut into the horse's chest. If it is adjusted longer, it will not come into play quickly enough to work effectively. Its one advantage is that it can easily be added to any kind of pair harness.

2. Trace buckle attachment. This type of breeching connects on both sides to the trace buckles at the collars. This is a very nice arrangement that functions correctly and also looks quite neat. (See the figure on page 241.) Its only drawback is that the harness must be designed specifically for this type of breeching. The trace buckles and keepers must be larger to accommodate two straps.

• TRAINING THE PAIR •

In years past, it was common practice to teach a young horse to drive by hitching him, right from the beginning, next to an experienced equine schoolmaster. Even if the green horse became very upset, the older horse would stay calm and help to hold back the panicky youngster. And many foals first learned about carriages from running next to their working mothers.

That might have been an effective method of creating a driving horse in those times where there was hardly any motorized traffic and very few frightening things to negotiate on the roads. Today, however, we don't feel comfortable with this method of training a pair; besides, how many people have that rare and wonderful schoolmaster at hand?

Many people say that pair driving is not as difficult as driving a single horse, because it is easier to keep the horses straight and they can reassure each other. This is true, to some extent, but if both horses become upset, you have to hold two horses. And holding two horses who want to bolt is a *lot* harder than holding one!

Confirm the Single Skills First

Pair driving is the art of driving in harmony two horses who already know how to drive well as singles. We make a point of training every horse thoroughly in single driving before we introduce him to pair driving. He must know all his rein and voice commands and must be very safe and reliable as a single driving horse. Then, we ground-drive the two horses together by connecting their collars in front.

With some horses, you may have to do this only once. With others, it may take several sessions for them to become accustomed to bumping against each other and to the feeling of the cross reins.

When they are confirmed in their single driving and confirmed in ground-driving as a pair, then you can hitch them to the pair carriage. Do this first in an arena with two helpers at hand in case something goes wrong. Usually, there is no problem at all. Some horses may be a little nervous at first about the pole, and there may be a few misunderstandings about having to pull together, but since they trust you and know all their commands things should quickly begin to go smoothly.

Once we feel the horses are comfortable together, we go right out onto the familiar trails to give them long stretches of straight pulling. If we think they're not quite confident in this new role, we'll stay in the ring for a few more sessions. Working in the ring is more demanding for them, but better for everyone from a safety standpoint.

When you do have both horses driving as a pair, you may realize that their single training was not quite as confirmed as you thought it was. As a matter of fact, they may have forgotten everything you taught them about putting their heads down and bending. This is a common response.

Don't insist immediately on the same level of obedience and suppleness as a pair that they demonstrated as singles. Continue their single driving sessions, concentrating especially on work in the ring to better establish the right muscles and reinforce all the goals of good training.

Work them as a pair no more than twice a week, and if the ring work is still atrocious don't insist on drilling them; all you will do is teach them bad habits. Take them on the trails, let them become thoroughly used to the different tugging on their bodies and let them find their rhythm together.

Remember also that the cross rein gives both horses a chance to escape your precise rein actions; don't let them know about this if you can avoid it! And don't go to a more severe bit unless you absolutely must for control.

If, after several weeks or months (depending on how much time you can invest in their training and how regular your schedule is), the pair's acceptance of the bit hasn't improved at all and their heads are still way up in the air, you can put your sliding side reins on for a few ring sessions. You must figure out how to attach the side reins so they don't interfere with the yoke, but it can be done. Usually you won't need the sliding side reins more than once or twice; once the horses figure out what you're asking them to do, they will remember how to work better.

If only one of the horses gives you trouble and you feel it may be because of the cross rein's different pressure, you might want to try running another single rein directly to this horse's inner side to help correct him. This requires some practice and skillful rein handling, but it can really help a horse who seems confused by the cross reins.

You may also want to try switching sides with your pair. Some horses just work better on one side than the other.

If you feel that one of your horses has developed a general disrespect for his bit, you can try a slightly more severe one. But make sure it is a broken-mouth bit (preferably double-jointed). Straight bar bits can make attempts at bending far more difficult. (See Chapter 3, The Bit.)

Common Problems in Pair Driving

1. Horses "pole off," with both looking to the inside with their bodies moving away from the pole as much as the traces allow. Horses often do this because their inside reins are too short or, if they are being driven with a pole-strap arrangement, the strap is pulling them too close to the pole in front. If they are hitting the pole, they may "pole off" to try to escape it. They may also have sore shoulders or are traveling crooked because it is easier for them to throw one shoulder against the weight than to pull it straight with both shoulders.

To solve this problem, you need to figure out the cause. First, go over the harness for possible pressure points. See if the bellygirths are rubbing the elbows or the traces are of different lengths. Try hitching them a little farther from the pole; if hooked too close, they may feel too restricted.

Check the length of the reins. If lengthening the inside reins and applying the whip on the outside shoulders does not help, try switching the horses. If they exhibit the same crookedness after you've switched them, it's probably some part of the equipment that is bothering them. If you can't find the cause of the problem by correcting the equipment or switching the horses, your training might be at fault. Drive them singly again and sort out any basic problems with straightness.

2. Horses crowd towards the pole. They may do this if their inside reins are too long. Also, the footing may be at fault. If you are traveling on trails that have deep ruts, the horses may try to stay out of those ruts by crowding the pole.

An insecure horse may also look for the support of his partner, and try to lean closer to him for security. If this is the case, more time and a general increase in confidence will solve the problem.

3. One horse won't bend but throws himself over the inside shoulder.

First, review your equipment and hitching to be sure you are making it possible for them both to bend. If your horses both know how to bend well when they are driven singly, and if they seem reasonably relaxed and working towards the bit as a pair, you may try shortening the direct rein (the right rein on the right horse or the left rein on the left horse) by making an additional hole at the bit for the rein buckle.

For instance, if your right horse is giving trouble in right turns, shorten the right rein and then drive a 30-meter circle to the right. Take both reins into your left hand and try to keep both horses out on the line of the circle. Then use your whip behind the girth until the right horse reacts by moving away from it. (You may have to support your left hand at times with your right hand to keep the horses under control.)

As soon as the right horse yields in his ribs, take the right rein back into your right hand and try to increase and secure the bend. Take and give on the right rein until his head moves to the inside.

Stay on this circle for two or three minutes, then move onto a straight track and then try it again on another 30-meter circle to the right. Make sure you praise the horse lavishly when he does respond well.

If you don't get any correct response, and all you seem to be doing is upsetting the horses, stop, put the sliding side reins on and try again. Remember that once the longitudinal bend is established, the lateral bend should come easily—and if there are problems with the lateral bend, you should look first to the longitudinal bend for correction.

Once your horse has learned to respond correctly, return the rein to its former length. If you don't do this, you might keep pulling his head too much to the outside when you are going straight, or you might even overbend him in turns.

If you have problems with the left horse on a left turn, the same principles and method should apply; simply shorten the left rein and drive your 30-meter circles to the left.

If it is your outside horse that does not want to bend in a turn, you have more serious problems because your cross rein does not offer you much help. Often, a horse will settle down with experience and begin to follow his partner through a turn without much in the way of correction from the driver; if this doesn't happen, however, and the outside horse is still looking to the outside of the turn to explore his surroundings, you may have to work him with the additional single rein as explained above.

• IN CONCLUSION •

Pair driving—especially in the ring—is a far greater challenge for the driver than handling a single horse.

It is also a far more difficult task for the horses. Pair driving demands great patience, willingness and submission from them. A horse can never be as comfortable in a pair as he is in a single carriage, simply because of the restrictions of the equipment and the need to accommodate a partner. Since the rein aids can never be as precise or as subtle as with a single hitch, the horses must be able to forgive more and to work with somewhat less direction from the driver.

Driving a pair, however, can also be a tremendously satisfying experience. Finding two horses who work well together and will do their best for you is exciting because you have harnessed twice the power of a single turnout.

BOOKS:

Pape, Max. *The Art of Driving.* Explains the Achenbach method of rein handling, for single and multiple hitches.

Rabinowitz, Sandy. *Driving Dressage.* A detailed summary of the training, techniques and ADS competition rules of dressage as they apply to driving.

PERIODICALS:

The Carriage Journal, 177 Pointers-Auburn Road, Salem, NJ 08079, www.caaonline.com

Draft Horse Journal, P.O. Box 670, Waverly, IA 50677, www.drafthorse journal.com

Driving Digest, 211 West Main Street, P.O. Box 110, New London, Ohio 44851-0110, www.drivingdigest.com

The Whip and *The Wheelhorse,* official publications of the American Driving Society, 2324 Clark Road, Lapeer, MI 48446, www.american drivingsociety.org

ASSOCIATIONS:

US Equestrian Federation, 4047 Iron Works Parkway, Lexington, KY, 40511, www.usef.org

The Carriage Association of America, 177 Pointers-Auburn Rd Salem, NJ 08079, www.caaonline.com

The American Driving Society, 2324 Clark Road, Lapeer, MI 48446, www.americandrivingsociety.org

US Driving for the Disabled, 8110 Elk Lick Falls Road, Lexington KY 40515-9322, www.horsejourney.com

INDEX

HEIKE BEAN is a Lifetime Member of the American Driving Society, where she was Chairman of the Dressage Committee for many years. Starting in 1986, she quickly rose to the top level of driving competition, winning many firsts at Gladstone and Myopia Combined Driving Events. She brought to carriage driving concepts of using dressage that broke new ground in the sport and significantly improved the performance of horses and drivers, adding to both safety and speed. In conjunction with the committee, she wrote the first manual on driven dressage and produced the video used to train drivers and educate judges. She has traveled widely, teaching driving clinics throughout the United States and Argentina. In her native Germany, she is licensed as an instructor by the German Equestrian Federation. The first edition of *Carriage Driving* became a bible in the sport. She is also a lifetime member of the American Morgan Horse Association and USA Equestrian. She lives in Vermont with her husband and her retired competition horses, a pair of Pinto Saddlebreds and a pair of Trakehners.

SARAH BLANCHARD is a professional horse trainer and riding instructor, licensed in Massachusetts where she lived for several years. While in New England, she had a career in corporate marketing and e-commerce management. Since moving to Hawaii, she has become a popular clinician and instructor in dressage and jumping. She serves on the board of directors of the Hawaii Isle Dressage and Combined Training Association and is chairman of the Panaewa Equestrian Center Development Group, where she works with local residents and county officials to expand the equestrian opportunities on the island. She is a member of the US Dressage Federation, the US Equestrian Federation, the Red River Regional Sidesaddle Association's Advisory Panel in Texas, and the Hawaii Quarter Horse Association. She teaches business writing at the University of Hawaii in Hilo. Her articles have been published in *Equus, Dressage and Combined Training, Horse Illustrated,* and *Horseman's Yankee Pedlar.*